The Evangelist

Lewis Drummond

WORD PUBLISHING

NASHVILLE

A Thomas Nelson Company

Produced with the assistance of The Livingstone Corporation, Carol Stream, IL, and the following individuals: Janet and Geoff Benge, who adapted and condensed chapters 1 to 13; Barbara Kois, who researched and adapted chapter 14; and Joan Guest, project manager.

ISBN 0-8499-1620-8

Printed in the United States of America

01 02 03 04 05 BVG 9 8 7 6 5 4 3 2 1

*This book is dedicated to my dear wife
and companion of over fifty years,
Betty Drummond: faithful friend, my
strength, and one deeply loved.*

Contents

Foreword by John R. W. Stott   vii

Preface   xi

1. An Epic Begins   1

2. The Holy Spirit   17

3. The Full and True Gospel   35

4. The Sovereignty of God   51

5. The Centrality of Christ   65

6. The "Social Gospel"   77

7. Billy Graham and Suffering   89

8. A Man of the Bible   105

9. Boldness   119

10. Godliness   129

11. Revival   143

12. A Worldwide Ministry   153

13. The Church   167

14. The Lasting Legacy   177

   Appendix A: Books and Booklets by Billy Graham   207

   Appendix B: The Lausanne Covenant   209

   Appendix C: The Manila Manifesto   219

   Appendix D: The Amsterdam Declaration   241

   Appendix E: Corporate Statements of the BGEA   257

Notes   271

Foreword

It was, I believe, an Episcopal clergyman who lodged a complaint against Billy Graham during the 1949 "Christ for Greater Los Angeles Crusade." His criticism was that Billy Graham had set back the cause of religion a hundred years. Billy Graham's rejoinder was typical. "I did indeed *want* to set religion back," he said, "not just 100 years but 1900 years, to the Book of Acts, when first century followers of Christ were accused of turning the Roman Empire upside down."[1]

This quip of Billy Graham's is a good example of his innocent humor in the face of opposition, and of his ability to turn a critical comment to the advantage of the gospel. It is also an unselfconscious assessment of his ministry. He sees himself (and rightly so) as belonging to the mainstream of evangelical faith and witness, as it has continued down the Christian centuries. So in his opening address at the Lausanne Congress in 1974 he was able to claim that "the Congress stands in the tradition of many movements of evangelism throughout the history of the church."[2]

Dr. Lewis Drummond's purpose in this book is to test this claim and to consider Billy Graham's place in history. His twelve characteristics of evangelism constitute a cluster of essentials, which may also be found in the evangelistic message, methods, and motives of Billy Graham.

Readers will enjoy this opportunity to compare the contemporary with the historical, and to evaluate the extraordinary ministry of Billy Graham by these twelve criteria. They form a substantial picture of evangelism. One might perhaps sum it up as follows:

Evangelism begins in the loving heart and sovereign will of Almighty God, as revealed in Scripture. It is essentially a bold proclamation by word and deed of Jesus Christ, incarnate, crucified, risen, reigning, and returning. It is undertaken in obedience to the Great Commission, whatever the cost, and in dependence on the Holy Spirit. It summons all humankind to repent and believe, and then to live a new life of godliness in God's new community, the church.

More simply still, evangelism is the proclamation of the revealed Word of God the Father, focusing on His Son, Jesus Christ crucified and risen, in the power of the Holy Spirit. For authentic evangelism is Trinitarian evangelism, and Billy Graham is essentially a Trinitarian Christian, who stands in the central tradition of the church.

It is my conviction, however, that Billy Graham will go down in the history of the church as more than an evangelist. First, and foremost, he is a *Christian*, determined by grace to follow in his Master's footsteps. In the increasingly permissive society of the last half of the twentieth century, Billy Graham has refused to bow down before the winds of public opinion. He has maintained his personal integrity. He has walked humbly with his God. He has loved his enemies who have vilified him, bearing the pain and declining to retaliate. In sexual self-control and financial accountability (areas in which other evangelists have fallen), Billy Graham has been above reproach. In brief, he has embodied the gospel that he has proclaimed. The Manila Manifesto declares that "nothing commends the Gospel more eloquently than a transformed life."[3] Billy Graham's testimony has been eloquent indeed.

Second, Billy Graham will be remembered as a *churchman*. He has never been a lone evangelist. He believes in the church. He has cooperated with the churches as much as he could. He has also called the church back to its mission. He has often said in my hearing that if the church were faithfully evangelizing, there would not need to be a person like him. He was exaggerating, of course, for there will always be some Christians whom God endows with the charisma of an evangelist. Nevertheless, we take his point. If every individual Christian were a faithful witness, and if every local church were diligently reaching out into its own neighborhood, mass evangelism would not need to be so prominent as it has been in our generation.

Third, Billy Graham has been an *internationalist*. Although he is a patriotic American citizen, he has never been a nationalist or been infected by the spirit of nationalism that has been so pervasive in his day. In visiting 185 countries, he has always been respectful of other cultures. From the beginning of his ministry he has opposed racism and refused to hold a racially segregated crusade. His internationalism has been acknowledged by world leaders, and he has been granted an audience by innumerable heads of state. Moreover, in these interviews he has always had the courage to go beyond protocol to testimony.

Fourth, Billy Graham has been a *statesman*. He has been wonderfully liberated from a preoccupation with his own ministry and has gladly recognized the importance of others' work. In consequence he has brought training and encouragement to multitudes of fellow evangelists throughout the world. His concern for them culminated in Amsterdam 2000. There, in July and August, 10,000 evangelists assembled from 209 countries. It is said to have been the most representative gathering, secular or religious, in the history of the world. What a vision! Although Billy Graham was unable to attend owing to ill health, his influence brooded over the assembly, as evangelists the world over look to him for inspiration. He was also the pioneer spirit behind the numerous congresses on evangelism (international, regional, and national), in particular Lausanne I (1974) and Lausanne II in Manila (1989). Nobody else could have created such a widespread and substantial evangelical unity.

I venture to commend Lewis Drummond for undertaking the task that has resulted in this wide-ranging book. He has thoroughly researched the evangelistic ministry of Billy Graham in order to ascertain his place in history. Although Drummond never descends to the level of hagiography, I prophesy that a careful reading of his book will convince us that, by God's providential grace, no single person in the twentieth century has been more influential for Christ than Billy Graham.

JOHN R. W. STOTT
December 2000

Preface

❦

It may seem redundant, if not presumptuous, to produce another volume on the ministry of Billy Graham and the Evangelistic Association he has led for more than half a century. A myriad of accounts, biographies, and books of many varieties on the evangelist and his work have been written. Why, then, another?

As strange as it may appear, Billy Graham and his ministry have never been placed and evaluated in the context of the sweep of evangelical church history and the contributions he has made to the church and the kingdom of God. The question should be raised: Do Graham's evangelization efforts find a worthy place in that historical, biblical context, and have his life and ministry contributed to Christ's cause in the world? Many realities suggest the ministry should be investigated from the historical perspective to discover an answer to these important issues. For example, no single evangelist has preached the gospel to more people in the entire scope of the Christian movement. Nor have more people responded positively to the gospel call from one man. Around the world he is known, respected, and loved. Having preached in more than 185 countries and territories, and preached to more than 210 million people in countless cultural settings, year after year polls recognize him as one of the ten most respected personalities in the world. He has been honored by governments, a myriad of organizations, not to mention multiplied churches and countless people. It would seem an investigation and evaluation of his ministry as related to its historical, contributory perspective surely stands in order.

The value of such an investigation can hopefully answer the issue as to the integrity, historical authenticity, and genuine impact of the Billy Graham phenomenon. If he and his association fulfill the principles of biblical, historically authentic evangelism, then he not only has his place in the sweep of church history, his ministry and contribution stand vindicated and he deserves the respect of succeeding generations. That is important for the present hour and for years to come.

Therefore, with such a rationale for another volume on the Graham epic, this work undertakes a journey to discern the essential principles of acceptable evangelism from an evangelical perspective along with an in-depth investigation of Graham's work with the view to discover whether or not the basic principles of authentic evangelical evangelism can be found in his ministry. If such be the case, Graham's contribution truly deserves an important place in history.

Honesty and objectivity have guided the entire investigation. Positive and negative discoveries alike are set forth. Historical integrity demands that approach.

Many have given invaluable help in producing this work. Dr. and Mrs. Graham graciously shared of their time to help this author attain a grasp of the many issues raised. Graham team members and others who gave interviews and presented their insights concerning Billy Graham's ministry proved most helpful. To all these I express my profound gratitude. A sincere word of appreciation goes to the Billy Graham offices in Minneapolis, Minnesota, and Montreat, North Carolina. Also, the Billy Graham Center in Wheaton, Illinois, provided significant resources. The personnel of all those institutions were most cooperative and helpful. And to Joseph Paul, executive vice-president and editor-in-chief of Word Publishing, I express appreciation; his council likewise proved invaluable. Dr. David Bruce gave of time and council that aided the work tremendously. I must also thank the secretaries who spent hours on the computer putting the manuscript in order: Michelle Joiner, Sherrill Hallquist, Tina Braswell, Mario Escobedo II, Lisa Tucker, Kathy Jauch, and Gail Gough. Gratitude must also be expressed to evangelist Frank Harber and his research students at Southwestern Baptist Theological Seminary. Several of my students at Samford University did excellent research as well. They saved this author many hours of labor. Above all, full honor goes to God for His graciousness in allowing this author to undertake the work and to sense His help and leadership. May He be glorified thereby and the Graham ministry find its proper place in posterity.

1

An Epic Begins

"Do the work of an evangelist."

— 2 Timothy 4:5

Can this really be happening? We've never seen anything like this before! Do you think this is truly of God? I don't know. Will it last? Such were the questions and exclamations that surrounded the phenomenon taking place in late September, 1949, on the corner of Washington Boulevard and Hill Street at the edge of the skyscraper district of Los Angeles, California. A large tent, affectionately called the Canvas Cathedral, had been erected on the site and people were flocking to it by the thousands. A casual observer might have thought that because of its proximity to Hollywood a magnificent entertainment program was in progress. Nothing was farther from the truth. Incongruously, the tent housed an evangelistic campaign being conducted by a thirty-year-old North Carolina farm boy named Billy Graham.

THE BEGINNINGS AND BACKGROUND

It had all begun some months earlier through the means of a concerted prayer effort for California. A local Lutheran minister, Armin

Guesswein, who had shared in the 1937 religious revival in Norway, challenged evangelical believers in the Los Angeles area to give themselves to prayer. He said, "Whenever God is going to do any kind of work, He always begins with prayer."[1] Another lesser-known personality who was significant in helping stimulate this prayer effort in Los Angeles was a young Baptist minister by the name of Joe Stevens. Others also had leadership roles in creating an atmosphere of prayer. They had discovered the secret that God moves in reviving power essentially in answer to prevailing prayer. As the old biblical commentator Matthew Henry said, "When God is about to pour out unusual blessings, He first sets His people a-praying." Los Angeles, in many respects, had fallen on its knees.

In the same general time frame, a group of Christian laymen felt a concern and burden that Los Angeles needed an evangelistic crusade, somewhat comparable to the former Billy Sunday meetings in the earlier decades of the twentieth century. They met and formed a committee to investigate such a possibility. Their critics saw it as a futile effort. The prevailing temperament of many Christians after the end of World War II centered in the conviction that the days of mass evangelism were over. Many argued that the world would be addressed with the gospel primarily through personal witness and by the ministry of local churches. The great American evangelists of the past such as Jonathan Edwards of America's First Great Awakening, Charles Finney of the Second Revival, and well-known evangelists like D. L. Moody and the aforementioned Billy Sunday were now relics and icons of the past. The days of people meeting en masse to hear the gospel preached seemed to have ended.

Yet it can be correctly said that all forms of mass evangelism had not ceased. Youth for Christ rallies were being held across America during the war and in the immediate postwar period. Young people were responding at these rallies. Yet while there were a number of evangelists ministering during these years, no significant personality had arisen that epitomized crusade evangelization as had happened in the past. Were the critics right? Was the time for that brand of evangelism really over?

Unperturbed by this question, the Los Angeles committee invited Billy Graham to come and hold an evangelistic crusade.

As we look back now and reflect on this effort at mass evangelism in Los Angeles four years after the fall of Germany and Japan, we see that God was once again about to do a marvelous work of grace. Exciting days lay ahead. But who was this evangelist named Billy Graham whom God was about to raise to world prominence?

THE EVANGELIST

Billy Graham had no unusual background to commend him to the task; at least so it would seem. Born into an ordinary Presbyterian farming family in 1918, Billy Frank, as his family and friends called him, grew up on the family dairy farm. He was reared in the typical Southern culture of Charlotte, North Carolina. He came to faith in Christ in an evangelistic crusade in September 1934, under the preaching of evangelist Mordechai Fowler Ham. Sixteen-year-old Billy Frank experienced a truly transforming conversion. In the same crusade in Charlotte, two friends, brothers Grady and T. W. Wilson, stepped out in a new commitment to Christ. God in sovereign grace began, even at this early stage, putting together a team that would have an ultimate impact on the globe.

When Billy Graham finished high school, he went for a short time to Bob Jones College in Cleveland, Tennessee. But he soon left Bob Jones and enrolled in Florida Bible Institute at Temple Terrace, a suburb of Tampa. Dr. Bob Jones, founder and president of the college in Tennessee, was disappointed and disturbed with Billy Graham's decision to leave his school. The president told the young man, "Billy, if you leave and throw your life away at a little Bible school, chances are you will never be heard of. At best all you could amount to would be a poor country preacher somewhere out in the sticks."[2] How wrong he was.

One night, while at the Bible institute in Temple Terrace, Billy wandered out onto the golf course. On the eighteenth green he fell to his knees and fully surrendered himself to do God's will, to preach His gospel, and to follow the Lord Jesus Christ wherever He may lead. God got His man!

EARLY MINISTRY

Billy Frank finished his studies at the Bible institute in Tampa and moved to Wheaton College west of Chicago, Illinois. There he received his Bachelor of Arts degree in anthropology. At Wheaton he also met his future wife, Ruth, a medical missionary's daughter. After college, Billy became pastor of a small Baptist church in Western Springs, Illinois. His life seemed set. A definite call to preach had come and now God had opened the door for him to become a pastor. Before long, however, he threw himself into the evangelistic rally ministry of Youth for Christ International. He began to travel extensively in America as well as serving as pastor of the Baptist congregation in Western Springs. He also started broadcasting *Songs in the Night*, a religious radio program that featured George Beverly Shea as vocalist. The program met with success. In the mid 1940s, Billy also traveled to England, extending his ministry of itinerant evangelism overseas.

As Billy Graham's involvement with Youth for Christ developed further and demanded more of his time, he became convinced that he should leave the Western Springs church and devote himself entirely to itinerant evangelism. His wife, Ruth, had longed to go back to the Far East and serve in Tibet, but Billy felt no such call and gave himself more and more to evangelism.

At the same time, Dr. W. B. Riley, pastor of the First Baptist Church of Minneapolis, Minnesota, urged him to accept the presidency of the Northwestern Schools that Riley had founded. Somewhat reluctantly, Billy Graham agreed and became an educational administrator along with his itinerant evangelistic ministry.

Around this time, at a spiritual life conference in North Carolina, Billy met Cliff Barrows. Cliff led the singing for the conference and he and Billy quickly became friends.

The ties between Billy Graham and the Wilson brothers also continued to deepen, with Grady Wilson also spending a year studying at

Wheaton College. In Grady Wilson, George Beverly Shea, Cliff Barrows, and Billy Graham, a team was coming together, and things were ready to erupt to the glory of God in Los Angeles. Yet, a significant spiritual step in the young Billy Graham's ministry took place just before the Los Angeles crusade opened.

A NEW STEP

Billy Graham had another close friend, a fellow Youth for Christ evangelist named Charles Templeton. He, too, was a young man with outstanding ability and a keen intellect. Although Billy himself had previously assumed he would go on to seminary after graduation from Wheaton College, his ministry developed so rapidly that he never made the decision to acquire further theological training. On the other hand, Charles Templeton felt convicted that the message they had been preaching was far too simple and they had to sharpen their respective theological swords. Templeton enrolled in Princeton Theological Seminary and pressured Billy to follow him. This threw Billy Graham into a quandary of indecision. Should he pursue his call to evangelism, or should he seek further training?

To compound the problem, in discussions with Charles Templeton and others, Billy had begun to entertain some doubts about the total truthfulness and authority of the Scriptures. That was on an intellectual level, but on a practical level Billy noticed that when he quoted the Bible in a sermon, convicting power gripped people in the audience. The Bible had a power over people that was impossible to explain outside of the notion that it contained God-generated words. Billy Graham grappled with the conflict between his conscience and his sharp inquiring mind. He knew he had to come to a definitive resolution; either the Bible was the Word of God, or it was just words about God.

Just before the Los Angeles meetings in 1949 were scheduled to begin, Billy served as a featured speaker in a student conference at Forest Home, a retreat center in the San Bernardino Mountains near Los Angeles. At Forest Home, Billy again faced his friend Charles

Templeton, who was also a speaker. The two men debated the validity of the Bible, but the discussion only deepened Billy's inner conflict.

In turmoil one evening, Billy Graham went for a walk in the pine forest surrounding the retreat center. He trudged about fifty yards off the main trail and sat down on a large rock. He spread his Bible out upon a tree stump in front of him. Struggling with his doubts, he had to face the question of the validity of the Scriptures and make a decision. In a spirit of absolute surrender before God, in something of the same spirit he exemplified on the eighteenth green at Temple Terrace, he cried out, "Oh, God, I cannot prove certain things. I cannot answer some of the questions Chuck is raising and some of the other people are raising, but I accept this Book by faith as the word of God."[3] Billy Graham made his choice. Faith became the key component, the factor that allowed him to accept the Bible as the fully truthful, authoritative Word of God. And with that decision, his ministry was transformed. The stage was now set for what took place in Los Angeles a few days later in September 1949.

Billy made his way to Los Angeles to start his campaign in the Canvas Cathedral. The eruption of God's mercy that occurred in that tent shook Los Angeles in a fashion that had not been seen since the dynamic days of America's First and Second Great Awakenings.

THE CRUSADE

The great Los Angeles crusade was scheduled to last for three weeks. The organizers wisely pitched the tent in a strategic location, a well-known intersection. There a large tent could not but catch the attention of passersby. Still, few expected what actually transpired, least of all Billy Graham and his team.

Although Armin Guesswein had challenged believers in Los Angeles to fervent prayer, Grady Wilson, when he arrived on the scene, really got the prayer chains organized. As well, prayer groups were established in churches, and entire days for prayer were set aside. There were also all-night prayer meetings, as well as much fervent individual prayer. The Spirit of God was setting the stage.

As the evangelistic services began to unfold, nothing of particular significance appeared to take place. But as one week followed the other, things picked up considerably and it began to become clear that God was starting to move. Encouraged, Billy Graham wrote in a letter to a friend: "We are having by far the largest evangelistic campaign of our entire ministry. You would have been thrilled, if you could have seen the great tent packed yesterday afternoon with 6,100 people and several hundred turned away, and seen the scores of people walking down the aisle from every direction accepting Christ as personal Savior when the invitation was given."[4]

The "Christ for Greater Los Angeles" campaign, as it was called, faced an important decision: Should the services end on a high note or should they carry on? As the committee addressed the issue, several felt the effort should stop. They reasoned it would be best to end on a positive note. Others, however, felt convinced that the work should be continued. People were still responding, and there seemed to be an ever-rising interest. The committee referred the question to a subcommittee of three. They in turn left it to Billy.

The evangelist found himself in a state of hesitation. He really did not quite know what God wanted him to do. He and Cliff Barrows prayed earnestly that the Holy Spirit would show them His will in an unmistakable way. They did as Gideon in the Old Testament ventured to do; they "sought a sign." They put out a fleece, praying and watching for a sign from heaven. And it came. Not with a wet fleece as in Gideon's case, but with a telephone call in the early hours of the morning.

THE "WET FLEECE"

Stuart Hamblen was a most unlikely candidate to become God's "fleece." Hamblen was a massive Texan in his late thirties, who had become one of the most popular radio stars on the West Coast. This was before television emerged as the main media, and his program was the most listened to radio broadcast in California. Tens of thousands of people tuned in to his program every day. He rose to become something of an icon to Westerners. He had also won the Pacific rodeo, was a successful racehorse owner, a big gambler, and a heavy drinker. His father had been a Methodist preacher in Texas, but when Stuart moved West he said he left it all behind. Yet his radio program was called the *Cowboy Church of the Air*. This made Hamblen a hypocrite, a fact he would gladly acknowledge later.

Stuart Hamblen's wife, Suzy, was a dedicated Christian with a vibrant faith. She had prayed for her husband for sixteen years. When Henrietta Mears started the Hollywood Christian Group for Bible study, Suzy Hamblen enticed her husband to attend the sessions from time to time. When Billy Graham's crusade began in September 1949, Hamblen promised his wife that he would go hear the young evangelist. Stuart Hamblen, though, tried to back out, which led to a bitter argument with his wife.

Suzy eventually won the argument, though she got the time of the service wrong, causing them to arrive an hour early for the meeting. For some unknown reason, Billy Graham also found himself at the tent an hour early, and the two men got to talking. While Billy found Stuart Hamblen to be loud and uncouth, there was something likable about him, something that reminded him of his Southern roots.

As the tent began to fill, Stuart Hamblen made Billy Graham an offer: "Come and be on my radio show. I can fill your tent . . . for you."

The next day Billy Graham went down to the Warner Brothers studio for a live interview on KFWB. After the interview Stuart Hamblen summed up by urging his audience to go to the tent meeting. He added, "I'll be there too."

True to his word, Stuart Hamblen showed up at the tent that evening. He enjoyed the sense of power he gained when many of his listeners showed up for the service. Later that night he took the entire Billy Graham team out to China Town for dinner.

As Hamblen continued to attend the meetings, he became very agitated. Conviction was setting in. Everything Billy Graham said seemed to be directed at him. When Billy said, "There is somebody in this tent who is leading a double life," Hamblen felt publicly exposed.

One night he could take it no longer. He retreated to the Sierras to go hunting and did not return until the supposed final Sunday of the crusade.

That night a grumpy Stuart Hamblen was back in the front row. As the service proceeded he found fault with everything. The singing was off key, the offering was emotional manipulation, and to top it all off, Billy Graham was only a few minutes into his preaching when he announced, "There is a person here tonight who is a phony." Hamblen could not stand it any longer. He shot out of his seat, shook his fist at Billy Graham and stormed out of the meeting.

Away from the crusade, Stuart Hamblen stomped defiantly from bar to bar. Alcohol, though, did not soothe his conscience. Finally, as he headed for home, he conceded that Billy Graham was right, he was a phony and he needed to get right with God.

About 2 A.M. Billy Graham's phone rang. On the other end was a drunk, sobbing man. Graham told him to get his wife to bring him over. Stuart Hamblen arrived at the door a few minutes later. He wasted no time with niceties. "I want you to pray for me," he blurted out.

Billy shook his head. "No, I'm not going to do it," he said.

Hamblen clenched his fists, fighting the urge to take a swing at the evangelist.

"Now come in, Stuart, and I'll tell you why," Graham went on.

When they were all seated, Billy Graham explained to Stuart Hamblen that he could not pray for him just so he could clear his conscience. Conversion is a total change of direction in life, and Billy was not sure that Stuart was ready to take that kind of a step. "I don't believe in a selfish, easy faith," he told the radio star. "Go on back home. If you're not going to go all the way and let Jesus Christ be the actual Lord of every area of your life, don't ask me to pray with you, and don't waste anybody else's time."

Stuart Hamblen refused to budge, and around 5 A.M. he promised to give all to Christ. A loud prayer meeting began. Billy Graham knelt down beside Stuart's chair. "Lord," he prayed, "You're hearing a new voice this morning."

That day Stuart Hamblen told his radio audience he had given his life to Christ. "I've quit smoking and I've quit drinking," he said. He also said he would sell all his racehorses except one, which he would never race again. "Tonight, at the end of Billy Graham's invitation, I'm going to hit the sawdust trail."

Stuart Hamblen's conversion was Billy Graham's "fleece." God had obviously spoken. People were flocking to the tent. The campaign would continue.

As the crusade went on, other celebrities showed up to see for themselves what was happening. The crowds grew too. They gathered hours early and swarmed into the tent to get a seat. As well, reporters and photographers recorded Billy Graham's every move. This was all totally unexpected and distracting. Indeed, in the middle of one of Billy's sermons he had to ask a newspaper photographer to climb down from a stepladder that had been placed right in front of the pulpit!

At the end of the week, someone said to Billy Graham, "You've been kissed by William Randolph Hearst." This meant that the Hearst newspapers were carrying the news of the Billy Graham crusade in a prominent and positive manner. Indeed, both the *Los Angeles Examiner* and *Herald Express* carried banner headlines. News of the revival in Los Angeles was soon picked up by the Associated Press and Billy Graham's name and reputation went national.[5]

THE MEDIA

The story of William Randolph Hearst committing his newspaper kingdom to publicizing the Graham crusade presents a fascinating tale in itself. The story goes that Hearst, at the urging of one of his house servants, got interested in Billy Graham. He liked what he heard and as a result penned a two-word note to his reporters: "Puff Graham." Some members of the family, however, later said that Hearst would not have expressed it that way. Regardless, the reporters were given some word from the newspaper tycoon and they began to publicize Billy Graham's ministry in an almost fanatical fashion.

ANOTHER CONVERT

At this stage another significant conversion took place. The West Coast "godfather" of syndicated crime at that time was Mickey Cohen. He became known as the Czar of the Los Angeles Underworld. Although many of his henchmen had been successfully prosecuted, authorities could not get enough evidence on Cohen to indict and convict him. One of his fellow crime masters was an electronics genius by the name of Jim Vaus. Vaus had been an officer in the U.S. Army during the Second World War and had developed outstanding electronic skills. But even while in the army, he had tampered with army equipment and was court-martialed. President Truman pardoned him, however, and thus he got off the hook.

Jim Vaus had a fascinating background. Being the son of a Baptist minister, to please his parents he attended a local Bible school for a period of time, but did not enter into the spirit of the institution. He became editor of the yearbook his senior year and embezzled the funds and was expelled. From there he went into the military and carried on his escapades. Upon discharge, Mickey Cohen hired him to set up electronic surveillance and various other electronic means of gathering information. Vaus developed a wiretapping system whereby all he needed to know was the telephone number in a given area and he could tap into the conversation. He did not need to attach wires; he would just sit in his hotel room and listen to any conversation in the city if he knew the telephone number. As can be imagined, many Hollywood stars engaged him in this enterprise. He also developed an electronic mechanism that would interrupt the teletype messages transmitted from New York to Los Angeles, interpret them and then feed the message back into the wire service without either party on the East or the West Coasts knowing their message had been intercepted and read. The purpose of this was to find out what horse had won a race on the East Coast, place a bet on the winning horse on the West Coast and then send the message back through the wire service. Using this system, large sums of money could be illegally won. Jim Vaus truly was a genius. And being close to Mickey Cohen, he had a great future in crime!

Like Suzy Hamblen, however, Jim Vaus's wife was a dedicated Christian. With all the notoriety Billy Graham received after Stuart

Hamblen's conversion, she talked her husband into attending one of the crusade meetings with her.

Jim Vaus attended the crusade the night before Billy Graham's thirty-first birthday. Vaus had to admit that it was hard to find fault with Billy Graham's method or preaching style. There was nothing new or radical about what he said; indeed, Jim Vaus had heard the gospel message proclaimed many times before. Surprisingly, there were no jokes or funny stories in Graham's sermon, just Bible stories. Yet something resonated in Jim Vaus's heart. He had to admit that the message that night had the ring of truth to it.

When Billy Graham gave the invitation at the end of his message, Jim Vaus fell deeply under conviction. He resisted for all he was worth, but somehow his legs would not carry him out of the tent. He had to stay. As he stood there, he heard Billy Graham say, "There is a man in this audience who has heard this story many times before, and who knows this is the decision he should make. Yet again he is saying no to God. He is hardening his heart, stiffening his neck, and he is going out of this place without Christ. And yet this may be the last opportunity God will give him to decide for Christ."[6] These words thrust Vaus into a deeper conflict of heart and mind. Graham continued, "This is your moment of decision."

Jim Vaus's heart raced. He broke into a cold sweat. Finally, grudgingly, he muttered, "I'll go." The battle was over. Vaus headed for the front. He was taken up to the small counseling tent. There he committed his life to Christ. "Lord, I believe this time from the bottom of my heart. . . . It's going to be almost impossible to straighten out this bewildered, tangled life of mine. But if you will straighten it up, I will turn it over to you, all of it," he prayed.[7]

The *Los Angeles Examiner* and *Herald Express* headlines the next morning read: "Wire Tapper Vaus Hits the Sawdust Trail." The news flashed across America. Armin Guesswein, on a train from Minneapolis to Chicago, heard the report on the train radio news bulletin. As soon as he reached Chicago, he called Billy Graham. "Armin," said Billy Graham on the other end of the line, "you had better get out here fast.

Something's happened and I don't know what it is. It is way beyond me."[8]

Of course the answer was that God had come in genuine reviving power.

MORE VICTORIES

There were other significant conversions too. Louis Zamperini, a track star who had won Olympic gold medals, came to Christ. This also made headlines. Los Angeles was stirred. Billy Graham's name was heralded across the country.

The Christ for Greater Los Angeles crusade turned out to be a startling event—an epic. But how did it come about? In the real sense of the word, it was the sovereignty of God, and Billy Graham's commitment to the Word of God and his faithful preaching of the gospel. As a result, the Holy Spirit fell. God's hour had arrived. As Billy Graham himself would later observe: "All [this] the Spirit has done, because the work has been God's and not man's. I want no credit or glory. I want the Lord Jesus to have it all."[9] The rest is history.

THE HISTORICAL QUESTION

From Los Angeles, Billy Graham had gone from strength to strength. But the statement "the rest is history" raises a significant issue: Is the ministry of Billy Graham a genuine historical phenomenon that finds itself in the mainstream of evangelical thought and the evangelistic credibility that has manifested itself throughout two thousand years of church history? Is the Billy Graham phenomenon in the latter half of the twentieth century something that will fade away and be forgotten, or will it find a legitimate place in the historical sweep of what God has done through two millennia of gospel proclamation? Has it made a contribution to the kingdom of God—and the world? If so, what precisely are Billy Graham's beliefs, methods, and principles in relation to evangelism, and how do these relate to evangelism through the ages?

The purpose of this book is to attempt to discover the answers to these questions. It must be understood at the outset that the Graham ministry unfolds in what has been termed "evangelicalism." Billy Graham is an evangelical evangelist. This calls for a definition of what sort of biblical Christianity evangelicalism is. A succinct definition is given by D. A. Carson, an able theologian, but it is rather academic.[10] Let me offer his definition (given in the footnote) in simpler terms. *Evangelical* refers to Christians who espouse a certain truth and who hold to a particular heritage. The truth that we espouse is that the Bible is the accurate, authoritative, and final Word of God. The heritage that we hold stems from the historic Protestantism from which evangelicals came. This heritage affirms several values:

- Christ is both God and man.

- Salvation is gained exclusively through personal faith in the finished work of Christ on the cross.

- Christ's death was planned by God the Father as payment for human sin, victory over Satan, and the inauguration of the kingdom of God.

- God is revealed in Jesus' life, death, resurrection, and ascension such that if we reject Jesus we are rejecting God.

- Jesus has sent us God the Holy Spirit as the "down payment" for the inheritance we will receive when Christ finally returns.

- The Spirit is displayed in the lives of God's people who are saved by grace—grace alone—that is accepted by faith alone.

- We respond to God's saving grace by reaching out to others in compassion and ministry.

This list joins what we mean by *evangel*—the gospel of Christ—to *evangelical*. It is out of this tradition that Billy Graham ministers.[11]

From this understanding of evangelicalism, twelve basic biblical, historical principles emerge by which we can investigate Billy Graham's evangelism. Right at the heart of all evangelical evangelism we find a balanced emphasis on:

1. The Holy Spirit

2. The call and the gospel

3. The sovereignty of God

4. The centrality of Christ

5. Holistic ministry

6. The Christian approach to suffering

7. The Bible

8. Boldness

9. Godliness

10. Revival

11. Worldwide ministry

12. The church

These twelve principles give biblical and historical authenticity to any evangelist who incorporates them into his or her ministry. That is how we evaluate such ministries, and that is how we will evaluate the historical and biblical authenticity of Billy Graham. These topics also provide an outline for this book.

Finally, one last word is called for before we delve into the Graham ministry. What do we mean by the word *evangelism*? Missiologist D. T. Niles defined the discipline as "one beggar telling another beggar where to find bread." That simple word does get to the heart of the matter. A more developed definition that fills out Niles's basic statement would be this:

Evangelism is a concerted, self-conscious effort to confront the unbeliever with the truth about and the claims of Christ with a view to leading that unbeliever into repentance toward God and faith in the Lord Jesus Christ. Thereby the new believer would also be brought into the fellowship of a local church where spiritual maturation can begin and be nurtured. There the new believer will find opportunities for service in and through the body of Christ, service that is aimed at establishing God's kingdom in the lives of as many as the Lord God will call.[12]

Evangelism is an important task and a vital role for the believer to fill. As has been said, evangelism is not just the *task* of the church, it is its very *nature*.

With these realities before us, we shall attempt to discover what the life, ministry, and impact of Billy Graham and his Evangelistic Association are all about and whether or not they truly measure up to authentic contributory evangelism.

2

The Holy Spirit

⤶∞⤷

"Without that wooing of the Holy Spirit, you can't come to Christ . . ."

— BILLY GRAHAM

Twenty-eight-year-old Billy Graham thrust his hands into his pockets as he walked off the stage at his third Youth for Christ crusade meeting in the small Welsh town of Gorseinon. As he walked down the stairs, just ahead of his chorus director, Cliff Barrows, Billy thought about the service that had just concluded. It had been like so many others he had held back in the United States, but somehow it had lacked something. But what? He grappled for a word. *Power.* Power was the closest he could come to describing what was missing. The meetings he had held so far were discouraging. The number of people gathered was small, and they fidgeted and whispered to each other while he preached. Billy Graham was well aware that he was in Wales, home to some of the greatest revival preachers of all time, and that his style was very different from what the Welsh were used to. But he had felt called to come to Wales, and God provided the money needed to get there.

He had felt this call soon after returning to the United States with

Torrey Johnson. In the spring the two men had been commissioned to go to Europe and establish the ministry of Youth for Christ. Billy had been discouraged by what he saw in Europe, particularly in England. The land of William Carey, Charles Spurgeon, and William Booth had become spiritually lethargic, and Billy Graham had seemed to lack what was needed to wake it up.

In late summer, Billy spoke at the Maranatha Bible Conference in Michigan. A man by the name of Clarence Benware heard him share about the great spiritual need in Europe, especially Great Britain. Benware came to Billy Graham after the service and gave him one hundred dollars saying, "You must go back."

This had struck a responsive chord in the evangelist's heart and he determined to return to Britain as soon as possible.

Now here he was in Wales, but so far things had not turned out as he had hoped. He had not been able to penetrate the tough Welsh exterior.

That night, lying in bed, Billy began to seek more of God. As he did so, a man kept coming to mind. The man was Steven Olford, a Welsh evangelist whom Billy and his small team had stopped to hear in Gravesend on their way to Wales. In that brief encounter Billy sensed Steven Olford had something in his life he desperately wanted. There was a dynamic exhilaration about Olford that bubbled over to all he talked to.

Steven Olford lived only eleven miles from where Billy Graham was currently staying. The next morning the evangelist determined to track him down and ask some serious questions about the power behind his ministry.

Delighted to hear from the young American evangelist, Steven Olford invited Billy to meet at a small hotel in the nearby village of Pontypridd. The two men began talking about spiritual things immediately. Billy soon learned that Steven Olford was the son of missionaries and had been raised in Africa. Olford's father had been led to Christ under the preaching of R. A. Torrey, while Steven himself had been led into a rich experience of the Holy Spirit under the influence of the Keswick movement in Great Britain. The Keswick movement emphasized the Spirit-filled life of total dedication to Christ.

Soon both men had their Bibles open and were down on their knees in their little hotel room. They sought God's heart and power for Billy Graham and his ministry. The hours rolled by as they turned pages together and shared the truths of God's Word.

By the end of the first day, Steven Olford had introduced Billy Graham to the concept of the "quiet time." Olford urged the young American to develop a life of prayer and Bible study that was consistent and disciplined and emanated from a hunger for God's best. The next day Olford led Billy Graham in a Bible study that expounded the power that comes into the life of the believer who is willing to submit moment by moment to the sovereignty of Christ and the authority of the Word.

At the end of the study, Steven Olford began to pray for Billy Graham. Billy prayed silently for a while and then, like Jacob of old he cried out, "Lord I will not let Thee go except Thou bless me."

Steven Olford testified to how God had completely turned his life inside out through experiencing the fullness and anointing of the Holy Spirit. As he spoke, Billy Graham replied with tears streaming down his face, "Steve, I see it. That's exactly what I want. It's what I need in my life." He then began pouring out his heart in a prayer of total dedication to the Lord.

Finally, he turned to Steven Olford. "My heart is so aflood with the Holy Spirit, I want to laugh and praise God all at the same time," he said. Graham then got up and began pacing back and forth across the narrow room declaring, "I have it. I'm filled." Finally he turned and grasped Steven Olford's hand. "This is a turning point in my life," he said, his eyes shining brightly.

On the third day, the two men went their separate ways, though Steven Olford promised to return for Billy's evangelistic meeting that night.

That night, for some unknown reason, the hall where Billy Graham was scheduled to preach was filled to overflowing, unlike the other nights when only a smattering of loyal churchgoers had shown up. From the moment Billy opened his mouth to preach, Olford sensed something was different. Billy preached a sermon he had preached before on the feast of Balshazzar. Yet this time it was delivered with a power and authority Billy had longed for, but never quite achieved. As soon as he gave an invitation to come forward, working men and women jammed the aisles, jostling to be the first to the front.

Later Steven Olford confessed that he was so moved by the change in Billy's demeanor that he could hardly concentrate on the road as he drove home. At home Olford's father took one look at his son and blurted out, "What on earth has happened?"

Olford sat down at the kitchen table and said, "Dad, something has happened to Billy Graham. The world is going to hear from this man. He is going to make his mark in history."

Billy Graham himself reflects back on that day as the definitive turning point in his ministry of evangelism. The experience has to a significant degree influenced Billy's whole understanding of the work of the Holy Spirit in evangelism. But just what are the foundational issues relating to the Holy Spirit in evangelism as Billy Graham sees them?

THE PERSON OF THE HOLY SPIRIT

In the years since his experience in that hotel room in Wales, Billy Graham has given much serious study and thought to pneumatology (the study of the Holy Spirit), and has produced a rather extensive book on the subject. His book, *The Holy Spirit*, was written some thirty-two years after his meeting with Steven Olford. *The Holy Spirit* presents a clear insight into Billy Graham's general view of the work of the Holy Spirit as it relates to evangelistic ministry. He begins, as one would expect, with the question, "Who is the Holy Spirit?"

The raising of this question and the practical issues that naturally follow is extremely timely. Numerous movements such as the Keswick movement, the Pentecostal-Charismatic movement, and the whole ethos that has been called the Third Wave have been building a resurgence of interest in pneumatology in the second half of the twentieth century that has almost been unparalleled in the history of the church.

Billy Graham firmly believes that there are two great gifts God gives to His born-again children. The first centers in the gift of forgiveness that brings one into a proper relationship with God, while the gift of the

Holy Spirit becomes the second. In this, Graham holds to the example of the Apostle Peter. Peter preached on the Day of Pentecost, "Repent, and let each of you be baptized in the name of Jesus Christ for the forgiveness of your sins; and you shall receive the gift of the Holy Spirit" (Acts 2:38). Billy Graham expresses it this way: "The work of the Son of God *for* us, and secondly the work of the Spirit of God *in* us, constitutes the essence of the spiritual experience."[1] He also declares, "To the gift of forgiveness God also adds the great gift of the Holy Spirit."[2]

Graham believes that Christian living depends on an understanding of the person and the work of the Holy Spirit. In this context he quotes a friend who said, "I need Jesus Christ for my eternal life and I need the Holy Spirit for my internal life."[3]

In light of the fact that the Lord Jesus Christ laid strong emphasis on the promised coming of the Holy Spirit, when that climactic event took place on the Day of Pentecost, the church was readied to launch the evangelistic thrust that has been going on now for two millennia. But who is this Holy Spirit according to Bill Graham's understanding?

The first major point that Graham makes is that the Holy Spirit must be understood as a *Person*. He must never be viewed as a mere "force for good." He is a Person; thus He should not be addressed as an *it*. The Spirit possesses an essential personhood. This can be demonstrated, Graham contends, because of the various actions that are attributed to Him in the Scriptures. The evangelist points out:

- He speaks (Acts 13:2).
- He intercedes (Romans 8:26).
- He testifies (John 15:26).
- He leads (Acts 8:29; Roman 8:14).
- He commands (Acts 16:6–7).
- He guides (John 16:13).
- He appoints (Acts 20:28).
- He can be lied to (Acts 5:3–4).

- He can be insulted (Hebrews 10:29).
- He can even be blasphemed (Matthew 12:31–32).

Each of these activities obviously speaks of personhood. The Holy Spirit is not an impersonal influence but is a Person. His actions and character, the Bible makes clear, demonstrate that the Spirit possesses a divine nature. He stands as a member of the Trinity. In a word, He is God. This leads Graham to a second listing of scriptural verification of this most important claim:

- The Spirit is eternal (Hebrews 9:14).
- The Spirit is all-powerful (Luke 1:35).
- The Spirit is everywhere present (Psalm 139:7).
- The Spirit is all knowing (1 Corinthians 2:10–11).
- The Spirit is called God (Acts 5:3–4; 2 Corinthians 3:18).
- The Spirit is Creator (Colossians 1:16–17).

It appears quite correct, Graham contends, to deduce from these scriptural attributes that the Holy Spirit is God.

Of course, this raises the mystery of the Trinity. Billy Graham is at times confronted with the question of the Trinity. He confesses, "When I first began to study the Bible years ago the doctrine of the Trinity was one of the most complex problems I had to encounter. I have never fully resolved it, for it contains an aspect of mystery. Though I do not totally understand it to this day, I accept it as a revelation of God." He goes on to say, "Thus there is nothing that God is that the Holy Spirit is not. He is very God of very God." And, of course, Graham says the same for the Son, Jesus Christ. But it still remains that the doctrine of the Trinity is shrouded in mystery, for the Bible declares that these Three are One. We simply cannot fully grasp that Trinitarian concept with our finite, rational minds. The Bible, which Billy Graham holds as the primary authority in Christian thought, declares it to be so. Thus we must "walk by faith, not by sight" (2 Corinthians 5:7). Graham brings it together in these words: "All of the essential aspects of deity belong to the Holy Spirit. We can say of Him exactly what was said of Jesus Christ. So we bow before Him, we worship; we accord Him every response Scripture requires to all-mighty God. Who is the Holy Spirit? He is God."[4]

But from the practical perspective, what does this imply relative to the Holy Spirit's work in this world, especially among people?

PRACTICAL OUTWORKING OF THE SPIRIT

It is one thing for the believer to have the Holy Spirit dwelling within him or her. Few theologians would disagree with that notion. But how does the Holy Spirit work out through our lives and what are His goals and intentions?

Billy Graham contends there are three main expressions in the Old Testament that speak of the work of the Holy Spirit in and through human beings.

1. The Holy Spirit came upon people (2 Chronicles 24:20).

2. He rested upon people (Numbers 11:25).

3. He filled people (Exodus 31:3).

All of these works of the Spirit speak primarily to the impact of the Holy Spirit in forming godliness and holiness in the believer and equipping them for service.

In summary, Billy Graham's understanding of the Old Testament work of the Holy Spirit can be capsulated in these words: "The Holy Spirit was at work before the world began. Then He renewed and fed this creation. He was active throughout the Old Testament, both in the world of nature and among people, guiding and delivering them through the judges, prophets, kings, and others."[5]

NEW TESTAMENT REALITIES

Billy Graham, moving to the New Testament revelation, points out that the Spirit's work in the four Gospels can be clearly seen as centering in the person and work of Jesus Christ. A further list surfaces from Graham's study of the four Gospels and related passages. Jesus was:

- Begotten of the Spirit (Luke 1:35).
- Baptized by the Spirit (John 1:32–33).
- Led by the Spirit (Luke 4:1).
- Anointed by the Spirit (Luke 4:18).
- Empowered by the Spirit (Matthew 12:28).
- Offered as an atonement by the Holy Spirit (Hebrews 9:14).
- Resurrected by the Spirit (Romans 8:11).

For these reasons Billy Graham insists that the Holy Spirit was fully operative in and through the entire life and work of Christ, beginning with His miraculous virgin birth. Although the doctrine of the virgin birth is disputed by some, Graham tenaciously holds that "any suggestion that God the Holy Spirit was not capable of bringing the virgin birth to pass is nonsense. If we believe that God is God—and that He rules the universe—nothing is too great for his limitless power. At all times God does whatever he chooses."[6] The Holy Spirit filled and operated in and through the entire "Christ event." And He works in people's lives today, pointing them to Jesus Christ.

THE SPIRIT AND SALVATION

How does Billy Graham view the Holy Spirit's work in bringing people to Christ? We get a clear indication in an interview with David Frost where Graham states, "I believe that when the Gospel is preached, however badly or however many mistakes . . . the Holy Spirit is the communicatory agent; that people are really not listening to me after about ten or fifteen minutes if I'm really preaching the Gospel. I think they're listening to another voice inside, the voice of the Holy Spirit, and the Holy Spirit is applying and communicating."[7]

Graham insists that the spiritual birth is the Spirit's work, and his early book *Born Again* attests to this fact. In that book Billy Graham writes, "Only God can give us the new birth we so desperately . . . need."[8] He also points out that the Lord Himself saw spiritual regeneration as the accomplishment of the Holy Spirit.

Billy Graham invariably turns to the third chapter of the Gospel of John, declaring that this passage constitutes one of the most relevant passages in the Bible concerning the work of the Holy Spirit in the new birth of salvation. Graham clearly contends that this radical change, being born again, stands as the most vital need in the inner being of every person. If it was true for Nicodemus, a religious leader of the Jewish people (John 3:1), it certainly is true for all. Moreover, this change cannot be earned or accomplished in one's own strength. Nor can anyone else effect this experience in a person's life. Graham argues that the new birth is solely the work of the Holy Spirit, and it comes about because of the death and resurrection of Jesus Christ.

Graham sees the Holy Spirit playing both a convicting and calling role in the new birth. The Holy Spirit first convicts of sin (John 16:7–11). As Graham says, "The Bible tells us . . . of the work of the Holy Spirit. What does He do? We are told that He convicts people of sin."[9] He pleads: "You cannot come to Jesus Christ unless the Spirit of God brings you and unless you yield to the prompting and urging of the Holy Spirit. I beg of you to come to Christ while there is yet time."[10]

Contemporary New Testament scholars agree. For instance, George Beasley-Murray has said that John in his Gospel "underscores the necessity of the spirit's illumination to grasp the revelation of God in and through His Son."[11]

In his autobiography, Billy Graham confesses of his own ministry of evangelism, "I am absolutely helpless and only the Holy Spirit can penetrate the minds and hearts of those who are without Christ . . . all I am doing is sowing seed. It is God—and only God—who can make the seed bear fruit."[12]

Billy Graham, by the Holy Spirit, gives such a heart call because he realizes one of the most devastating effects of human sin resides in its ability by Satan to blind people to its destructiveness. He points out that Paul made this clear in 2 Corinthians 4:4: "In whose case the god of this world has blinded the minds of the unbelieving, that they might not see the light of the gospel of the glory of Christ, who is the image of God." The Holy Spirit alone can remove the blinders and enable people to see their sin and need. Thus the Holy Spirit is called "the Spirit of truth" (John 14:17).

In the context of conviction, the Holy Spirit uses the Word of God. Thus apart from the convicting, convincing ministry of the Holy Spirit, no one could ever clearly see their sin, much less the truth of Jesus and His power to forgive sins and create new life. Therefore, says Billy Graham, a solemn warning must be heralded on this issue, because the Bible declares that a point can be reached in the hardening of one's heart against the Spirit's conviction where He will no longer strive. Proverbs 29:1 states, "A man who hardens his neck after much reproof will suddenly be broken beyond remedy."

But as the Holy Spirit enlightens concerning "sin and righteousness and judgment," He then calls and draws the sinner to the Savior. He reveals the risen Christ as one's only hope. He leads the open-hearted person to repentance and faith as he or she embraces the Lord Jesus Christ for all He is and all He has done. As Graham declares in his prophetic book, *Approaching Hoofbeats,* "It would be completely futile for me to preach the gospel, as I have done to many people every year for the past generation, if the Holy Spirit were not convicting the hearers of their sin and prompting them to open their hearts to Christ."[13] As Billy Graham has stated, "The Holy Spirit is the great communicator. Without His supernatural work, there would be no such thing as conversion."[14] But there is more.

THE APPROPRIATENESS OF SALVATION

Billy Graham goes on to address issues concerning the agency of the Holy Spirit in the life of the believer after he or she has been led by the Spirit to redemptive faith in Jesus Christ. He points out that we live in a time when contention concerning the inner work of the Spirit of God abounds. The advent of the Pentecostal-Charismatic movement has helped to precipitate the issues that have arisen. Though much good has come out of this and similar movements, considerable uneasiness and misunderstanding have also developed. Therefore, Graham feels that he must state his convictions concerning the work of the Holy Spirit in areas of the baptism of the Holy Spirit and the infilling of the Holy Spirit.

THE "BAPTISM"

When addressing what has basically come out of the holiness and perfectionist movements known as "the baptism of the Holy Spirit," Billy Graham expresses his understanding of the issue by referring to a personal illustration. While still a young student in Bible school in Florida, a preacher asked him, "Young man, have you been baptized with the Holy Spirit?"

Billy replied, "Yes sir."

"When were you baptized with the Holy Spirit?" the preacher asked.

Billy Graham replied, "The moment I received Jesus Christ as my Savior." Although the preacher disagreed with him, the reply states Billy's basic and ongoing conviction. He holds that the baptism of the Holy Spirit, although it was initiated at Pentecost, becomes the experience of all who have received Jesus Christ as Lord and Savior. He contends that all true believers are baptized in the Spirit, and he quotes as a scriptural reference 1 Corinthians 12:13: "For by one Spirit we were all baptized into one body."

THE INFILLING

Billy Graham goes on to point out that there are additional experiences of the Holy Spirit, in particular being "filled with the Spirit" (Ephesians 5:18). We have seen this principle at work in the opening illustration of this chapter. Graham expresses his position as "one baptism but many fillings." That is to say, when a person is saved they are baptized in the Holy Spirit. But the fact that the Ephesians 5:18 passage is a present imperative implies that God expects and commands people to experience the Spirit's continuing fullness. Billy grants there may be some differences in opinion that are merely semantic, but this particular approach he contends is foundational to the inner work of the Holy Spirit in believers. He confesses, "During my ministry I have known many Christians who agonize, labor, struggle, and pray to 'get the Spirit.' I used to wonder if I had been wrong in thinking that having been baptized by the Spirit into the body of Christ on the day of my conversion I needed no other baptism. But the longer I have studied the Scriptures the more I have become convinced that I was right."[15] From this position he draws several conclusions.

He holds that a person is "baptized in the Spirit" on conversion, but he or she can also certainly be "filled with the Spirit." The gift of the Spirit can encompass both at the new birth. Therefore, no Christian needs to strive or "pray through to get the Spirit." He or she has already received the Holy Spirit when they invited Christ into their life through repentance and faith. This becomes clear as exemplified in the experience of Philip and the Ethiopian eunuch recorded in Acts 8. It certainly is true in the case of Paul's encounter with the Ephesians who only had a partial understanding of the Gospel (Acts 19). Thus Billy Graham concludes that all true believers share in the Pentecostal event, as he states, "Since the baptism with the Spirit occurs at the time of regeneration, Christians are never told in the Scriptures to seek it."[16]

Using this as a starting point, Graham shares that he has become convinced that many of the things some attach to the so-called *baptism* of the Holy Spirit actually belong to the experience of being *filled* with the Spirit. He lays much importance on the infilling of the Spirit for believers. In stressing being Spirit-filled he goes so far as to say, "I think it proper to say that anyone who is not Spirit-filled is a defective Christian. Paul's command to the Ephesian Christians, 'Be filled with the Spirit,' is binding on all of us Christians everywhere in every age."[17]

Why should it not be seen as an option? Because in the final analysis being filled with the Spirit is no more or no less than complete surrender to Christ's lordship in daily living. As Graham has said, "To be filled with the Spirit is to be controlled by the Spirit. It is to be so yielded to Christ that our supreme desire is to do His will . . . as we grow in Christ, our goal is to be controlled by the Spirit."[18]

At the same time, Billy Graham does not wish to be divisive. He strongly emphasizes that the Holy Spirit creates unity. The Pauline passage on which he has relied so heavily, 1 Corinthians 12:13, speaks of the unity of the Spirit. He contends that the doctrine of the Holy Spirit should be a unifying factor, not a discordant one. In the final analysis, the Holy Spirit's primary work in the believer centers in creating a life of holiness. And all Christians would certainly agree to that. But Graham does contend that the life of holiness comes about by the infilling of the Holy Spirit. What does he mean by this?

HOLINESS

As is clear, Graham argues that any believer who does not walk in the Spirit's fullness becomes a defective Christian. This is predicated upon the fact that Paul's admonition in Ephesians 5:18 is a command. To fail here creates a pattern of carnality in the Christian's life. The devotional life tends to be erratic, the Word of God becomes neglected, prayer is a chore, and as with Lot in Sodom, sensitivity to sin is bludgeoned, with known sins remaining unconfessed. He concludes, "There are no exceptions. We must conclude that since we are ordered to be filled with the Spirit, we are sinning if we are not filled. And our failure to be filled with the Spirit constitutes one of the greatest sins against the Holy Spirit."[19]

Not only are these realities evident in the epistles of Paul, but the Lord Jesus Christ emphasized these principles as well. In our Lord's dialogue with the woman at the Samaritan well, He said He would impart to believers a well of water springing up to life (John 4:13–14). In John 7, Jesus went on to say in verse 38, "He who believes in Me, as the Scripture said, 'From his innermost being shall flow rivers of living water.'" As Billy Graham puts it, "This is not a pond of water, but an ever-flowing spring."[20]

The purpose behind all this rests in the fact that when believers are filled with the Holy Spirit they become a vessel of blessing to the world. And whether that service is large or small in the eyes of the world, God smiles upon it.

Billy Graham points out, however, that one must be careful to avoid overstressing the ongoing work of the Holy Spirit. Much unbiblical terminology and many unbiblical ideas are bandied about today like, "the second baptism," "the second blessing," or "the second work of grace." He points out that these terms cannot be found in the Scriptures. He contends that the Holy Spirit's work is not a second or a third or a thousandth. The Spirit operates on a continual basis in the Christian experience. Moreover, the central thrust of the idea revolves not around getting more of the Holy Spirit, but the Holy Spirit getting more of the believer. Paul's admonition to be filled with the Spirit means to be dominated, controlled, and utterly possessed of the Holy Spirit. Thus one becomes an instrument in the hands of God for ministry and service to the glory of Christ.

MATURITY

Billy Graham further sees the experience of the fullness of the Spirit as a vital necessity for spiritual growth and maturity. The Holy Spirit operates as the one who sanctifies. That is, He makes the believer holy. When a person first comes to faith in Christ, their spiritual capacity and understanding is quite limited. But the Spirit-filled believer grows rapidly, and Christian maturity develops. Peter urged us to "grow in the grace and knowledge of our Lord and Savior Jesus Christ" (2 Peter 3:18). That is accomplished by the inner working of God's Spirit.

However, Billy Graham injects another word of caution, stating that the actual experience of walking in the fullness of the Holy Spirit must not necessarily be equated with a deep emotional experience. He grants that at times the Holy Spirit may come in a forceful emotional fashion, yet at other times it may be no more emotional than a consciousness of His presence and blessings. As long as the basic price of commitment is paid, then the emotions that follow rest in the hands of God and one should not seek for mere emotional experiences.

There are certainly times, though, when God does give a person a special touch. Billy Graham remembers well one such time in his own life. In 1954 Graham and his wife, Ruth, set sail for England for his famous Harringay crusade. The crusade became a memorable moment in the history of British evangelism. Some would say that it was the nearest thing to true revival that London had seen since the days of Wesley and Whitefield.

However, unaware of what was about to happen, Billy Graham struggled in a deep spiritual battle as his ship crossed the Atlantic. He was all but overtaken with a sense of depression and a frightening feeling of inadequacy. He gave himself to prayer night and day. Later, he said he learned what the Apostle Paul meant when he admonished God's people to "pray without ceasing" (1 Thessalonians 5:17). He related the event this way: "One day on the ship I was in a prayer meeting with my wife and colleagues, and a break came. As I wept before the Lord, I was filled with the deep assurance that power belonged to God and He was faithful. I had been baptized by the Spirit into the body of Christ when I was saved, but I believe God gave me a special anointing on the way to England. From that moment on I was confident that God the Holy Spirit was in control for the task of that 1954 crusade in London."[21] The Holy Spirit *baptizes, fills*, and, at times for special needs, *anoints* His people. But why does God do this gracious work in believers?

REASONS

It is clear, according to Billy Graham, that God fills His people with the Spirit for a purpose. This purpose essentially centers in serving Jesus Christ. In the case of the evangelist it is to empower the proclamation of the gospel for salvation. Graham often quotes Paul's statement to the Corinthians: "And my message and my preaching were not in persuasive words of wisdom, but in demonstration of the Spirit and of power, that your faith should not rest on the wisdom of men, but on the power of God" (1 Corinthians 2:4–5). Billy Graham grants the possibility to seek the fullness of the Holy Spirit for the wrong reasons, such as self-enjoyment of self-glorification. The ultimate and final purpose of the Spirit's infilling for any believer is that his or her service might be effective and bring honor and glory to Jesus Christ. The Westminster Confession has it correct: "The chief end of man is to glorify God and enjoy Him forever." The Lord Jesus Christ Himself said, "He [the Holy Spirit] shall glorify Me; for He shall take of Mine, and shall disclose it to you" (John 16:14). The Holy Spirit does not even glorify Himself; He glorifies Jesus Christ.

Given this, Billy Graham asks: Why do we need the fullness of the Holy Spirit? He answers, "Because only in the power of the Spirit can we live a life that glorifies God."[22] The Holy Spirit becomes the Agent whereby a person can bring glory to God through a life of effective service, evangelism, and holiness. Little wonder Graham also says, "I am convinced that to be filled with the Spirit is not an option, but a necessity. It is indispensable for the abundant life and for fruitful service. The Spirit-filled life is not abnormal; it is the normal Christian life. Anything less is sub-normal; it is less than what God wants and provides for his children."[23]

The question then arises: According to Billy Graham, what are the prerequisites for this level of Christian living? His answer is embodied in three concepts: *understanding, submission,* and *walking by faith.*

Understanding serves as the first step in being filled with the Spirit—understanding that God has given His Holy Spirit and deeply desires His people to be filled with all His fullness. Furthermore, one must recognize that such a blessing is not a mere option, but a command. Not only that, it must be clearly grasped that unconfessed sin cannot be tolerated. Indeed, Billy Graham says, "Before we can be filled with the Holy Spirit we must deal honestly and completely with every known sin in our lives." He goes into considerable detail in this respect. Sin has to be dealt with in the area of the offense through confession, restitution, and a genuine broken spirit before God. The entire process of seeking the Spirit's fullness reduces itself to this: Who controls life, self or Christ? Anything less than absolute submission to Christ is sin and must be confessed and forsaken before the richness of the Holy Spirit will be experienced. This leads to the second point—submission.

Billy Graham sees two steps in the concept of submission. The first step centers in the area of confession and repentance as stated above. Anything in which the Holy Spirit has been grieved must be acknowledged and surrendered to God so that the blood of Christ may cleanse that particular sin (1 John 1:9). In the second step, we must yield ourselves utterly and completely to the will of God. Paul points this out very clearly in Romans 12:1–2: "I urge you therefore, brethren, by the mercies of God, to present your bodies a living and holy sacrifice, acceptable to God, which is your spiritual service of worship. And do not be conformed to this world, but be transformed by the renewing of your mind, that you may prove what the will of God is, that which is good and acceptable and perfect." Billy saw this clearly in the little Welsh hotel with Steven Olford.

Graham holds that surrender is a definite and conscious act on the part of the believer in obedience to the Word of God. In one sense, this act constitutes the heart and essence of the entire human-divine encounter. To be filled with the Spirit means to be dominated by the Spirit, and that means being in submission to Him in all things. In a word, obedience assumes a central place in the Christian's life. Right there the third prerequisite arises.

The Bible tells us that cleansed, obedient believers walk by faith. Billy Graham sees this as essential to the Spirit-filled life. Moving into the Spirit's fullness does not necessarily mean copious quantities of agonizing and interceding and pleading with God. Rather it rests upon reaching out in faith and bidding Him to fill us. Graham puts it this way,

> Now when we yield ourselves to Christ and follow Him as Lord of our lives, we know that something has happened. The Holy Spirit has taken over our lives, to guide and empower us. We are now to walk by faith, reckoning ourselves to be dead to sin and alive to God. We are filled with the Holy Spirit; now we are to live in light of this truth. This is not pretending; it is acting on God's promise.[24]

Billy Graham stresses that the experience rests in faith upon one's identification with Christ in death and resurrection. Quoting Paul, he states that we are to "consider [ourselves] to be dead to sin, but alive to God in Christ Jesus" (Romans 6:11). Paul brings this all together in

Galatians 2:20 when he says, "I have been crucified with Christ; and it is no longer I who live, but Christ lives in me; and the life which I now live in the flesh I live by faith in the Son of God, who loved me, and delivered Himself up for me."

In concluding his emphasis on the faith aspect of the Spirit's fullness, Graham points out that if we are knowledgeable and understanding of our needs, and have every known sin confessed and are submitted to God, then we can reach out in faith and say, "I know I am filled with the Holy Spirit." And that is not presumption, it is simply taking God at His Word (Luke 11:13).

In light of all these truths concerning the work of the Holy Spirit, the evangelist sets out his understanding of the wonderful biblical truth that God by the Spirit lives within all believers and leads them into godliness, spiritual maturity, and effective service. And that surely relates to evangelism.

THE SPIRIT-FILLED MAN

Few disagree that Billy Graham fills the criteria of the Spirit-filled evangelist as exemplified by the Apostle Peter. Several things can be said in this regard. First, from a traditional evangelical perspective, he has a sound biblical theology of the Holy Spirit. There are, however, those who disagree with his views. Yet he falls within the bounds of what the evangelical church has held and taught for over two millennia. He has a basic historical, biblical, evangelical understanding and authenticity.

In turn, Graham has made a significant contribution to the body of Christ in heralding the truth of the Holy Spirit in the life of the believer. This truth has transformed more than a few churches.

Moreover, countless people have been challenged by Billy Graham's teaching and ministry, and consequently have been enriched and brought into the fullness of the Spirit-filled, Spirit-led, and Spirit-empowered life.

Finally, and of most importance, millions have been converted to Christ through Billy's Spirit-filled preaching of the gospel. This leads to the next chapter on Billy's call to preach the Good News of Jesus Christ.

3

The Full and True Gospel

"I'm going to preach His birth, death, and resurrection. I'll preach it until Jesus comes."

— BILLY GRAHAM

Billy Graham gave his typical invitation; unfortunately, few people responded. He had been experiencing "good" results in his services up until this time, but the lack of response this night bothered him. Later, as he was being driven back to his hotel, he wondered what he could have done differently to encourage the decision he was asking people to make. "What happened? Why did so few come forward?" he wondered out loud.

The driver of the car, who had been at the meeting, thought for a moment and then said simply, "You did not preach the Cross."

Immediately Billy Graham fell under conviction. Why hadn't he seen it before? As soon as he got back to his hotel room, Billy fell to his knees and made a promise to God, "I'll never preach again without stressing the Cross."

From that moment on, the cross of Christ has remained central to the preaching of Billy Graham. In relation to this, Graham tells the following story: "Mother always told me to preach the gospel, and keep it simple. Two weeks before she went to be with the Lord she admonished me with the same words. I said, 'Mother, I'm going to preach His birth, death, and resurrection. I'll preach it until Jesus comes.' She squeezed my hand and said, 'I believe it.'"[1]

Billy Graham's mother was right, and he has not deviated from his promise to her. His closest associate, T. W. Wilson, has said, "I have never heard him compromise. He is committed to the exclusiveness of the Gospel."[2]

But many people say they preach the gospel. Indeed the Apostle Paul warned believers, "But even though we, or an angel from heaven, should preach to you a gospel contrary to that which we have preached to you, let him be accursed" (Galatians 1:8). The pure, unadulterated full gospel must be tenaciously held at any cost. But what is this gospel, and does Billy Graham truly preach it? Does he deserve an honored place among those we celebrate as having proclaimed that gospel down through two thousand years of evangelical church history?

The answer to assessing this full gospel can be found in the Greek word *kerygma*. Briefly stated, *kerygma* is the public declaration of the gospel to the non-Christian world with a view to converting that world. New Testament scholar C. H. Dodd says in his classic book *The Apostolic Preaching and Its Development*: "For the early church, then, to preach the gospel was by no means the same thing as to deliver moral instruction or exhortation. While the church was concerned to hand on the teaching of the Lord, it was not by this that it made converts. It was by *kerygma*, said Paul . . . that it pleased God to save men."[3]

Paul's gospel, according to C. H. Dodd, can be summarized as follows:

1. Prophecies are fulfilled, and the new age is inaugurated by the coming of Christ.

2. Jesus was born of the seed of David.

3. He died according to the Scriptures to deliver us out of the present evil age.

4. He was buried.

5. He rose on the third day according to the Scriptures.

6. He is exalted at the right hand of God, as Son of God and Lord of the quick and dead.

7. He will come again as Judge and Savior.[4]

C. H. Dodd is not the only scholar who has discussed the meaning of *kerygma*. Another prominent scholar who has made an extensive study of the subject is Michael Green. Green suggests three basic points as being essential to the word of salvation for all peoples of all times. First, the early church preached a Person. Their message was unapologetically Christ-centered. They dwelt not so much on Jesus' life and public ministry; but rather on His death and resurrection.

Second, Michael Green holds that the infant church proclaimed the gift of forgiveness, the gift of the Holy Spirit, and the gift of adoption and reconciliation. This kind of grace made "no people" the "people of God."

Third, the first-century church looked for a positive response on the part of its hearers. The apostles were anything but shy in asking people to decide then and there, for or against Jesus Christ. These early preachers declared all people must do three things in the light of the gospel:

They must repent. This stands first.

They must exercise faith. A continuing life of faith is called for, but it must begin by a "leap of faith." Moreover, true faith must be viewed as inseparable from repentance.

They must be baptized. This act of obedience serves as the seal on God's offer of forgiveness and the essence of one's overt response to that offer in repentance and faith.

More recently, in his helpful book *A Faith to Proclaim*, James Stewart declares the first axiom of evangelism to be that the evangelist must be sure of his message. He then presents what he believes constitutes relevant gospel proclamation. According to Stewart the following five principles must be found in all evangelistic proclamation. An evangelist must proclaim:

- The Incarnation.
- Forgiveness of sin.
- The Cross.
- That Christ has been raised from the dead.
- Christ Himself. Moreover, the message presented must never be just a cold, conceptualized theology or philosophy. Christianity is the experience of a vital relationship to the living Christ, and the message needs to reflect this vitality.

Perhaps the best summation of *kerygma* can be found in Peter's sermon preached on the Day of Pentecost along with the surrounding events as recorded in Acts 1 and 2. Ten basic principles emerge in this context. These principles are a "litmus test" to the faithfulness of the gospel preached by any evangelist of any age as he or she attempts to fulfill their calling. These essential principles are as follows:

1. Jesus Christ of Nazareth is the fulfillment of Old Testament prophecies concerning the coming of God's kingdom and salvation through His Messiahship (Acts 2:16–21).

2. The incarnation of the Son of God (Acts 2:22).

3. Jesus lived a sinless, revealing, perfect life doing many glorious miracles (Acts 2:22).

4. Jesus Christ was crucified on the cross to make atonement for the sin of the world (Acts 2:23).

5. Jesus Christ was raised bodily from the dead, thereby triumphing over sin, death, hell, and the grave (Acts 2:24), and ascended into heaven to be at the Father's right hand (Acts 1:9).

6. Jesus Christ is coming again to usher in the fullness of the kingdom (Acts 1:11).

7. The call comes to repent and believe and follow Christ in commitment to life as symbolized in baptism (Acts 2:38).

8. The one who responds receives the promise of forgiveness of sins (Acts 2:38).

9. That one receives the gift of the Holy Spirit (Acts 2:38).

10. A whole new life is experienced by the one who responds (Acts 2:42).

If these points are the litmus test for the authentic gospel, then where does the gospel as preached by Billy Graham fall in relation to them? Is it the authentic, historical, evangelical gospel? Let us take a closer look and see.

JESUS CHRIST THE FULFILLMENT OF THE MESSIANIC PROMISE

C. H. Dodd makes the point that the messianic reign was fully prophesied in the Old Testament and is a part of the gospel message. It constitutes an important element of the message. Billy Graham agrees with this assessment. He says, "His [Jesus'] death had been prophesied."[5] He elaborates further on this point. "Fulfilled prophecies witness to the Bible's accuracy hundreds of years before Christ." It was predicted that He would:

- Be born of a virgin (Isaiah 7:14; see Luke 2:26–35).
- Be born in Bethlehem (Micah 5:2; see Luke 2:4–7).
- Live a sinless life (Isaiah 53:9; see 2 Corinthians 5:21).
- Be put to death (Isaiah 53:5, 7; see Matthew 27:35).
- Cry from the cross, "My God, my God, why have you forsaken me?" (Psalm 22:1; see Matthew 27:46).[6]

Through these points we can see that Billy Graham clearly believes Jesus Christ is the fulfillment of many Old Testament prophecies, thus sealing Christ as the legitimate Messiah of both Jews and Gentiles.

THE INCARNATION

The basic issue of the entire Christian faith ultimately is this: Was Jesus truly God robed in human flesh? Is the Incarnation a true historical reality? Or should Jesus be seen as no more than just a very gifted spiritual leader who had "more of God in Him" than most?

Billy Graham is unequivocal on the subject of the Incarnation. He makes it clear exactly where he stands in such statements as: "At the heart of that good news is Jesus Christ. He is God in human flesh"[7] and "Jesus Christ made the astonishing claim that He was God. Either Christ was God, or He was a blasphemous liar, or a maniac."[8]

One of Graham's fullest statements on the issue is as follows:

You cannot read the New Testament without realizing that Jesus claimed—frequently and clearly—that He was the divine Son of God, sent from Heaven to save us from our sins. It is also clear from the Gospel accounts that His disciples did not believe His claims at first, but only gradually came to understand and accept them (particularly after the resurrection, which proved beyond doubt that He was who He claimed to be). . . .

Anyone could claim to be divine, of course, but did Jesus do anything to backup His claim? Yes! His miracles, which were witnessed by thousands, were an evidence of His unique nature. His resurrection verified His claim. But why is this important? It is important because only a divine Savior could truly save us from our sins. If Christ were just a great religious teacher, He would have no power to bring us forgiveness. But because He was God's only Son, He could die as a perfect and final sacrifice for our sins. Have you accepted the gift of forgiveness He offers you?[9]

From this it is obvious that Billy Graham accepts the traditional historical evangelical view on the Incarnation. Not only does he accept and believe it, he preaches it as part of the gospel. He continually reminds his audience that, as Paul says to the Philippians, "He [Jesus] existed in the form of God, did not regard equality with God a thing to be grasped, but emptied Himself, taking the form of a bond-servant, and being made in the likeness of men" (Philippians 2:6–7).

CHRIST LIVED A PERFECT LIFE

If we take seriously the fact that the incarnate Christ is the final revelation of God, then the life He lived on earth must have been incredibly different from any other life ever lived. As we study the Scriptures in this regard, three things become apparent. First, Jesus never sinned "nor was any deceit found in His mouth" (1 Peter 2:22). Second, Jesus Christ came and revealed God. His perfection in spirit, in attitude, and in word showed us what God is like. Jesus was conscious of this role and said to Thomas, "He who has seen Me has seen the Father" (John 14:9). Third, He lived victoriously. That is to say, He succeeded where Adam failed. These are important points, and Billy Graham affirms each of them. He says, "These essential truths concerning the humanity of Jesus I positively affirm."[10]

CHRIST DIED ON THE CROSS

As we learned in the opening paragraphs of this chapter, Billy Graham discovered his message had the most power when he preached the message that Christ died on the cross. This is further illustrated by a quote from his book *Peace with God*. He says,

> Man's only salvation from sin stands on a lonely, barren skull-shaped hill; a thief hangs on one cross, a murderer on another, and between them a man with a crown of thorns. . . . The blow that crucified Christ became the blow that opened the gates for man to become free. Sin's masterpiece of shame and hate became God's masterpiece of mercy and forgiveness. Through the death of the Lamb of God upon the cross, sin itself was crucified for those who believe in Christ. His death is the foundation of our hope, the promise of our triumph![11]

From this there can be no doubt that Billy Graham has a firm grasp of the importance and meaning of the atoning death of Christ as understood by historic Christianity.

THE RESURRECTION

Billy Graham holds and preaches most emphatically the bodily resurrection of Jesus Christ. He calls the Easter event the foundation of faith. In his popular work *How to Be Born Again,* he writes, "The basis for our belief in Jesus Christ is in His resurrection." He also cites theologian Karl Barth as saying that without the "physical resurrection of Jesus Christ there is no salvation." Graham goes on to declare, "If Christ were entombed someplace in a grave near Jerusalem where millions who visit Israel each year could walk by a grave and worship Him, then Christianity would be a fable. The apostle said, 'If Christ has not been raised, then our preaching is in vain and your faith is in vain. . . . If Christ has not been raised, your faith is futile and you are still in your sins' (1 Corinthians 15:14; 17 RSV). . . . Without the resurrection, the cross is, meaningless."[12]

Graham contrasts the Christian faith in the Resurrection against other world religions such as Judaism, Islam, and the like, and states, "Only Christianity claims resurrection for its founder."[13] He then goes on to show the evidence for the resurrection of Jesus, listing realities like the empty tomb and the testimony of reliable witnesses. He quotes philosopher and theologian C. S. Lewis: "The first fact in the history of Christendom is a number of people who say they have seen the Resurrection. If they had died without making anyone else believe this 'gospel' no gospels would ever have been written."[14] Obviously, Billy Graham believes that without the resurrection of Jesus Christ the Christian religion is a sham. He has said, "All of Christianity as a system of truth collapses if the Resurrection is rejected . . . resurrection is central to the Gospel." Further, he points out that a personal salvation experience is directly related to belief in the Resurrection.[15]

Moreover, Billy Graham is emphatic about the *bodily* resurrection of Jesus. He says, "The resurrection was not disembodied, it was physical."[16]

John Stott has expressed in a personal interview that he would like to see Billy Graham emphasize the resurrection of Christ more. Be that as it may, Graham holds tenaciously to the fact of the Resurrection. He has said, "This event was unique in human history and is fundamental to

Christianity."[17] Beyond any wisp of doubt, Billy Graham believes in and preaches the bodily resurrection of Jesus Christ, and understands that it is an essential point in the proclamation of the gospel. And, of course, with that truth is the fact of Jesus' ascension to the Father. This leads us to the next major point.

JESUS IS COMING AGAIN: KINGDOM FULLNESS

"He is coming. One of these days the sky is going to break open and the Lord Jesus Christ will come back. He will set up His reign upon this planet, and we're going to have peace and social justice. What a wonderful time that's going to be."[18] With these words Billy Graham takes his stand on the biblical declaration that Christ will return to earth. He understands the promise of Christ's second advent very literally. He knows that on Ascension Day (Acts 1) the angels emphatically promised that "this Jesus, who has been taken up from you into heaven, will come in just the same way as you have watched Him go into heaven" (Acts 1:11). A new heaven and earth await the believer in Christ on the glorious day of Jesus' return (Revelation 21–22).

Graham presents five reasons for believing in the return of Christ:

- The prophecies of the Old Testament state it.
- Jesus' own statements confirm it.
- Satan must be dealt with.
- The present world is in crisis.
- The dead must be raised. He believes that all true Christians will be resurrected from the grave and Jesus will usher in, as he expresses it, "peace and social justice." All this then leads to the call for a response by those who hear the call to repentance and faith.

REPENTANCE

Repentance and *faith* must not be seen as synonyms. In this respect Billy Graham defines *repentance* and *faith* clearly when issuing a call to Christ and conversion. We begin with the call to repentance and Graham's understanding of what this means. Billy Graham has written:

What did Jesus mean by the word *repent*? Why does it appear over and over throughout the Bible? If you look in a modern dictionary you will find that repent means "to feel sorry for, or to regret." But the original words that Jesus spoke meant a great deal more than that. They meant a great deal more than just regretting and feeling sorry about sin. The biblical word *repent* means "to change, or to turn." It is a word of power and action. It is a word that signifies a complete turnabout in the individual. When the Bible calls upon us to repent of sin, it means that we should turn away from sin, that we should do an about-face and walk in the opposite direction from sin and all that it implies.

Too many modern Christians have lost sight of what the Bible means when it talks about repentance. They think that repentance is little more than shaking their heads over their sins and saying, "My, but I'm sorry I did that!" and then continuing to live just as they have lived before.

True repentance means "to change, to turn away from, to go in a new direction."[19]

Graham then points out that repentance is not *mere* emotion. There are three aspects of true turning from sin to God. "First, there is a knowledge of sin. . . . Second, emotions are involved . . . true emotions and depth of feeling. . . . Third, repentance involves the will . . . [and] only the Spirit of God can give you the determination necessary for true repentance."[20]

This is a large order to be sure, and Graham regretfully states: "There are thousands of people in America who have their names on church rolls . . . but they have never really expressed true repentance."[21]

Billy Graham must be seen as one who fully understands the biblical meaning and call to repentance. In his crusades he faithfully issues the call to turn from sin to God. In this respect he is preaching the authentic gospel.

FAITH

The Bible stresses faith as a vital exercise in coming to know God. Scripture passages that drive this reality home appear on almost every page of the Bible. The following are a few of the many verses Billy Graham cites when explaining the importance of faith.

John 14:11—Believe Me that I am in the Father, and the Father in Me; otherwise believe on account of the works themselves.

Acts 16:31—Believe in the Lord Jesus, and you shall be saved, you and your household.

John 1:12—But as many as received Him, to them He gave the right to become children of God, even to those who believe in His name.

Romans 5:1—Therefore having been justified by faith, we have peace with God through our Lord Jesus Christ.

Ephesians 2:8–9—For by grace you have been saved through faith; and that not of yourselves, it is the gift of God; not as a result of works, that no one should boast.

When he preaches, Billy Graham always makes certain to point out that a person is not saved by faith; rather, they are saved by *grace* through *faith*. Thus faith becomes the channel through which the saving grace of God flows. Then comes a whole new life, beginning with forgiveness.

FORGIVENESS

Billy Graham strongly stresses the fact that forgiveness and its attending peace of heart can be fully experienced: "You can lose your despised and sinful self and step forth a new person, a clean and peaceful being from whom sin has been washed away."[22] In the book *How to Be Born Again*, he puts it this way: "In place of a broken relationship between God and the sinner, 'atonement' results and 'he shall be forgiven' by God."[23] He brings it all together in summary fashion with these words:

"Your sins are forgiven you for His name's sake" (1 John 2:12). What a stupendous promise! Throughout the New Testament we learn that the one who receives Christ as Lord and Savior also receives, immediately, the gift of forgiveness. God's forgiveness is not just a casual statement; it is the complete blotting out of all the dirt and degradations of our past, present, and future. . . . God's goodness in forgiving us goes even further when we realize that when we are converted we are also declared just, which means that in God's sight we are without guilt, clothed forever with Christ's righteousness.[24]

These key statements certainly cover the issue. In Christ we are forgiven. We find peace at last. Guilt is gone. This is part of the authentic gospel. But there is more involved in the full gospel than forgiveness of sins, as important as that obviously is.

THE GIFT OF THE SPIRIT

When people come to Christ in repentance and faith, they receive the gift of the Holy Spirit. The previous chapter has been devoted to this truth, but a reminder of what Graham says about the gift of the Holy Spirit is appropriate here. He has preached: "Each Christian has the Holy Spirit . . . (and) when we are yielded to God and His will, we are filled with the Holy Spirit." He emphasizes, "It is not how much of the Spirit we have, but how much the Spirit has of us."[25] This also is a wonderful truth that emerges in the gospel message (Acts 2:38).

A NEW LIFE

A whole new life is the consequence of salvation. Billy Graham has written an entire book on this theme under the title *The Secret of Happiness*. He sees the Christian life as one of victorious joy even in the midst of trials, tribulations, and sorrow. He has declared:

> Too many think of happiness as some sort of will-o-the-wisp thing that is discovered by constant and relentless searching. Happiness is not found by seeking. It is not an end in itself. . . . Jesus once told His disciples: "seek first the kingdom of God and His righteousness; and all these things shall be added unto you" (Matthew 6:33). . . . There, if we will take it, is the secret of happiness.[26]

HEAVEN

Finally, Jesus Christ will usher Christians into His glorious presence forever. Billy Graham has also written an entire book on life after death. He preaches that there is an eternity to be faced that will be brought in all of its fullness at the Second Coming of Jesus Christ. Of heaven Graham has said, "Heaven is a place, designed by the greatest Architect, and it is promised that there we will receive our glorious inheritance. I don't know exactly what kind of inheritance I will receive in heaven, but I know it will be magnificent."[27] He goes on to make several points about heaven found in the Bible. He tells us:

- Heaven is the city of our God.[28]

- In heaven there will be no fear.[29]

- In heaven there will be no night.[30]

- In heaven there will be no more suffering.[31]

- In heaven we will recognize and be recognized.[32]

- In heaven there will be no more sorrowful separations.[33]

- In heaven we will have a superhuman body.[34]

Billy Graham also tells us that in heaven we will be like Jesus in knowledge, in love. But "the supreme benefit, the one which surpasses all others, is that we will be with Jesus Christ."[35]

That is heaven, and Graham urges us to be ready for the day when we leave this temporal life and face eternity. If Jesus is our Savior and Lord, heaven will be our home.

All these wonderful realities explain why the message of Christ is Good News. But the news is not so good for those who have rejected Christ.

THE BAD NEWS

"Now we know that God is a God of love," says Billy Graham. "We know that God is a God of mercy, but the Bible also teaches that God is a God of wrath."[36] There is a heaven to gain and a hell to shun. Graham believes in a literal separation from God forever, which constitutes the essence of judgment and hell. As an evangelist he has said, "Jesus specifically states that nonbelievers will not be able to escape the condemnation of hell" (Matthew 23:33). Graham points out that one of the most graphic descriptions of hell in the Bible is given by Jesus in His parable of the rich man and Lazarus. The rich man was sent to hell and was in torment. His is a graphic description of the unbeliever's sufferings apart from God, sufferings that were "fixed" or permanent. There was no second chance.[37]

This doctrine, though, has raised questions, and Graham points out some of the deviations from this truth as Jesus taught it:

- Universalism: Everybody will eventually be saved.

- Annihilationism: Nonbelievers will just cease to exist.

- Second Chance: There will be the opportunity to be saved after death—Purgatory.

All of these deviations are errors and Graham rejects them. He believes hell is a real, eternal place of torment for the damned. And the essence of the torment is, as he states, "separation from God. Hell is the loneliest place in the universe."[38] This is no doubt why, as Graham points out, "Jesus Himself spoke frequently about hell. He warned of a hell to come. . . . There is no fellowship in hell except fellowship of darkness."[39] The judgment of God is a reality that cannot be escaped. The "wages of sin is death" (Romans 6:23). The writer of Hebrews tells us that first comes *death*, and then the *judgment* (Hebrews 9:27).

All of these principles and truths place in high profile the fact that people stand in desperate need of salvation. If Christ died and rose again for the problem of human sin, then in God's economy sin must be a problem of great proportions. What does Billy Graham have to say about the issue of sin?

HUMAN SIN

The Bible says, "All have sinned and fall short of the glory of God" (Romans 3:23). Graham says that is how we know that we are sinners. "But there is a second reason. . . . Any person who is not fully as good as Jesus Christ is a sinner. He alone is the world's only example of one who was without sin," says Billy Graham.[40] He then goes on to point out that the problem of sin all began in the Garden of Eden when Adam and Eve disobeyed God's specific command. Graham says, "This was the test. . . . Adam made his choice . . . [and] the Bible states very clearly that the results of Adam's sin shall be visited upon every one of his descendants. [Thus] sin entered the human race through Adam."[41] But what constitutes our personal sins today?

Billy Graham defines the sins of which we are all guilty:

- Lawlessness; the transgression of the law of God.
- Iniquity; deviating from the right.
- Missing the mark, falling short of the goal that has been set.
- Trespass, the intrusion of self-will into the sphere of divine authority.
- Unbelief.[42]

In light of these truths and the fact that "all have sinned," it is little wonder that Billy Graham insists there is only one remedy. He states, "Man's only salvation from sin stands on a lonely barren skull shaped hill."[43] It was there Jesus died, where He became "sin on our behalf, that we might become the righteousness of God in Him" (2 Corinthians 5:21). Jesus alone saves. And that, as Graham argues, explains the reason why the gospel message is so powerful and must be heralded worldwide. In a word, every living person needs to experience forgiveness and salvation. Thus it is understandable why Graham said, "The motto I have taken for my life is 'To evangelize the world in this generation, that every person might hear the Gospel once before the others have heard it twice.'"[44]

The all-inclusive word that defines the salvation experience is *conversion*—the change to a new life to enjoy.

CONVERSION: NEW LIFE IN CHRIST

Billy Graham understands the connection between repentance and conversion, and he often quotes the following scripture, "Repent ye therefore, and be converted" (Acts 3:19, KJV). He follows up this admonition by Peter with a statement: "To be a Christian means to be Christ-like, and we cannot be like Him in any degree unless we are changed, *converted*."[45] And that is life in its God-given fullness.

These sobering truths should motivate any Christian to present the gospel to those around them. They have clearly motivated Billy Graham to preach Christ around the world in over eighty countries. His heart yearns to see conversions.

Billy Graham has been in the trenches sharing the gospel for more than half a century. And, as we have seen in this chapter, the message he shares is the full, biblical gospel, as outlined for the church by Peter and Paul in the first century. Rare is the evangelistic sermon from Billy Graham where he does not set forth the whole gospel in the power of the Holy Spirit. That is what primarily leads to the amazing response people have to his preaching. Therein he has made his great contribution and given his evangelistic ministry the ring of biblical, historical authenticity.

4

The Sovereignty of God

❦

"I believe in the sovereignty of God."

— BILLY GRAHAM

As we have seen in the last two chapters, the work of the Holy Spirit and the power of the gospel are operative in the life of Billy Graham. These two foundational principles were epitomized and personified in the first-century apostles Peter and Paul. The work of the Holy Spirit was demonstrated through Peter on the Day of Pentecost (Acts 2). Paul made clear the importance of the pure gospel at the Jerusalem conference (Acts 15). These men and events laid the groundwork for anyone who would want to be described as an evangelist called by God. We have shown that Billy Graham falls in that noble tradition.

Now we move on biblically and historically to address two more vital evangelistic principles, namely, the sovereignty of God and Christology—the Person and work of Christ. Two of the early church fathers who held tenaciously to these biblical, historical principles were Augustine (sovereignty) and Athanasius (Christology). But we will begin with an intriguing contemporary story.

On November 5, 2000, three elderly men stood together at a pulpit before a large stadium crowd. They looked at each other for support. The tallest of the three began to sing, "This little light of mine, I'm going to let it shine." The other two men joined in, their voices surprisingly tuneful. When they got to the chorus the trio became animated. "Hide it under a bushel? No!" they belted out. The audience sat in respectful silence until the song was over, then all seventy thousand people erupted into exuberant cheers. A photo of the three men singing made the front page of the Jacksonville *Florida Times-Union* the following morning.

Three old men singing a children's song is not normally front-page news, nor does it often inspire a standing ovation from a packed football stadium. Clearly these were not ordinary men. They were Billy Graham, age 81; George Beverly Shea, age 91; and Cliff Barrows, age 77, a trio who have worked together for over fifty years. It was this long track record of working together that the audience was undoubtedly responding to. In our fast-paced, cutthroat, "corporate-takeover" world, Billy Graham and his team of workers are perhaps the happiest and most longstanding example of how a ministry can be true to its foundations and its staff.

God's Sovereignly Chosen Team

Billy Graham sees the call and commitment of each founding member of the Billy Graham Evangelistic Association as evidence of the sovereignty of God at work. What else explains the fifty years of constant service these men have offered so willingly and competently? Graham did not go out of his way to recruit these men; he believes God handpicked each one and sent him along at just the right time. For instance, one of Graham's early ventures in Youth for Christ was as a speaker at a large rally in Minneapolis. This event forged a lasting bond between Billy Graham and George Wilson, who would later become Graham's business manager. When Graham was still serving as pastor of Western Springs Baptist Church, another "divine coincidence" occurred. The evangelist enlisted as soloist on his radio program, George Beverly Shea. He has been working with Billy Graham since that time. Then in the summer of 1945, while Graham was speaking at the Ben Lippen conference center in Asheville,

North Carolina, someone urged him to enlist the help of Cliff and Billie Barrows, two young musicians who were actually on their honeymoon. Cliff Barrows led the music and Billie played piano at the conference, and their talent impressed Billy Graham. In this way God sovereignly brought together the central members of a team that has remained together and active in the ministry of evangelism to this day, some fifty-plus years later.

THE PARADOX OF SOVEREIGNTY

Yet while God sovereignly brought this team together, they also chose to be together. And one can say that Billy Graham exercised good judgment in choosing these people to work with him. While these statements may seem at odds, they are, in fact, all true. And in the fact that they are all true lies the wonderful paradox of the sovereignty of God and the free will of man.

But the sovereignty of God and human free will, as shall be seen, are involved in more than just bringing together a team to share in ministry, as wonderful as that is. The issue of God's sovereignty and our human ability to choose lies at the very heart of evangelism. Every time Billy Graham stands to speak in a crusade rally, he must reckon with these two paradoxical realities. Therefore, to gain a fuller understanding of the message and practice of Billy Graham's evangelism, we must take a closer look at what he thinks and believes in relation to the sovereignty of God and human responsibility.

To introduce the theme, Billy Graham has said, "I believe God has prepared the hearts of certain people in every audience I speak to. I never think about the results. I know there are people that God has prepared their hearts, and in that sense they are chosen by God. I have total relaxation, I just know something is going to happen that God has planned."[1] He goes on to use the often-repeated illustration of a person walking up to the gate of salvation and seeing on the threshold a sign reading, "Whosoever will may come." Eagerly the person enters and turns around to see another sign on the inside of the threshold that reads, "Chosen from the foundations of the world." Graham gladly acknowledges the tension of divine sovereignty and human responsibility.

Furthermore, he admits to being absolutely committed to this paradox. He believes unequivocally in the sovereignty of God: "I have sensed the sovereignty of God in my life, ministry, in all."[2] He also states, "Christ comes . . . and says, 'I am Lord! There is no circumstance beyond My power, and you can trust Me.'"[3] Concerning his ministry in relation to God's sovereignty, Graham has said, "I have no other answer. . . . Sheer sovereignty chose me to do this work and prepared me in His own way."[4] Thus it becomes clear where he stands on that issue. This primary principle will be discussed in more detail as this chapter unfolds.

God's Sovereignty and Billy Graham's Evangelistic Ministry

New Testament scholar Beasley-Murray, in his commentary on the Gospel of John, uses the phrase "the saving sovereignty of God" countless times. By this he means salvation operates under God's sovereignty. Billy Graham, well aware that God has been sovereignly at work in his ministry, essentially agrees with Murray. "The longer I work in crusades the more convinced I am that salvation is of the Lord," he says.[5] He also states, "I've learned my greatest lesson. It's not by power or might or any fancy sermon, it is wholly and completely the work of the Holy Spirit."[6] Graham acknowledges that in his earlier years he did not entertain strong convictions about the sovereignty of God and the work of the Holy Spirit. He confesses, "I used to think that in evangelism I had to do it all, [now] I don't believe any man can come to Christ unless God has drawn him."[7] Having witnessed the sovereign work of the Spirit of God through the years, the evangelist now fully realizes and acknowledges, "The Lord is sovereignly directing His own work of redemption."[8] Moreover, his basic conviction has deepened concerning the salvation experience itself. He says that in salvation, "the new birth is a divine work."[9] "Salvation is all of God."[10] This is consistent with the doctrine of the sovereignty of God as found in the works of Augustine.

In a very practical, down-to-earth sense we see the sovereignty of God at work right at the beginning of Graham's crusade in Los Angeles. For no apparent reason, William Randolph Hearst sent out a memo to his reporters to publicize Graham's crusade. The result was the groundbreaking ministry of 1949. The sovereignty of God then became forcefully evident in the London Harringay crusade of 1954. In some respects this crusade remains the highlight of Graham's ministry. Concerning this outpouring of the Holy Spirit and the sovereign grace of God, Graham has said, "I am sure that all of you that have been to Harringay have become aware that the atmosphere has been charged with the power of the Holy Spirit. . . . I felt like a spectator standing on the side watching God at work, and wanted to get out of it as much as I could and let Him take over."[11]

Such experiences have ingrained in Billy Graham an utter dependence on the saving sovereignty of God. This principle is not only reflected in his theology but in his whole approach to evangelism. On one occasion Billy described the error of some believers as digging little trenches and saying, "God, You work right here; and if You don't work here then I won't work with You." We try to put God in a corner, but before long God comes out of the corner—the mighty, sovereign God works in His own way.[12]

This understanding of God's sovereignty in the work of evangelism has created a genuine spirit of humility in Billy Graham. At a London crusade, in a conversation between Billy Graham and Sir Winston Churchill, the then British prime minister said, "I want to congratulate you for these huge crowds you've been drawing."

Graham replied, "Oh well, it's God's doing, believe me."

Churchill remonstrated, "That may be, but I dare say that if I brought Marilyn Monroe over here, and she and I went together to Wembley [stadium], we couldn't fill it."[13]

Graham had a similar encounter with President Nixon. When the president congratulated the evangelist on filling a stadium for a crusade, Graham instantly replied, "I didn't fill the place, God did it. God has done this, and all honor, credit and glory must go to Him."[14]

As a case in point, Sterling Houston, North American crusade director for Billy Graham, tells the story of the Washington, D.C., crusade in May 1986. The date was set and the civic center booked. One day Houston received a telephone call from the director of the center saying that the Convention Bureau of Washington had double-booked an event at the same time as Graham's crusade was to begin. Realizing that the BGEA had more "clout" than the competing party for the venue, Houston chose not to use that clout. Instead, in prayer the situation was laid before God, whereupon it was felt they should go ahead and let the other group use the venue. A new day was set for the Billy Graham crusade. The decision to reschedule resulted in getting use of the facilities at half price, and they were also able to book the large outdoor stadium for a rally. The masses came, and many found Christ. Clearly God was at work in His sovereignty once again.

THE SOVEREIGNTY OF GOD IN REDEMPTION

The most controversial issue in God's sovereignty revolves around God's action and our human response in salvation. In an interview with David Frost, Billy Graham reveals a basic insight into his view of the sovereignty of God in relation to the salvation experience. Regarding God's action in redemption he said, "He'll take over. And He won't make any mistakes. There is not going to be anybody in hell who was not supposed to be there, and there's not going to be anybody in heaven who wasn't supposed to be there. And I'll leave it at that."[15] God does elect and predestine to salvation. It must be said, however, that the evangelist does not accept the concept of so-called "double predestination." That refers to the doctrine that God predestines some to salvation and heaven and then predestines others to damnation and hell. God predestines to the heavens but never to hell. People make their own choices to reject God's offer of redemption in Christ. Graham states concerning predestination, "This does not imply that if a person is lost, God ordained it so."[16] Graham also accepts the concept of eternal security, or as it is better termed, the perseverance of the saints. He says, "Christian conversion is the transformation which we experience when we are born again. Since one is not born over and over again, we must think of Christian development in two phases: birth and growth."[17] Further, he states, "The Holy Spirit seals us or puts His mark on us [;] we are secure in Christ."[18] That, too, rests in the sovereignty of God.

While Graham declares that "salvation is of God," as an evangelist he makes a strong appeal for a human response to the gospel (as we discussed in a previous chapter). He calls for repentance and faith. He is committed to full human freedom and responsibility. Thus he seems quite content to rest in the paradox, holding steadfast to the sovereignty of God and human choice as well.

THE BASIS OF THE DOCTRINE

Graham predicates his view of God's sovereignty on the fact of His work in creation:

> The only possible answer is that all these things and many more are the work of a Supreme Creator. As a watch must have a designer, so must our precision-like universe have a great designer. We call him God . . . the Bible declares that the God we talk about, the God we sing about, the God from whom all blessings flow is the God who created this world and placed us in it.[19]

The creative hand of God must also be seen in bringing about the salvation of straying mankind.

But God in His infinity remains inscrutable. "God is a spirit, infinite, eternal, the unchangeable. That definition of God has been with me all my life, and when a man knows in his heart that God is infinite, eternal and unchanging spirit it helps to overcome the temptation to limit Him."[20] Although this great God transcends all, He is by our side to help, guide, strengthen, and meet needs. He is hidden, yet imminent. In the words of Frances Shaeffer, He is the "God who is there." This principle, too, has practical and historical precedents.

Biblical scholar Wayne Stanley Bonde contends that among the theological assumptions that constitute the basic tenets of Protestant evangelism is belief in "the sovereignty of God over human life."[21] Bonde states that the principle was held by many historical evangelistic luminaries such as Roger Williams, Thomas Hooker, George Whitefield, and Jonathan Edwards. Moreover, the position has a history of *effective* evangelism behind it. Bonde argues that "in the doctrine of the sovereignty of God, classical Protestantism rests on the Bible; as found in Augustine, Aquinas, Luther and more dramatically associated with John Calvin." He quotes from Calvin's *Instructions in Faith*: "We contemplate, therefore, in this universality of things, the immortality of our God, from which immortality have proceeded the beginning and origin of all things . . . for, the seed of the word of God takes root and brings forth fruit only in those whom the Lord, by his eternal election, has predestined to be children and heirs of the heavenly Kingdom."[22]

Bonde, in his understanding of Billy Graham, sees the evangelist adhering to this basic reformed view. But at the same time he is quick to point out that historic evangelism has also contended "that man has freedom of will to choose the grace of God."[23] Recognizing the enigma of divine sovereignty and human responsibility, he contends that Billy Graham rests in the historic theological stream with its practical applications.

Billy Graham's prayer is "Our Father and our God, we pray that the Holy Spirit will draw those to Thyself whom *Thou hast chosen in Christ*" (italics mine). From this, and many similar prayers, it seems that Graham's theology of divine sovereignty and human responsibility maintains the biblical balance that traditional evangelicalism has espoused through the centuries of church history. The evangelist feels comfortable talking about "the Father's sovereign will"[24] and at the same time contends, "We must all enter the Kingdom of heaven with the simple faith and trust as a child."[25] Billy Graham lives with the ultimate, supra-rational truth that God is sovereign in salvation but all mankind must respond in their free choice of faith and repentance. And that makes for a firm, biblical, workable evangelism.

SALVATION IN, THROUGH, AND TO THE GLORY OF GOD

Billy Graham brings it all together as he visualizes God working sovereignly in evangelism in a threefold way. One, evangelism is *of* God. Two, evangelism is *through* God. And three, evangelism is to the *glory* of the sovereign Lord.

Evangelism Is in God

As the Apostle Paul wrote to the Romans, "For from Him and through Him and to Him are all things. To Him be the glory forever. Amen" (Romans 11:36). As previously stressed, Billy Graham resonates with this principle. He says, "It is impossible for man to turn to God to repent, or even to believe without God's help! All you can do is call upon God to turn you. . . . When a man calls upon God, he is given true repentance and faith."[26] And everyone is free and responsible to call upon God. This simple equation gets to the heart of Billy Graham's grasp of personal salvation. He is fully committed to the principle Paul elucidates in 1 Corinthians 1:26–29: "For consider your calling, brethren." God does call to salvation. The Scriptures forthrightly declare it. And Billy Graham believes it. "In the Bible God has spoken verbally, and this spoken word has survived every scratch of human pen," he says.[27] For Billy, the Bible says it, and that settles it.

Evangelism Is through God

The supreme power for evangelism rests in the moving of the Holy Spirit through the communication of the gospel. This means two things as Graham sees it. One is that the Holy Spirit's work in the life of the unbeliever leads that person to salvation. As John puts it in his Gospel, "When He comes, [He] will convict the world concerning sin, and righteousness, and judgment" (John 16:8). Billy Graham is fully aware of this truth. In his autobiography, concerning the London crusade, he says, "I was almost filled with fear. In my entire life, I had never approached anything with such a feeling of inadequacy as I did in London. If God did not do it, it could not be done."[28] He goes on to say, "As the crusade gained momentum, I found myself becoming more and more dependent on God. I knew that all that we had seen happening in Britain was the work of God."[29] Graham fully acknowledges the work of the Holy Spirit in the context of God's sovereignty in addressing the gospel to people. As pointed out, this accounts for Graham's deep humility.

Further, the Holy Spirit not only works in the lives of unbelievers in convicting them of sin, righteousness, and judgment, but the Holy Spirit also moves in and through the life of the evangelist in the task of communicating the gospel effectively. John quotes Jesus as saying, "But the Helper, the Holy Spirit, whom the Father will send in My name, He will teach you all things" (John 14:26). As seen in the previous chapter, Billy Graham testifies to this principle saying, "I rarely leave without attempting to explain the meaning of the Gospel."[30] He knows that the gospel becomes the instrument the Spirit of God uses to bring the truth of Christ to the human heart. Therefore, the evangelist must explain the Good News to people. At the same time, however, Graham confesses, "Now I know that I may preach it [the gospel] rather poorly and I know that maybe some evening I may not be feeling up to par physically and all the rest of it and I leave out many things that I wanted to say. But . . . God uses even that simple presentation that might have been poorly done and he applies it to the human heart because salvation, the Bible says, is of God."[31] Graham sees his proper role: "I was merely the preacher, the messenger. None of what was happening could have happened apart from God."[32]

Billy Graham realizes that not only he, but also the members of his team, must understand this principle and serve on the basis of it. And they do. Walter Smyth, for many years Billy Graham's director of international crusades, once said, "We can waste a lot of time and effort, we can promote, we can do all kinds of things; but if we don't have the blessing of almighty God, our work's going to be in vain . . . so it's not the work of a man—it's the work of the Spirit of God."[33] Smyth's reaction is typical of those in Graham's team. Indeed the evangelist has said of his team members, "With each passing year . . . [we feel] more dependence on the power of the Holy Spirit."[34] God is the supreme power for evangelism. Evangelism is *through* Him.

Evangelism Is to the Glory of God

The culmination of biblical evangelism must be the glory of God. Great glory accrues to God when His people, evangelist or layperson,

submit themselves to His sovereignty and share the gospel with unbelievers. God is exalted when people in their need and in their sin come
through the path of repentance and faith and experience the transforming power of Christ. As Jesus said, "By this is My Father glorified,
that you bear much fruit, and so prove to be My disciples"(John 15:8).
The Bible even goes so far as to say that there is more joy in heaven
over one sinner who repents than over ninety-nine righteous persons
(Luke 15:7). When sinners repent, God's grace is magnified and He is
thereby glorified. The angels rejoice with exaltation in the salvation
that is of Him, through Him, and finally to Him.

MOTIVATION FOR EVANGELISM

The natural outcome of these essential truths means that the task of
evangelism must ultimately be motivated by seeking the praise and
honor of God. That becomes the prime motivation. John Stott, in his
book *Our Guilty Silence*, outlines three motives to evangelize. One,
God commands us to do so. Two, unbelievers are in great need. Three,
of most importance, for the glory ascribed to God. As the Apostle Paul
said to the Corinthians, "Whether, then, you eat or drink or whatever
you do, do all to the glory of God" (1 Corinthians 10:31).

But can it be said of Billy Graham that the glory of God is his basic
motivation in evangelism? It surely has been made clear that such is
the case. Graham is very conscious of the fact that God "is not going to
divide His honor with anybody."[35] It would be easy for the evangelist to
take credit for himself. With all the accolades he has received, the
temptation must surely be there. But Graham does not give in to such
temptation. Instead he says, "We could not help but be overwhelmed
by the response we had seen almost everywhere. . . . But [it was] a
response we could only attribute to God."[36] He told one writer, "There
is something here with depth that is beyond me—it can only be God
at work."

Of course, there are those who criticize Billy Graham for his extensive
crusade publicity and what some would see as the exalting of his persona.
Yet the evangelist has clearly stated a number of times that he wishes he

could dispense with all the advertising using his name. However, Graham recognizes that we live in a day, especially in the Western world, where people are drawn to personalities. Thus it seems wise to utilize this mentality for the good of the crusades. As a result, he reluctantly lets his name go forward. But his inner circle is very conscious of his genuine spirit of humility. Billy Graham truly desires that the honor and glory for what occurs in his evangelistic ministry go to God.

IN PERSPECTIVE

Billy Graham thus strives to keeps a biblical, historical perspective in relation to the sovereignty of God, affirming that God is sovereign in all things. There is nothing God does not know, no place He does not occupy, and nothing He cannot do. God is in control. No event transpires that He does not sanction, no human action He does not allow. This world is His creation and He rules and runs it.

Granted, as shown, this truth possesses an inherent paradox that will not be fully understood by human beings this side of eternity. Until that day, Billy Graham urges us to walk by faith. As Paul tells us, "We walk by faith, not by sight" (2 Corinthians 5:7). Indeed, Graham orders his life and evangelistic ministry on this basis.

And because he walks in faith and holds steadfast to the truth of God's sovereignty, God can be seen at work in the ministry of Billy Graham in so many ways: calling him to evangelism, putting the team together, keeping the team secure and free from tragic blunders that would undo their ministry, protecting them in the many onslaughts that have come their way, honoring the ministry with blessings and many people won to Christ, keeping the team intact.

The ultimate crux of the matter reduces itself to this: Is there a practical, legitimate contribution made to the church as a result of God's sovereign activity in the ministry of Billy Graham? The answer is *yes*. Several things surface to verify this contention:

- It has given Graham a spirit of humility that is a challenge and a witness to others.

- It has inspired the faith of many to rest in God's sovereignty in the extreme circumstances of life.

- It has put God where He belongs in the thinking of many.

- It has guided the entire Graham team, and God has been pleased to bless the ministry to millions.

- It falls in line with the history of evangelism that gives it veracity.

- It has brought glory to God, which always blesses others.

Thus Billy Graham displays his biblical and historical authenticity in standing firm on the full sovereignty of God in his evangelistic work. Now we must move on to see if the evangelist falls in step with history in his views on the Person and work of Jesus Christ.

5

The Centrality of Christ

⟨∞⟩

"It is simple: Jesus is God."

—Billy Graham

In October 1974, Billy Graham preached to a crowd of over 200,000 people in Rio de Janeiro, Brazil. Dominating the landscape of the city and clearly visible from the arena where the crusade was being held, was the famous statue known as the Christ of the Andes. The statue depicts Jesus looking longingly over the city, His hands outstretched in welcome. As the evangelist surveyed the masses, he declared, "Do not look here, at me—look up there." It was a gesture that encapsulated his entire message.

Billy Graham is arguably one of the most well-known people in the world. For the last twenty-five years he has consistently been named among the ten most admired men in the world in polls conducted among Christians and non-Christians alike. It would be easy for a man of his stature to fall into the trap of thinking that people were coming to see the messenger, rather than to hear the message. But in a remarkable feat spanning fifty years, Billy Graham has refused to allow fame to corrupt him or his message. In Rio de Janeiro, as in every other place he preaches, his goal is to point people to Christ, "who takes away the sin of the world" (John 1:29).

Who is this Christ that Billy Graham proclaims? The church father Athanasius settled the issue in his day; what does Graham espouse concerning Jesus Christ today?

BILLY GRAHAM'S CHRISTOLOGY

Anthropologists estimate that over the course of human history about four thousand distinct religions have been practiced throughout the world. Billy Graham is often challenged by people of other religions who want to know what right he has to come to their country and preach the gospel message; after all, they have their religion.

But Graham is tenacious. In the book *Storm Warning*, Graham states, "I have spent my lifetime proclaiming one central truth: there is good news for the people of the world. At the heart of that good news is Jesus Christ."[1] As David Lockard in his insightful book on the evangelist, *The Unheard Billy Graham*, has pointed out, a "Christ-centered message presupposes a strong Christology."[2] Graham agrees. He has said, "At the heart of that good news is Jesus Christ."[3] However, the same words can mean different things to different people, and so we must look closer to discover what constitutes Billy Graham's basic assumptions about Jesus Christ and how they affect his ministry. Even though some of these issues have been touched on in other chapters, it is helpful to explore them in more detail here and see how they relate specifically to Graham's understanding of Christology. So the question again becomes: According to Billy Graham, who is Jesus?

THE INCARNATION

Quite naturally, the truth of the incarnation of the Son of God begins with His birth. Billy Graham is fully committed to the concept of the virgin birth of Jesus Christ. Along with verbal affirmation of this position, he has written, "The Bible claims he was born of a virgin. I believe that, and I believe it is important for our faith to believe it."[4] Graham not only strongly emphasizes the uniqueness of the birth of

Jesus Christ, but he is also convinced many Protestants, particularly evangelicals, do not give due respect to Mary who bore Jesus. Unquestionably, many evangelical Protestants react against what they consider an unbiblical view of the person and position of Mary held by many Roman Catholics. But even if that is true, Graham contends it constitutes no legitimate reason for refusing Mary the proper place she should have. She was highly chosen of God, she became the one through whom the Son of God entered into the world. That is unique and unprecedented, and Mary will always stand alone as the "most blessed among women."

But Mary aside, the primary issue centers in the truth that the divine Son of God Himself actually did come into this world. Billy Graham expressed it forcefully when he wrote, "God walked upon the Earth in human flesh."[5] Graham takes seriously Paul's words when he says, "Have this attitude in yourselves which was also in Christ Jesus, who, although He existed in the form of God, did not regard equality with God a thing to be grasped, but emptied Himself, taking the form of a bond-servant, and being made in the likeness of men. And being found in appearance as a man, He humbled Himself by becoming obedient to the point of death, even death on a cross. Therefore also God highly exalted Him, and bestowed on Him the name which is above every name, that at the name of Jesus every knee should bow, of those who are in heaven, and on earth, and under the earth, and that every tongue should confess that Jesus Christ is Lord, to the glory of God the Father" (Philippians 2:5–11).

Billy Graham expresses Paul's principle succinctly when he states,

You see, God has not left us wandering around guessing whether or not he exists or what he is like. Instead—and this is very important for you to understand—God has shown himself to us. How has he done this? He has done it in a way that staggers our minds. He did it by actually taking upon himself human flesh and becoming a human being. Do you want to know what God is like? Examine Jesus Christ, because Christ was God in human flesh. "He is the image of the invisible God . . . for God was pleased to have all fullness dwell in him" (Colossians 1:15, 19). Christ confirmed that he was the Son of God by rising from the dead after his death on the cross. I invite you to look with an open mind and heart at Christ as he is found in the New Testament.[6]

Graham reinforces this stance by stating, "Why is Christianity so different . . . ? The answer, folks, is not on a plan for living, but on the person of Jesus Christ: Jesus, the Son of God the Father and the second person of the Trinity."[7] This leads us to a closer look at Billy Graham's views on Jesus as part of the Godhead.

IS JESUS GOD?

Billy Graham is careful that the full message of the incarnate Christ be declared and understood. He writes, "It is actually the deity of Christ that above anything else gives to Christianity its sanction, authority, power and its meaning."[8]

When Billy was preaching in Nagaland, in northeast India, where many in the congregation were from Hindu, Muslim, or syncretistic backgrounds, he took great care to emphasize that the God he proclaimed was not "one of the gods," but "*the* God."[9] This did not prove acceptable to everyone attending given their diverse religious orientations, but in the three days the evangelist preached there, more than four thousand people made a decision for Christ.

In his well-known book *The Secret of Happiness*, Graham expresses the concept of the deity of Jesus quite pointedly: "Jesus was not only man, but he was God himself, come down from the glory of heaven to walk on earth and show us what God is like. Christ is 'the image of the invisible God'"[10] (Colossians 1:15). Given this, what does Graham say about Jesus' humanity?

JESUS THE MAN

It must be made clear that the statement of Billy Graham quoted above implies that Jesus Christ was also fully man as well as the infinite, incarnate God. Graham contends that Jesus walked among us and experienced life in a fully human sense. He brings this out in his book entitled *Death and the Life After*. Speaking of the humanity of Christ he writes, "He loved life on this earth. He enjoyed the pleasures of walking with his disciples, holding children on his knees, attending a wedding, eating with friends, riding in a boat, or working in the temple at Passover time."[11] Graham further points out that our Lord was human enough that "Jesus did not take delight in his approaching crucifixion."[12] He even prayed, "Let this cup pass from Me." From the human vantage point, Jesus experienced the pleasures and the traumas of this life, as does everyone else.

At the same time, Graham is very careful to state that, though human, Jesus never sinned. Concerning the sinless perfection of Jesus the evangelist declares, "All the days of his life on earth he never once committed a sin. He is the only man who ever lived that was sinless. He could stand in front of men and ask, 'Which of you convinceth me of sin?' He was hounded by the enemies day and night, but they never found any sin in him. He was without spot or blemish."[13]

When Jesus queried His critics, "Which one of you convicts Me of sin?" (John 8:46), there was no reply. Yet, in His sinless humanity, as Billy Graham points out, "He humbled himself as no other man has ever humbled himself."[14] Not only did Jesus empty Himself (Philippians 2:7), He died on the cross.

In Graham's continual emphasis on the cross of Christ, he makes the point that it may seem difficult to understand that Jesus, "who knew no sin," would have to "bear the sin of guilt of all men."[15] But that truth rests at the core of Christianity. The evangelist then quotes 2 Corinthians 5:21: God made "Him who had no sin to be sin on our behalf." This fact Graham emphasizes time and again. Jesus did not sin Himself, but God in unfathomable grace and infinite holiness heaped human sin upon His Son when He died on the cross, thus paying the penalty for our transgressions.

As Billy Graham preaches that Jesus Christ is human yet God, he resolves the paradox by lifting up the faith principle. He says Jesus "was more than God, he was man. He was as much man as he was God. He was as much God as he was man. He was the God-man" and there we must rest in faith, for it is a biblical Christology.[16] As Graham has declared, "All other things may change, but Christ remains unchangeable. In the restless sea of human passions, Christ stands steadfast and calm, ready to welcome all who will turn to Him and accept the blessing of safety and peace."[17] Billy confesses, "This is a staggering, almost incomprehensible truth."[18] But it is a truth, grasped by faith.

A second aspect of the gospel, one that emerges out of Christ's incarnate humanity, revolves around the dynamic life He lived. Graham has much to say in this area.

THE LIFE OF CHRIST

No one disputes the biblical truth that Jesus lived a dramatically different quality of life. His life was far more than just a life free from sin, as marvelous and miraculous as that obviously is. Billy Graham places a healthy stress on the fact that Jesus lived a life of sacrifice, love, and ministry profoundly touching the needs of others. "He went about doing good" (Acts 10:38). He spoke comfort to the sorrowing. He granted forgiveness to the erring. He gave food to the hungry. He imparted healing to the sick. He issued rebuke to the rebellious. He laid out the pathway of life and fullness to the seekers. He led people to their destiny with God. But such a listing scarcely tells the incredible life of ministry and teaching of Jesus. As has been said, Jesus was the "ultimate man." And He alone has the ultimate influence to change all people for the better. Graham believes that because of the exemplary life of Jesus Christ, "virtually every significant and social movement of western civilization—from the abolition of slavery to child labor laws—owes its origin and influence to Jesus Christ."[19] But ungrateful humanity crucified Him.

THE MAN ON THE CROSS

If Billy Graham has a motto, it is that of the Apostle Paul when he says, "God forbid that I should glory, save in the cross of our Lord Jesus Christ" (Galatians 6:14, KJV). The cross stands as the focal point of the Christian faith (coupled with the Resurrection, which will be discussed later). The spotlight of God's revelation shines brightly upon Calvary. The Bible lifts up the Cross as the focal point of all history. But what does the Cross actually mean? How does Billy Graham see the cross of Jesus Christ? What is his theology concerning the death of Jesus? The answer has been hinted at, and now we must see it in full.

Many theories of Christ's atoning work — for it was that — have been propounded through the years; concepts such as the moral influence theory, the dramatic view of the struggle between God and evil, and the ransom theory among others. The view espoused by a large community of evangelicals, however, and that to which Billy Graham gives basic assent, centers in the so-called governmental or substitutionary view of the Atonement. In simplest terms, the idea revolves around the fact of Jesus' bearing the sins of the world in Himself and dying on the cross as a *substitute* sacrifice for sinful humanity. "At the cross in holy love God, through Christ, paid the full penalty of our disobedience himself. He bore the judgment we deserve in order to bring us the forgiveness we do not deserve. On the cross, divine mercy and justice were equally expressed and eternally reconciled. God's holy love was 'satisfied.'"[20] Billy Graham forcefully preaches this truth. He is vividly aware of the agonizing suffering of the Cross. On one occasion he said, "I want you to see what happens. When Christ went to the cross, they took off his clothes, and they took a long whip of thongs with steel pellets in the end and lashed him across his back until his back was in shreds. They put a crown of thorns on his brow, until his face was bleeding. They spat on his face. They mocked him. They laughed at him."[21]

But Billy Graham sees more involved at Calvary than Jesus' physical suffering. In the same crusade in which he stressed the physical agony of Jesus, he also said, "You can't get to Heaven with your sins and the only way you can have your sins forgiven and be presented unblamable to God is through the death of Jesus Christ on the cross. That's what God did."[22] Graham gets to the heart of the matter when he says, "I preach the blood of Christ because on that day Jesus Christ shed his blood for the sins of mankind. . . . No matter how moving and emotional it may become, the real gospel is in the fact that Christ died for me as a substitute."[23] And what does that mean?

When Jesus cried out, "My God, my God, why hast Thou forsaken Me?" (Matthew 27:46), in that moment of time, in the inscrutable wisdom of God, all the sin of the world fell on the Son and He bore the judgment and punishment for humanity's evil that is the supreme agony of the Cross. The pure Son of God became sin for us. As vast as the depth of that sacrifice, as encompassing as the love it expressed, as difficult as it may be to grasp, the grace of God brought about the salvation of the world in that act. Jesus died for us! The atonement has been made. God has been reconciled to sinners and sinners to God. Eden has been restored. Life with God in time and eternity now stands available to all.

The Cross strikes at the essence of all reality. Billy Graham concluded a stirring sermon by stating: "I want you to see as they [the heavenly hosts] gather in the great council hall of God, and the Lord Jesus Christ, the second person of the Trinity, as He says to God the Father and God the Spirit, 'I will go and save the world. I will go and become man's mediator. I will go and become man's substitute. I will go and suffer and die.'"[24]

However, the Cross cannot be divorced from the Resurrection. Again we see the proverbial two sides of the coin. Christ not only died for sin; He was resurrected as the living Lord to bestow new life on all genuine believers.

THE RESURRECTED LORD

Billy Graham upholds the absolute necessity of Jesus' resurrection. As the substitutionary atonement stands vital for salvation, so does the Resurrection. In a message given by Graham and reproduced in *Decision* magazine, he writes, "Jesus Christ, who was crucified, has been raised from the dead. If Christ's bones lie decayed in a grave, then there is no GOOD NEWS, and life has no meaning. The headlines of the world would soon indicate that the world is coming to an end soon with no hope for the future and eternity if Jesus Christ had not been raised."[25]

Further in the same article Graham makes clear his stand on the bodily resurrection of the Lord: "Remember that after Jesus' resurrection, he came into all kinds of ordinary places to all kinds of ordinary people. He appeared to people near his tomb and to two men on the road to Emmaus; he came to others at the lakeside; he met with a group in a house. He shared their meals and their walks."[26] And later he states, "The New Testament teaches from one end to the other that Christ indeed is risen from the dead. The most thrilling fact of human history is the resurrection of Jesus Christ."[27] And then He will come back.

THE ONE WHO WILL RETURN

Few evangelicals would contest the fact that the Bible teaches the visible return of Jesus. At His ascension, angels appeared to the disciples and gave the promise: "And as they were gazing intently into the sky while He was departing, behold, two men in white clothing stood beside them; and they also said, 'Men of Galilee, why do you stand looking into the sky? This Jesus, who has been taken up from you into heaven, will come in just the same way as you have watched Him go into heaven'" (Acts 1:10–11). Billy Graham obviously takes this word literally. On many occasions he has made his position clear. In a sermon preached in 1962 entitled "Three Keys to Youthfulness," he stressed evangelist D. L. Moody's pronouncement that the world was soon coming to an end; and then he went on to say, "If the world seemed about to come to an end in Moody's time, how much closer must we be to the climax of history?" The climax of history for both Moody and Graham centers in the second coming of Jesus Christ, which the evangelist points out the Bible alludes to over three hundred times.

But at what moment in history does Billy Graham believe Christ will return? He is an unabashed premillennialist in that he believes in a "pre-tribulation rapture" and a literal reign of Christ on earth for a thousand years. Yet, Graham does not take an argumentative, dogmatic stance on this. While he holds to a literal return of Christ and the setting up of the millennial reign, he does it in the sense of motivating people to be ready for that day. He is first and foremost an evangelist, not a theologian, and the motivation behind all his preaching centers in creating a sense of urgency to be prepared for the hour when Christ does come again.

In Billy Graham's early days of public ministry he was prone to set dates on the Lord's return. He said on one occasion, for example, that Christ would probably come back within two years. But over time Graham has mellowed on setting dates and making pronouncements. He now contends, "It is wrong and unscriptural to try and set a date for Christ's return. God alone knows when He will come."[28] He states that even Jesus did not know the times, only God the Father knows (Matthew 24:36). He further argues that if one knew the date of Christ's return, it would destroy the air of expectancy. Still, Billy does declare the distinct possibility that Christ may come in the relatively immediate future. He preaches, "I would like to say with emphasis, I do believe we are now living in the closing period of history as we know it."[29] And he sees the return of Christ as a glorious hope, a utopia for the earth. He believes that when Jesus returns all the world's problems will be forever solved. War, famine, racial discrimination, social injustice, and the like will perish as Christ establishes His reign on earth. The kingdom is coming, and all will confess, "Jesus Christ is Lord" (Philippians 2:11).

LORD OF THE KINGDOM OF GOD

Often overlooked by many evangelists is the fact that one of the essential messages of our Lord centers on the establishment of God's kingdom. Jesus taught His disciples to pray, "Thy kingdom come" (Matthew 6:10). He preached, as did His predecessor John the Baptist, "Repent, for the kingdom of heaven is at hand" (Matthew 4:17). A person cannot hold to a well-rounded Christology unless due respect is given to Christ's emphasis on the arrival of the kingdom of God and His lordship in it. In light of this, the kingdom of God should be preached.

In relation to the kingdom of God, Billy Graham has said, "Men will never build the Kingdom of God on earth, no matter how hard they might try. Only God can do that—and some day He will when

Christ comes again."[30] He argues from the premise that when Jesus was crucified, "a superscription was written over Him . . . 'THIS IS KING OF THE JEWS.' He was then, and still is, King, but we have failed to acknowledge Him."[31]

Graham also makes it clear that when a person comes to salvation, he also enters into the kingdom of God. Our citizenship in Christ is in heaven, in the kingdom.

THE CENTRALITY OF CHRIST IN ALL

Billy Graham obviously holds to a high Christology: Jesus Christ was the God-man. This truth can only be grasped and held by faith. Recognizing this, Billy Graham rests in faith and trusts the day will come when the shadows will disappear in the glorious light of the full revelation of the Lord Jesus Christ.

As he awaits that day, Graham preaches Christ in all his fullness. In his writings, service, and preaching he exalts the principle uttered by Paul, "Jesus is Lord" (Romans 10:9, KJV). For Billy, Christ is central, all in all. There is no question about this in his mind, and he employs every means at his disposal to spread that truth. In so doing, he is in step with the flow of evangelism as it has been practiced down through church history. Therein Graham has made his great contribution in his day as did Athanasius and others in theirs.

6

The "Social Gospel"

"I have preached on every conceivable social issue."

— BILLY GRAHAM

As the 1957 New York crusade was drawing to a close, a series of federal court orders were established to end school segregation. In Charlotte, North Carolina, Billy Graham's hometown, there was a fifteen-year-old African-American girl named Dorothy Conts. Her father was a pastor, and her family had determined she should be one of the first African-Americans to enroll in the newly integrated Harding High School. When Dorothy arrived at school she was repelled by white students and their parents pelting her with rocks and sticks.

When Billy Graham heard of Dorothy's difficulties he was very moved. He wrote the following letter to her mother: "Dear Mrs. Conts, Democracy demands that you hold fast and carry on. The world of tomorrow is looking for leaders and you have been chosen. Those cowardly whites against you will never prosper because they are un-American and unfit to lead. Be of good faith. God is not dead. He will see you through."[1]

In September the year before, a similar incident had erupted at

Central High School in Little Rock, Arkansas. Governor Orbal Faubus called out the National Guard in an effort to stop Black students' attempts to integrate the high school. On this occasion Billy Graham had also stood with the oppressed. He wholeheartedly urged the White citizens of Little Rock to submit to the court order desegregating the school, telling them, "It is the duty of every Christian, when it does not violate his relationship to God, to obey the law. I would urge them to do so in this case."

Two years later in September 1959, Billy Graham was invited to hold two large crusade rallies in Little Rock. The Ku Klux Klan and the White Citizens Council distributed thousands of leaflets attacking him for his views on integration and for inviting Martin Luther King Jr. to take part in the New York crusade. Even though Graham had asked that seating at the rallies be integrated, when he arrived on the first night he found that some areas were cordoned off for African-Americans. Billy got off the stage and tore down the barriers himself.

A few years later, in volatile Birmingham, Alabama, Graham scheduled a large evangelistic rally at Legion Field, the football arena for the University of Alabama. It proved to be a very explosive situation indeed. The FBI had to assign guards to the Billy Graham Evangelistic Association (BGEA) office workers. Threats poured in, and they were taken seriously in light of what had just happened at the Sixteenth Street Baptist Church. There the notorious "Bessemer bombers" had bombed the building, killing four young African-American girls.

On the day of the rally, the stadium was packed to overflowing with thirty thousand people, in a ratio of about 50 percent Blacks and 50 percent Whites. After the invitation was given a stream of people from both races made their way to the altar. Biographer John Pollock describes it as "the most completely integrated public meeting in Birmingham's history, and the beginning of a new day."[2] No incident occurred and Birmingham took a major step forward.

Throughout his lifetime Billy Graham has taken a stand on many other social issues besides racism. Poverty, both at home and abroad, is deeply troubling to him, and he has initiated many actions to relieve people's suffering. Dr. John Corts, president of the BGEA, tells of Graham's traveling to southern India after a devastating monsoon season. The pitiful plight of the people deeply moved him. He stepped in and shipped tons of food and clothing to the area. The local people were so grateful they changed the name of their small village to "Billy Graham."

Graham was so moved by that grateful response that in his Minneapolis crusade in July 1973, he instigated an offering of food for the hungry. Over the years this has grown into a ministry called Love in Action. Christians still bring canned goods, nonperishable food, clothing, and the like to Graham crusades to be distributed to the needy in their city. Untold boxes of clothing and truckloads of food have been collected and distributed through this simple approach. Better still, many of these programs continue in various forms long after the crusade has packed up and left a city.

The BGEA also formed the "World Emergency Fund" in 1973. This fund has helped to alleviate suffering and privation when war and natural disasters occur. In 1995, for example, the fund sent more than $335,000 to needy areas around the world. BGEA officials make it clear that every dollar contributed to the World Emergency Fund goes directly to relief projects. Nothing is siphoned off for administrative expenses.

POLITICS

What about the political views of Billy Graham? In what ways does Graham involve himself in politics in order to help alleviate human suffering?

Graham is clearly aware of the fact that the state cannot reform people and give them a new heart; only Christ can do that. One of the contemporary problems in a country like America (as well as some countries in Europe), is that an attitude has developed that the state can solve all problems. But this view falsely assumes that people's hearts are always altruistic. As Billy Graham has said:

We have been trying to solve every ill of society as though society were made up of regenerate men to whom we had an obligation to speak with

Christian advice. We are beginning to realize that, while the law must guarantee human rights and restrain those who violate those rights, whenever men lack sympathy for the law they will not long respect it even when they cannot repeal it. Thus the government may try to legislate Christian behavior, but it soon finds that man remains unchanged.[3]

This statement implies two principles. First, harking back to Graham's initial philosophy, the human heart must be changed before any lasting cultural problems can be finally resolved. Second, the law does have a role to play and concerned Christians should involve themselves in the political arena to get the right kinds of laws passed. Graham is careful in this regard, though. He feels that as a Christian leader he should not alienate people on political issues that do not have a moral or ethical element. When Christian principles are not at stake he advocates a neutral stance. However, when Christian principles are at stake, a stand must be taken. In light of this, Graham takes a firm position when moral and ethical Christian principles are at issue.

The evangelist has been supportive of many aspects of American foreign policy. For example, his concern for needy people, especially in emerging nations, has made him a strong supporter of certain forms of foreign aid. He feels that government policy should reflect Christian values, and he lets this view be known.

While Billy Graham is reluctant to involve himself in partisan politics, some issues are of such moral importance that he has felt the need to speak out. One such occasion was in June 1967, when Graham went to Washington, D.C., to make his influence felt and give his full support to the antipoverty program of President Lyndon B. Johnson. In that setting he spoke to two hundred influential people at a luncheon meeting and gave a strong affirmation for doing all that was humanly possible individually and collectively as a nation to alleviate the misery of poverty in America. At the luncheon meeting he made the following statement: "This is the first time in seventeen years that I have come to Washington to speak for or against a government program. But now I have come to speak to various Congressmen, in favor of the poverty program."[4]

Johnson's poverty program passed Congress and the president signed it into law. It became a revolutionary new approach to meeting America's needs. President Johnson was so impressed with Billy Graham's passion for the poor that he urged the evangelist to come to Washington and head the new poverty program. Graham toyed with the idea, but declined in favor of continuing his crusades.

THE WHOLE GOSPEL

Such things as standing against racism, fighting world hunger, and clothing the poor would appear to be the epitome of Christianity, yet surprisingly Graham has come under attack for involving himself in some of these activities. Some of the most vitriolic attacks have come from fellow clergy. How can this be? How in the late twentieth century can speaking out against oppression be viewed by many as outside the mandate of Christianity? To answer the question we need to go back to the early decades of the twentieth century.

At the beginning of the twentieth century, the modernist-fundamentalist controversy, which had been raging in Europe for decades, spilled over into American Christianity. Simply put, the controversy revolved around the fact that the fundamentalists accepted the inerrancy of the Bible, and the modernists did not. It had been a rancorous debate in Europe and had devastating effects on the church in North America.

Prior to this time, preaching the gospel and attending to the physical needs of people were considered two sides of the same coin. This amalgamation of social action and evangelism had held true through the history of the church as portrayed in the lives of such people as St. Francis of Assisi. In more recent centuries, evangelists such as John Wesley fostered significant social movements. He became the loudest voice in Britain calling for prison reform. When evangelist Charles Finney became professor of theology and president at Oberlin College in Ohio, he saw to it that Oberlin served as a major station in the North for the Underground Railroad, where runaway slaves could find freedom. Oberlin became the first coeducational college in America and would accept students of all races. Finney even had a health plan for students at the college. Charles Spurgeon's church in London ran more than twenty social and evangelistic ministries. And no one involved himself more in the temperance movement of the early twentieth century than evangelist Billy Sunday.

Then came the modernist-fundamentalist controversy and the polarization of views. The liberal strata in American Christianity lost much of its evangelistic fervor and devoted itself to social action. Those in this camp apparently equated pietistic evangelism with obscure fundamentalism. On the other hand, those in the conservative camp began to equate social action with the new liberal theology modernists held. However, in rejecting this new theology, those on the conservative side threw out the baby with the bath water. They rejected a purely social action ministry and gave themselves solely to evangelism. The upshot was the divorce of evangelism from social action. In the United States, evangelism became equated with fundamentalism, and social action became synonymous with modernism.

In his ministry, Billy Graham has always sought to repair this split. He sees the divide between the two theological viewpoints as artificial:

> The Gospel is both vertical and horizontal. The vertical signifies our relationship to God. The horizontal signifies the application of the principles of the teachings of Christ to our daily lives. At least a third of my preaching is spent encouraging and teaching people to apply the principles of Christianity in their personal and social lives. . . . I would like to say emphatically that any Gospel that preaches only vertical relationships is only a half-Gospel.[5]

Billy has also said, "I firmly believe in the application of the Gospel to the social order, for the Gospel must relate to the social concerns of our day."[6]

He is insistent that the new life in Christ can be brought into maturity only by the inner work of the Holy Spirit. In this context, the Spirit of God transforms the individual person, and through changed lives

He changes the church and hence a force is developed that can transform society as well.

Graham's major premise on social and ethical concerns has its roots in individual people coming to new life in Christ. He is convinced that social needs cannot be fully and totally met by governments and the passing of new laws, or even the benevolent ministry of the church. The *individual* must be changed. He sees two aspects of conversion; the first being *from* the world to Christ. The second is *with* Christ back to the world. As he puts it, "The fruit of a new life is love for one's neighbor, which leads to social action."[7]

A whole new perspective on life must be generated in people. The basic social problems in various cultures are a manifestation of individual sinfulness, selfishness, and lack of a relationship with God. Graham has said, "If we today could only realize that a nation can rise no higher, can be no stronger and no better than the individuals which compose that nation! There is nothing wrong with the world. The trouble lies with the world's people. If the world is bad, it is because people are bad."[8]

This strong contention centers in Billy Graham's argument that "bad people" become "good people" only when they experience new life in Christ. When that takes place and a Christian world-view is adopted, a person is motivated to meet the needs of others in the love of Christ. This alone will inexorably change the world and solve its perplexing social problems. As Jesus said, His followers are the "salt of the earth" and the "light of the world." Only true "salt" and "light" can permeate the pollution and the darkness of the world's sin and social ills and give birth to a new society. Changed lives lead to a changed society.

When interviewed in England before a crusade, Billy Graham openly confessed, "I am going to insist that honesty and integrity pay in individual lives. I am calling for a revival that will cause men and women to return to their offices and shops to live out the teachings of Christ in their daily relationships."[9] As a result, Graham reaches out to people in an attempt to not only lead them to Christ, but to also lead them into a more fulfilling, ethical life. He is convinced that Christ alone can create in the human heart the spirit that eventually can transform society.

HOW FAR IS TOO FAR?

Billy Graham does not shy away from issues that affect people's lives. He has spoken out on AIDS, urging Christians to get informed about the facts of the disease and the organizations fighting this worldwide epidemic, or to volunteer to help those suffering from it.

Abortion is another areas where Graham feels he must speak out, though he is grieved that it has created such a wedge between various Christian groups. He is a strong advocate of birth control, but he is not in favor of abortion. He was deeply disappointed in 1996 when President Clinton vetoed legislation banning partial birth abortions. Of this he said, "I think the president was wrong in vetoing it. I had the opportunity of telling him that in person."

Billy Graham does feel, however, that violent activism in the anti-abortion camp goes too far. Such extreme actions cause hurt and draw the focus away from the issue itself and onto the personalities and tactics used to convey the message. He urges Christians everywhere to use prayer and open dialogue as their "weapons."

On the issue of war, Graham has said, "I am not a pacifist, nor am I for unilateral disarmament. Police and military forces are unfortunately necessary as long as man's nature remains the way it is. . . . From the Christian perspective, therefore, the possibility of a nuclear war originates in the greed and covetousness of the human heart [where] there is a tragic and terrible flow in human nature that must be recognized and dealt with."[10] He laments, however, the trillion or more dollars spent every year on armaments around the world while children are starving to death. Hunger moves him deeply. He declares emphatically, "War is not necessary."[11] Christians are to seek peace (Matthew 5:9).

RESULTS

The question arises, does the biblical and social philosophy espoused by Billy Graham *truly make a difference* in society? One of the leading professors and scholars in the area of Christian social ethics contends that it does. Professor T. B. Maston says:

> It also has been indicated that most world issues are basically moral and spiritual. This means that if Christianity does not have an answer for the major problems of the world, they will not be answered adequately. . . .
> *The Christians who have turned the world upside down have been men and women with a vision in their souls, the resurrected Christ in their hearts, and the Bible in their hands.*[12] (italics mine)

Billy Graham strongly affirms this argument. He contends that the new birth and the regenerating power of Jesus Christ not only transform a person spiritually, but socially as well. In this manner society can experience the radical change it needs. In his book *World Aflame*, Billy says:

> Thus the Bible teaches that man can undergo a radical spiritual and moral change that is brought about by God Himself. The word that Jesus used, and which is translated "gain," actually means "from above." The context of the third chapter of John teaches that the new birth is something that God does for man when man is willing to yield to God. Man does not have within himself the seed of the new life; this must come from God Himself.[13]

As is evident from this discussion, Billy Graham believes every Christian has two obligations. "One, to proclaim the Gospel of Jesus Christ as the only answer to man's deepest needs. Two, to apply as best we can the principles of Christianity to the social conditions around."[14] He is convinced that this approach makes a difference morally, socially, and spiritually.

Many of Graham's converts have embraced his view. Remember the story of Jim Vaus, the wiretapper converted in Graham's 1949 Los Angeles crusade, and recounted in chapter one? After his conversion, Jim Vaus spent the bulk of his Christian life ministering to wild young people in a storefront mission in a slum area of New York City. Vaus's conversion and subsequent turnaround have positively affected the lives of many poor teenagers in New York.

Billy Graham's stance on racism, particularly during the turbulent era of the 1950s, also bore fruit. In all these racial upheavals, Graham kept to his basic philosophy, saying, "We are ultimately not going to solve the race problems in America until men truly love each other. And this love can only be brought about by God, as we yield to Him."[15]

John Corts of the BGEA relates an example of the evangelist's principle of social action at work during an integrated crusade rally in the South. A certain woman, a top socialite in the community, came forward at the invitation to make a commitment to Christ. A black counselor talked with her and prayed with her. Afterward, the woman's irate husband said, "Didn't you realize you were speaking with a Negro counselor?" The woman replied, "You know, I didn't even notice the color of her skin." Of this Graham remarks, "You see, in the spirit of that moment, in a moment of dedication, racial consciousness was in the background."[16]

After the crusade in Little Rock, Arkansas, where Billy Graham was welcomed with a lambasting from the Ku Klux Klan and the White Citizens Council, Dr. W. O. Vaught, pastor of one of the largest Baptist churches in town, said of Graham's stand: "There has been universal agreement in all the churches and out across the city that your visit here was one of the finest things that ever happened in the history of Little Rock. So very many people have changed their attitude, so many people have washed their hearts of hatred and bitterness, and many made decisions who had never expected to make such decisions."[17] Many years later, Vaught still remembered the event well and wrote, "The influence of this good man was a real factor in the solution of our racial problems here in Little Rock."[18]

Billy Graham is gratified when he and his team are able to help bring about a regeneration of Christ's standards in a city or a country. Yet in all of this, Graham defines himself as the *evangelist*. He recognizes that the most profound human need is spiritual. He has never compromised or cut short his evangelization to do other ministries. Yet as he preaches the gospel, the love of Christ compels him to do all in his power to alleviate the pain and suffering of people in the world. And that is biblical and historical Christianity. Social concern and evangelism do go hand in glove. Jesus Himself epitomized that approach to ministry and so have countless others through two thousand years of church history. One wonders what society would be like were this not so. Graham has hit the right note—and may the contemporary church follow his lead. But such a stand entails suffering for the full gospel, as the next chapter shall show.

7

Billy Graham
and Suffering

❦

*"We accept each hurt, each problem,
each difficulty as from His hand."*

— BILLY GRAHAM

In the 1980s Billy Graham received a request from two reporters with Charlotte, North Carolina's daily newspaper, the *Charlotte Observer*. They had interviewed Graham before and had written positive articles about him, and so Graham did not hesitate to give them a full interview.

In the course of the interview, the reporters asked Billy Graham several questions about his work and then raised the question of what Graham planned for the future. He replied that he hoped to build a large building on the campus of Wheaton College that could be used as both a repository for his archives and an academic center for research into evangelism. He went further to state that he also hoped to build a conference center not far from his home in Montreat, North Carolina. The reporters asked how he intended to fund these two projects. Graham replied that he had set up a foundation to receive gifts and funds for the projects and as soon as it was sufficiently large enough, he would undertake the construction. The interview came to an end and no more was said about the future projects.

Over the next few days, though, the reporters investigated the foundation Billy Graham had established to fund the projects. They discovered that the fund was approved by the Internal Revenue Service and had been audited every year in accordance with the law. Nevertheless, a sensational headline appeared on the front of the Saturday edition of the paper. The headline announced: "Billy Graham's Secret $23 Million Fund." The story exploded across the nation. Television, radio, newspapers, and magazines blared the shocking news everywhere. Billy Graham had twenty-three million dollars secretly stashed away.

In reading the first paragraph of the article in the *Charlotte Observer*, it did sound questionable. However, reading on, noting all the facts, a thinking person would have cause to ask, "What's so bad about that?" It was no secret at all. In fact, Billy Graham had sent out a press release more than once regarding his plans and the foundation. But at the time, it was so inconsequential in the thinking of the media that no one had even bothered to publish it. The general feeling was that the foundation was legitimate, the two projects were worthy, and there would be no personal gain to Billy Graham. But when it came out that the evangelist had a "secret" twenty-three-million-dollar fund, one can imagine how less thoughtful people received the news.

The battle raged on for some time. As a case in point, on the first page of the daily newspaper in Orlando, Florida, there was a picture of a dollar bill with Washington's face removed and Graham's superimposed with the heading, "Billy Graham's Secret 23 Million Dollar Fund."

Finally, the board of directors of Graham's organization issued a decree that nothing illegal or unethical had been done. Billy Graham had deceived no one. Creating a foundation to hold the funds until the projects could be completed was a wise and ethical way to handle the matter.

Eventually the criticism of Graham faded away, and in the next few years the fund was sufficient to build the Billy Graham Center at Wheaton College, which sponsors programs supporting worldwide evangelism and houses the evangelist's archives. The building also serves as the graduate school of Wheaton College. The Cove, one of America's most respected Christian conference centers, was also constructed in North Carolina, where it has been a source of spiritual encouragement to many thousands of people.

At times, the press has been merciless in its pursuit of sensational headlines at Billy Graham's expense. Although Graham has not been called upon to wear a martyr's crown, it has not always been easy to endure such onslaughts, especially when these headlines proved to be wrong. As John Corts of the BGEA has said, "Mental suffering is greater than physical suffering."[1]

It is clear from the Scriptures and church history that "all that will live godly in Christ Jesus shall suffer persecution" (2 Timothy 3:12, KJV). Classic histories have been written on the theme of Christian persecution. Incontestably, those who have borne a fervent witness for the Lord Jesus Christ have often become Christian martyrs. As a case in point, Savanarola of Florence, Italy, was martyred for his clear Christian stand back in the fifteenth century. And it has been true of many who have stood fearlessly for Christ. But through their martyrdom, these people have inspired many others to faith in Jesus. Evangelism cannot be divorced from suffering. This has been true throughout the ages of God's dealings with rebellious humanity, and shall be so until the final trumpet sounds. As the Apostle Paul puts it, "For to you it has been granted for Christ's sake, not only to believe in Him, but also to suffer for His sake" (Philippians 1:29).

BILLY GRAHAM'S UNDERSTANDING
OF CHRISTIAN SUFFERING

Billy Graham, who has suffered harsh criticism, raises the issue of Christian suffering in his work. He points out that Jesus told His disciples in unmistakable language that discipleship meant a life of self-denial and bearing His cross. That is to say, Christ's cross was to become their cross. In his book *Storm Warning,* Graham says, "Jesus warned that the price of believing in him would be high mockery, laughter, persecution, even death would be common."[2] Thus the Lord urges those who would be His followers to count the costs carefully, lest they should turn back when they encounter the inevitable suffering and onslaughts of this world. Billy Graham points out that some Christians think just because they are believers their problems and suffering will vanish. He reminds us of Christ's words: "They will make you outcasts from the synagogue, but an hour is coming for everyone who kills you to think that he is offering service to God" (John 16:2). Moreover, Graham points out that the Apostle Paul reminded the early Christians at Lystra, Iconium, and Antioch that "through many tribulations we must enter the kingdom of God" (Acts 14:22).

Statistics make it abundantly clear that God's people suffer. In the 1990s alone, the martyrdom of some 290,000 Christians a year was recorded. Billy Graham well understands that suffering is the believer's lot. He contends that Christians should actually rejoice in the midst of their trials. After all, Christ says, "Blessed are you when men cast insults at you, and persecute you, and say all kinds of evil against you falsely, on account of Me. Rejoice, and be glad, for your reward in heaven is great, for so they persecuted the prophets who were before you" (Matthew 5:11–12). Paul also says that "the sufferings of this present time are not worthy to be compared with the glory that is to be revealed to us" (Romans 8:18).

Getting to the heart of things, Graham points out, "We are not surprised that the early Christians rejoiced in suffering, since they looked at it in the light of eternity. The nearer death, the nearer a life of eternal fellowship with Christ." In A.D. 110, church father Ignasius was put to death for his faith. He is said to have cried out, "Nearer the sword, then nearer to God. In company with wild beasts, in company with God." The Apostle Paul states the principle in Romans 8:17: "If indeed we suffer with Him in order that we may also be glorified with Him." Graham resonates with this when he says, "For Paul the Christian life was one of suffering."[3] He also says, "In all ages, Christians have found it possible to maintain the spirit of joy in the hour of persecution."[4] Why is this? According to Graham it is because "in the midst of the suffering, trials and temptations, He [God] will provide His peace, joy and fellowship."[5]

Billy Graham is well aware that many kinds of persecution arise. Suffering and persecution can certainly come in the guise of discrimination, being scorned, maligned, laughed at and rejected by friends and society. Mental and psychological suffering at times can be more painful than physical torture. A tragedy of this type of persecution is that it can even arise from within the ranks of those who profess the Christian faith. There are those Christians who inevitably shoot arrows of criticism and scorn at those who take valiant stands for Christ. As Graham has said, "There is no doubt that the Bible teaches that every believer who is faithful to Christ must be prepared to be persecuted at the hands of those who are enemies of the gospel."[6] And some of those enemies can be found within the church.

In light of this, the question becomes: Where does such persecution come from? What lies behind it?

THE SOURCE OF CHRISTIAN PERSECUTION

For Billy Graham, an insight into the source of the persecution and suffering that Christians endure came from one of his sons. The Billy Graham Evangelistic Association had been under particularly heavy attack. Graham was in conversation about the situation with his son Franklin, who at the time was enrolled in college. As he poured out his heart, his son challenged him. "Dad," said Franklin Graham, "you shouldn't even think about it. You know where these lies are coming from, don't you?"

"What do you mean?" asked Billy Graham.

His son replied, "Well, who's the father of lies?"

"The devil," replied the evangelist.

"So that's where they're coming from. You're in a spiritual battle."

Graham thought for a moment and then confessed, "I'm a coward."

Why did Billy Graham say this? As he told the story later, he said that Franklin's words made him realize that enduring criticism and ridicule was a part of spiritual warfare, and it was time to stand up for Christ against the wiles of Satan. Graham had got to the point where he had almost asked God to take the trial away from him. But now he understood that it was God's will for him to fight. He searched the Bible for renewed strength and found it in the following words: "Blessed are ye, when men shall revile you, and persecute you, and say all manner of evil against you falsely, for my sake." He read on triumphantly. "Rejoice, and be exceeding glad; for great is your reward in heaven."[7]

This gets at the essence of the matter. Billy Graham forcefully states that the ultimate source of all persecution and malignment that befalls Christians has its origin in the pits of evil and the devil. In a few words, he outlines this stand when he says, "The world, the flesh, and the devil are enemies."[8] Satan is the culprit. Graham contends that Satan, "the anointed cherub" (Ezekiel 28:14), enjoyed a high standing in the hierarchy of God's created beings. But being lifted up with pride he cried out, "I am a god, I sit in the seat of gods" (Ezekiel 28:2). In that moment the cherub Lucifer became Satan the devil, the adversary. Billy Graham believes from the Bible's teachings that in Satan's fall a host of angels, possibly a third of the heavenly host, fell with him (Revelation 12:4). And now there exists a hierarchy of demonic evil, superintended by Satan, with one goal: to thwart the expansion of God's kingdom.

Little wonder, then, that those who evangelize become Satan's special targets. In the midst of a world that has essentially given itself to Satan and the demonic forces, believers valiantly attempt to bear testimony for Christ and the gospel. John expresses the believer's battleground as "all that is in the world, the lust of the flesh and the lust of the eyes and the boastful pride of life, is not from the Father, but is from the world" (1 John 2:16).

If society truly is, as Billy Graham calls it, an upside-down world, then it stands to reason that when God's people confront the world in the power of the Holy Spirit with the gospel of Christ, many people cry out in consternation.

And because many in the world willingly, although perhaps unknowingly, give themselves to the satanic enterprise, they become pawns in the devil's hand to bring destruction upon those who serve Christ. As Billy Graham points out, "Herein lies the fundamental reason for Christian persecution. Christ's righteousness is so revolutionary, so contradictory to man's manner of living, that it evokes the enmity of the world . . . as long as Satan is loose in the world and our hearts are dominated by his evil passions, it will never be easy or popular to be a follower of Christ."[9]

Graham knows the reality of this truth all too well. Excerpts from his early diary confirm the fact: "Don't doubt for a moment the existence of the Devil! We see his power and influence everywhere. He is very personal and he is very real. And he is extremely clever." At the end of a long day of conferences preparing to open the All-Scotland crusade in Glasgow, he wrote, "Satan is very cunning. We recognize that on our way to Glasgow, as we are holding our meetings and planning our strategy and spending time in prayer that God will send revival, that Satan is also holding his councils, laying his plans to bring, if he can, God's work to naught." Prior to his mission in Cambridge University in the fall of 1955, he wrote: "During the past week I have felt the tremendous opposition of Satan. I seriously doubt if at any time in my ministry I have so felt the powers of darkness. It seems as though the demons of Hell had concentrated against this mission."[10] Were it not for the grace of God and the fact that Satan can do nothing apart from what God permits, the cause of Christ would soon fail.

WHY DOES SATAN HAVE POWER?

Much mystery surrounds the truth of Satan's hold on the world. The question constantly surfaces: Why does God permit him to have such a hold? How can God allow bad things to happen to good people? Why does He give Satan leave to do his ravaging work in the world? Indeed the issue becomes very personal: *Why do I have to suffer?*

Billy Graham answers such questions by granting that in the inscrutable and ultimate wisdom of God, when such problems arise, the final answer to the quandary must wait for eternity to reveal God's answer. In the meantime, God's people should arm themselves for the realities of Satan's attack and gird themselves in the power of the Holy Spirit, rejoicing in their suffering, knowing that it has an "eternal weight of glory" (2 Corinthians 4:17). As Paul brought it all together in Romans 12:21, "Do not be overcome by evil, but overcome evil with good."

The evangelist points out that believers are to "fight the good fight of faith" (1 Timothy 6:12). He says: "The world, the flesh, and the devil are our enemies. In times of war one hardly expects the good will of the enemy's forces. . . . A battle is also raging in the spiritual realm. The Bible says, 'We wrestle not against flesh and blood, but against principalities, against powers, against the rulers of the darkness of this world, against spiritual wickedness in high places' (Ephesians 6:12)."[11] Graham takes this spiritual battle very seriously when he states, "Jesus said that a cross is the Christian's lot" (Matthew 10:38).[12] Still, "The very fact that they, the persecutors, are inclined to persecute us is proof that we are 'not of this world,' that we are 'in Christ.'"[13] Therefore, Billy Graham sees all Christian suffering as "the privilege of persecution."[14]

He gives Christians some cautions, however. First, as Christians we may suffer because of our own poor judgment, stupidity, and blundering. He contends, "There is no blessedness in this."[15] Furthermore, Graham insists, "We must be careful not to behave offensively, preach offensively, and dress offensively."[16] And we must also never adopt or embrace a martyr's attitude. Graham contends that the patient suffering of Christians often precipitates the conversion of people who would perhaps otherwise remain untouched. Finally, persecution and suffering identifies us with Christ so that a martyr truly does become a witness.

TRIALS AND TRIBULATION FOR THE EVANGELIST

Billy Graham has had his share of suffering and persecution, even though he has not suffered physically for his faith. Graham's longtime friend and colleague Grady Wilson has pointed out, "People have tried to lump the BGEA with unsavory stereotypes of evangelism, especially in our early days. They accused us of being flamboyant and flashy, hypocritical Elmer-Gantry types."[17] As could be expected, persecution for Billy Graham has come often in the form of severe criticism and ostracism. As John Stott has said concerning Graham's trials, "Slander is a vicious kind of torture."[18]

FUNDAMENTALIST CRITICISMS

One of the attacks that grieved Billy Graham perhaps more than any other came from Dr. Bob Jones Sr. When Graham decided to leave Bob Jones College and attend a Bible institute in Temple Terrace, Florida, Dr. Bob, as the students affectionately called him, requested that Billy come to his office. There, Jones admonished him not to leave, warning that if he did so, he would never be heard of and would probably end up in some insignificant church having forfeited a much larger ministry.

When Billy Graham did become prominent, Bob Jones Sr. accused the evangelist of peddling a "discount type of religion" and "sacrificing the cause of evangelism at the altar of temporary convenience."[19] While Graham was still involved with Youth for Christ and serving as president of Northwestern Schools, the relationship between Bob Jones and Billy had been reasonably cordial. However, as Graham's fame increased, Jones's criticisms grew apace. At times, rather bizarre things took place in this context. For example, as preparations were being made for the New York Madison Square Garden crusade, a printing company in Greenville, South Carolina, the new location of Bob Jones University, was awarded the contract to do the printing for the New York crusade. Several Bob Jones University students were working part-time at the printing firm, and Bob Jones Sr. took issue with that work. In addition, Jones criticized students who dared to attend any of Billy Graham's services.

It must be said that Billy Graham did everything he could to heal this ever-widening breach, but to no avail. Bob Jones Sr. went to his grave denouncing Billy Graham, accusing him of having "led thousands into compromise and alliance with infidelity and Romanism" and "doing more harm to the cause of Jesus Christ than any living man."[20] Concerning this, Graham has said, "Fundamentalist is a grand

and wonderful word, but it has gotten off-track and into so many extreme positions. . . . I felt like my own brother had turned against me."[21] The evangelist points out that "one of the worst wounds we can receive or give is done with 'words.'"[22] But he also quotes evangelist D. L. Moody, who said, "If the world has nothing to say against you, beware lest Jesus Christ has nothing to say for you."[23]

Fundamentalist preacher Carl McIntire, as might be expected, also attacked Billy Graham quite viciously. McIntire, always outspoken, said that Graham's crusades could "very easily be the church of the anti-Christ, Babylon the great, the scarlet woman, the harlot church, described in Revelation 17–18."[24] Such ferocious attacks have constantly dogged Billy Graham, especially in his earlier years of ministry, though the attacks still flare up from time to time.

When Graham traveled to Northern Ireland during a very volatile time, Ian Paisley, an ultraconservative Presbyterian, wrote, "Is he [Graham] not so gracious? Is he not so kind? Is he not a lovely man? Satan can be transformed into an angel of light. And no marvel, for Satan himself is transformed into an angel of light. Therefore it is no great thing if his ministers also be transformed into ministers of righteousness, whose end shall be according to their works."[25]

SPIRITUAL WARFARE

Billy Graham is well prepared for such attacks. He knows suffering is inevitable for God's evangelists. The Bible says, "For our struggle is not against flesh and blood, but against the rulers, against the powers, against the world forces of this darkness and against the spiritual forces of wickedness in the heavenly places" (Ephesians 6:12). This warfare deeply involves people; the people of God and the people of darkness. It has always been so since the Garden of Eden (Genesis 3). As Graham says, "In his warfare against God, Satan uses the human race, which God created and loved. So God's forces of good and Satan's forces of evil have been engaged in a deadly conflict from the dawn of our history."[26] Regarding his Dortmund, Germany, crusade Graham said, "I felt in Germany that I was in hand to hand combat with the forces of evil, though I believe the victory was the greatest in the history of our work."[27]

The evangelist stresses the reality of warfare, pointing out that a well-known, highly visible pastor or evangelist is often a special target of Satan. At times he really has been "tried with fire" (1 Peter 1:7, KJV). For example, during the Chicago crusade in the early 1970s, a large number of Satan worshipers rushed into the auditorium and ran down the aisles chanting their satanic verses. A hymn was being sung at that moment, but Graham got up, went to the microphone, interrupted the hymn and said, "There are three or four hundred Satan worshipers here tonight. They said that they're going to take over the platform. Now I am going to ask you Christian young people to do something; don't hurt them; just surround them and love them and sing to them. And if you can, just gradually move them toward the doors." That was the end of the demonstration.

A PURITANICAL THROWBACK

Always sensitive to criticism, Graham stated during preparation for the New York crusade, "We face the city with fear and trembling. I am prepared to go to New York to be crucified by my critics, if necessary. When I leave New York, every engagement we have in the world might be canceled. It may mean I'll be crucified—but I'm going."[28] And he did receive severe criticism. The *Christian Century* derided the forthcoming crusade as a "trumped-up revival." The writer went on to say, "The Graham procedure . . . does its mechanical best to 'succeed,' whether or not the Holy Spirit is in attendance."[29] But Jesus told us that if they persecuted Him, they would also persecute us because "a disciple is not above his teacher" (Matthew 10:24). And as Billy Graham has said, "[This] points us to the suffering Savior as a pattern of how we as His believing people, should endure our suffering."[30]

The evangelist is always prepared for the inevitable attacks, especially from the left. And when they come he handles them in his typical Christ-centered manner. For example, he confesses that many consider him a throwback to Puritan times, hopelessly out of date. Of this Graham says, "Some extreme liberal and Unitarian clergies said I was setting back the cause of religion a hundred years. I replied that I did indeed want to set religion back—not just a hundred years but 1900 years, back to the book of Acts where first century followers of Christ were accused of turning the Roman empire upside-down."[31]

THE SECULAR PRESS

Billy Graham has been perceived by many in the secular world, especially in his early years, as a typical "hot gospeler" who employs high-pressure American salesmanship in order to "get people down the aisle." At one time he was known as "God's machine gun" by the press. In a typical case, the *London Evening News* castigated Graham as an "American hot gospel specialist" during the Harringay crusade of 1954.[32] The article called him an "actor-manager of the show," saying that "like a Biblical boebeker, he takes his listeners strolling down pavements of gold, introduces them to rippling-muscled Christ, who resembles Charles Atlas with a halo, then drops them abruptly into the Lake of Fire for a sample scalding."[33] The *Daily Worker*, another popular London newspaper, ran the headline "Atom Bomb Gospeler" just before Graham arrived for the Harringay crusade. Playing on Graham's fierce anti-Communist bent, the article went on to say, "We should be able to get some quiet fun out of Mr. Billy Graham when he gets here. . . . His mission is to cause a religious revival on the strength of scores of thousands of pounds provided by wealthy backers. . . . He will try to persuade us that the more atom bombs America piles up, the more certain is the victory of the Prince of Peace."[34]

Of course, the *entire* media has never been against Billy Graham. There have always been positive articles written about his crusades. Indeed, as mentioned earlier, he has been voted one of the ten most admired men in the world for over twenty-five years. That is unprecedented. The media, by and large, have come to highly regard Billy Graham.

At times, however, there have not only been attempts on the evangelist's reputation but also threats on his life. As a result, precautions must constantly be taken. Both before and during crusade meetings, tight security has to be maintained.

BILLY GRAHAM'S ATTITUDE TOWARD SUFFERING

Dr. Nelson Bell, Billy Graham's father-in-law, had a motto concerning attacks, criticisms, and suffering. The motto read, "No attack, no defense, proclaim the truth." This, too, has become Billy Graham's basic position. He takes two basic stands in the face of criticism. First, he refuses, except on rare occasions, to reply to his critics and detractors. Second, he seeks to love his detractors and desires reconciliation with them. As John Corts of the BGEA has stated, Graham always says, "Pray for them." This approach has been an inspiration to many. Dr. Frank Harbor, a young evangelist who admires Billy Graham's approach, says, "When attacks come, I ask myself, what would Billy do? How would he react?"[35]

Graham has learned through the years that to perpetuate an issue with some line of defense normally does nothing but deepen the problem. Those who want to believe the bad will do so regardless, and those who wish to be fair will make themselves knowledgeable of the true facts.

CONFIDENCE IN THE PROVIDENCE AND CARE OF GOD

Billy Graham is not a fatalist or a naive person who superficially takes everything that occurs as being from the hand of God. Nor does he always face suffering in a glib fashion. There have been times when suffering has thrown him into depression. He has said, "In my own life, the pressures at times, mentally, physically, and spiritually, have become so great that I felt like . . . lying down in the cemetery to see how I fit."[36]

Yet in the face of it all, Graham firmly believes that in the providence and care of God, nothing is going to happen to him that God does not permit. This does not mean there will be no suffering or heartache or death. He shared in an interview, "I get [death threats] quite often [but] I'm clothed in the armor of God . . . and if He wants me killed, I'm happy to be killed."[37] Christians who faithfully serve Christ must face these realities. Nothing occurs among His children that He does not, for some reason, permit. And if severe suffering, even martyrdom, does occur, there will be "stars in their crowns" that will far supersede anything that this world could possibly imagine. Billy Graham has been criticized for virtually everything imaginable. But to repeat what Paul said, "The sufferings of this present time are not worthy to be compared with the glory that is to be revealed to us" (Romans 8:18). That is a glorious hope.

David Frost, the well-known British interviewer, once asked Billy Graham, "How do you suggest that Christians get ready for the hard times ahead?" The evangelist's answer was classic Graham:

> The most important thing we can do is to grow in our relationship to Christ. If we have not learned to pray in our everyday lives, we will find it difficult to know God's peace and strength through prayer when hard times come. If we have not learned to trust God's Word when times are easy, we will not trust His Word when we face difficulties. . . . The Scriptures speak to us in those moments when we look to the Lord for sustenance and strength.[38]

Billy Graham lays out five points as to how believers ought to endure times of suffering. He urges fellow sufferers to:

1. Expect suffering. Don't feel surprised.

2. Don't look at anyone else and what he or she does or does not have to bear. Such comparisons are demoralizing.

3. Recognize that it doesn't take great wealth or social influence to be faithful. It takes patience and endurance.

4. Remember that one day all earthly suffering will end, and will not touch us.

5. Keep in mind that when one bears suffering faithfully, God is glorified and honored. The suffering Christian will be honored in a special way.[39]

When asked how he felt about his Parkinson's disease and if he considered God responsible for it, in typical Graham fashion he said,

> I don't know. He allows it. And He allows it for a purpose that I may not know. I think that everything that comes to our lives, if we are true believers, God has a purpose and a plan. And many of these things are things that cause suffering or inconvenience or whatever. But it helps to mature me because God is molding and making me in the image of His Son Jesus Christ. Jesus Christ suffered more than any man that ever lived because when He was on the cross He was bearing the sins that you and I have committed.[40]

Perhaps Billy Graham's basic attitude toward suffering is best summed up in his statement that Christians are not "exempt from the tribulations and natural disasters that come upon the world. Scripture does teach that the Christian can face tribulation, crisis, calamity, and personal suffering with a supernatural power that is not available to the person outside of Christ."[41] Simply put, over the decades, Billy Graham has faced difficulties, problems, criticisms, and attacks with a spirit of Christ that permeates his entire approach to life and reality. He stands victorious, as so many other Christians have done down through the ages. Graham contends that regardless of what may fall across one's path by way of affliction, Christians are to be patient and rejoice and become exceedingly glad (Romans 5:12).

Billy Graham stresses, "Christians can rejoice in the midst of persecution because they have eternity's values in view."[42] What will prepare us for the day of suffering? "The most important thing we can do is grow—in our relationship to Christ."[43] That, according to the evangelist, is the secret to victory over suffering. After all, as Paul promises, believers who live in Christ's intimate fellowship can be more than conquerors (Romans 8:37). Paul himself exuded this confidence when he said to the Corinthian church, "I am overflowing with joy in all our affliction" (2 Corinthians 7:4). He went on to say he was content with weaknesses, insults, hardships, persecution, and calamities (2 Corinthians 12:10).

"I have found in my travels that those who keep heaven in view remain serene and cheerful in the darkest day. . . . Victory for such does not come easily or quickly. But eventually the peace of God does come and with it is joy."[44] These words, uttered by Billy Graham, have been true of Christ-honoring evangelists down through church history. Graham is certainly one of their number. He has said, "I don't want to get to heaven without any scars."[45] He won't.

8

A Man of the Bible

⸙

"The Bible says . . ."

— BILLY GRAHAM

Martin Luther stood before the august leaders of the Roman Catholic Church at Worms, Germany. It was April 17, 1521, and the demand had come for him to recant his position. Faced with the threat of excommunication, Luther uttered the now famous words, "Here I stand, I cannot do otherwise; God help me." And this stand did cost him. Two years later he was thrust out of the Roman Catholic Church, whereupon he became the champion of the Protestant Reformation.

What caused Luther to take such a defiant stand? Why defy more than a thousand years of ecclesiastical history and the power of the established church? When John Eck, Luther's prosecutor at Worms posed this question to him, the young Luther replied: "Since then Your Majesty and your lordships desire a simple reply, I will answer without horns and without teeth. Unless I am convicted by Scripture and plain reason—I do not accept the authority of popes and councils, for they have contradicted each other—my conscience is captive to the Word of God."[1]

Luther contended that the Word of God alone forms the basis of divine truth and subsequent authority. On one occasion, when he was asked how he was able to effect such a spiritual revolution in Europe, he replied, "I simply taught, preached, wrote God's Word; otherwise I did nothing . . . the Word did it all."[2] For Martin Luther it was *Sola Scriptura:* the Scriptures only. He came to experience God's grace in Christ personally and set out at all costs to share the truth of the gospel with the world. In the pursuit of this goal the Reformation was launched. It was a thrust based upon the deep conviction that the Bible alone stands as the written revelation of Christian truth and experience.

GOD'S REVELATION

Every Christian, to some degree, is faced with the same question with which Luther wrestled: Can the Bible be trusted as the foundation for all faith and knowledge? It is certainly a question Billy Graham has had to grapple with. Indeed, his particular approach to understanding the nature and authority of the Bible did not come easily.

Although he had been reared in a Christian home where the Bible was regularly read, Graham encountered several struggles in his Christian walk, none greater than the question as to whether the Bible could be trusted in its entirety. The evangelist's struggle was brought to a head in an encounter, mentioned earlier in this book, with Charles Templeton concerning higher critical methods of Bible interpretation. The question became whether by faith to take the Bible at face value as the Word of God, or whether to probe deeper into theology looking for rational answers and definitive proofs. The encounter took place in 1949, and Billy Graham recalls it was "a crucial moment in my ministry."[3] Graham's old friend Steven Olford states that it was in this experience that was born Billy's most famous phrase, "the Bible says. . . ."[4] But several steps led to this critical moment.

Graham's first major step came when he realized that aspects of the Scriptures would never be reconciled on a purely rational level. He says, "As a Christian, I am under no obligation to attempt to reconcile the Bible teachings with modern philosophy. Biblical truth does not parallel human opinion of any generation; it usually opposes it."[5] Those who declare the Bible to be riddled with contradictions and myths project the implication that the gospel of Jesus Christ is anti-intellectual. Billy Graham rejects this position. In this regard he says, "It's a strange thing about this book (the Bible). There are many things in it I don't understand and can't explain. Some of the questions I have asked about it I am sure will never be answered this side of Heaven."[6] His argument sets forth the idea that Scripture transcends mere human intellectualism. As a result, one must rest in faith in a God that exists above finite human reason.

At the same time, Graham points out that "skeptics have attacked the Bible and retreated in confusion. Agnostics have scoffed at its teachings but are unable to produce an intellectually honest refutation. Atheists have denied its validity, but must surrender to its historical accuracy and archeological information."[7] There are reasons to believe. There are principles and precepts of apologetics that can be employed to convince the open-minded. In the case of the debate between science and religion, Graham declares, "There is never any conflict between true science and Christian faith."[8] Yet he simultaneously sees the Bible as essentially "a book of faith, not necessarily science."[9] He stresses, "The Bible is a book of redemption."[10] And science, as all acknowledge, is not a book of religion. Billy Graham contends, "The fact of the matter is: science and faith complement each other."[11] The Bible believer cannot be charged with naive anti-intellectualism, even though faith plays a vital role in the acceptance of biblical claims.

The evangelist's views can be summarized as follows: The Bible is totally inspired by the Spirit of God. Yet, one should not attempt to define the methodology by which God inspired the human writers. God brought the Bible together so that, in the form in which we have it today, it can be properly called the composition of God. Divine inspiration serves as the foundation for the validity and the authority of the Bible. Therefore, being God's Word, the Bible is always relevant to the human situation. The Scriptures not only spoke to the Jews of old and the first-century church, they are alive and have been relevant to every succeeding generation. Billy Graham believes this stands true because the Bible points the way to the answer to humanity's deepest needs and presents the solution in Jesus Christ.

As a result of this belief, Graham has not only built his ministry on the Scriptures, he has also contributed to the body of Christ by helping many Christians gain a new confidence in the Bible.

A CONFIDENT CONCLUSION

Billy Graham must be seen as a "revelationist" rather than a pure rationalist. For him, if God's revelation as we have it in the pages of the Bible conflicts with rational reason, he opts for revelation. As Martin Luther has said, "We must consider the Word alone and judge according to it."[12] While Graham fully agrees with this stand, he nonetheless maintains an appreciation for research. He has said, "Every scientific fact that man has so far discovered adds luster and testimony to the value and integrity of the Bible."[13]

Not only does the evangelist agree with Luther, but also with John Calvin. Calvin said, "Those who penned the Bible 'were sure and genuine scribes of the Holy Spirit,' and their writings are considered to be oracles of God. We, therefore, teach that faithful ministers are now not permitted to coin any new doctrine, but they are simply to cleave to the doctrine to which God has subjected all men without exception."[14]

Graham is emphatic that the Bible must be understood, assimilated, and lived out. He takes the Bible by simple faith, and argues that by faith alone we can grasp God's truth. "The Bible says!" is his clarion call. Indeed, for Billy Graham, the Bible serves as the essential foundational core in all his preaching. No instrument in the evangelist's ministry has played a more central role than the Word of God. As John Stott says of Graham, "He's a man of the Bible."[15]

BILLY GRAHAM'S VIEWS OF THE BIBLE

Billy Graham's basic view of the Bible and its relevance can be seen in his convictions concerning the actual nature of God's Word. He takes a positive stance on the Bible as being authoritative truth able to meet life's issues. He gives several reasons.

Inspiration

In the first place, Billy Graham holds a high view of the Bible because of his commitment to the proposition that the Scriptures are divinely inspired. When he speaks of inspiration, the evangelist speaks of *plenary* inspiration. That is, each *word* counts, and not just the idea behind the words. When the question is raised, "Do you believe in plenary, verbal inspiration?" Graham answers, "I do, for the mere, simple reason that the words are mere signs of ideas, I do not know how to get at the idea except through the words."[16]

Graham believes that God has spoken in a unique sense in the Scriptures. Therefore, the Bible stands as the revealed truth of God. The Bible is totally inspired by the Holy Spirit. It has the stamp of infallibility upon it, and thus the ring of authenticity. Billy Graham says, "I came to believe with all of my heart in the full inspiration of the Bible."[17] The evangelist, of course, is conscious that the human pen played its part in the creation of the Bible. But at the back of it all, God the Spirit moved the writers in such a manner that they wrote under His divine sovereignty. The end product is an inerrant transcript of the thoughts and truth of the triune God.

Billy Graham would again agree with Martin Luther when he declared that we are to read and wrestle with Scripture in such a way that one must understand it as God Himself speaking the words. The Bible is replete with the statement, "Thus saith the Lord." Graham sees such statements as a vindication of the inspiration and absolute truthfulness of Scripture. The Bible stands as the "God-breathed" Word of God. In this regard, Graham says, "God breathed life into man and made him a living soul, so also He breathed life and wisdom into the Word of God."[18] He goes on to elaborate, "I believe the Bible is the Word of God. By that I mean the full verbal inspiration of the Scriptures. I can accept no compromise with the teaching of the Scripture."[19]

The evangelist also holds to the view that the Holy Spirit has led and preserved the Bible in such a way that today we have in the canon of Scripture an authentic version of God's written revelation. Even though the original autographs are missing, we have in hand a fully reliable body of God's truth. Graham says, "God has spoken verbally, and His spoken Word has survived every scratch of the human pen."[20] This approach can be summarized in a statement Graham made while penning an article under the title "Ambassadors." He wrote, "Our generation, especially in the West, has occupied itself with criticism of the Scriptures and all too often questioning divine revelation. Don't make that mistake. Take the Bible as God's Holy Word."[21] In a word, Billy Graham adheres to the total verbal inspiration and infallibility of the Bible, and hence to the inerrancy of the Word. However, he prefers to use the word *infallibility* rather than *inerrancy* due to the baggage the later term has acquired. "I decided to use the word 'infallibility' . . . [still] they mean the same," he says.[22] This belief in infallibility in turn implies another principle: authority.

The Authority of the Bible

Billy Graham not only believes in the total inspiration of Scripture, but also in its absolute authority. And the authority of the Bible grows out of its God-breathed nature. On this point Graham writes, "There is a second word that we would discuss when we talk about the Bible. Not only is the Bible inspired, but it is 'authoritative.' When we say that the Bible is 'authoritative,' we mean it is God's binding revelation to us. We submit to it because it has come from God."[23]

The evangelist holds that the Bible's authority is expressed in a unique way. He believes not only that the original texts were inspired by the Holy Spirit, but also he is confident that the Spirit of God inspired the selection of the sixty-six books that comprise the canon itself. He grants, of course, that the choice of the books that make up the canon came through human hands. Yet it was certainly not a mere human choice. God worked in and through the scholars who fashioned and compiled the canon. What we have, therefore, is again an absolute authoritative Word.

All this implies a multiplicity of things, but it certainly means that the Bible is the final authoritative word in all matters of ethics, doctrine, and theology, and in formulating an understanding of life as a whole. It forms the core of the preaching of the gospel. Graham sums it up this way: "God 'designed' the Bible to meet the needs of all people and all ages."[24]

THE PRACTICAL ASPECTS OF GRAHAM'S VIEWS ON THE BIBLE

Billy Graham holds tenaciously to the principle of the Bible being authoritative in the totality of the spiritual experience, particularly as it relates to ethics and morals in Christian spirituality. He says, "Every area of our lives is to be under the Lordship of Jesus Christ. And that means the search light of God's Word must penetrate every corner of our lives."[25] He quotes John R. W. Stott's statement that "we submit to the authority of the Scripture. . . . Submission to Scripture is fundamental to everyday Christian living, for without it Christian discipleship, Christian integrity, Christian freedom, and Christian witness are all seriously damaged, if not actually destroyed."[26]

Turning to passages of Scripture such as John 15:3, "You are already clean because of the word which I have spoken to you," Billy Graham states that we "should be obedient to all of it—that is, the Word of God."[27]

Concerning the Bible's role in developing Christ-likeness in a person's spiritual life, Graham quotes George Mueller: "The figure of spiritual life will be in exact proportion to the place held by the Bible in our life and thoughts."[28] It is the Bible that instructs a person in making correct moral and ethical decisions. Graham says, "I believe that God never leads anyone contrary to the Bible. So if you have a feeling that is contrary, it isn't God, but it might be the devil."[29]

In summary, for Billy Graham the development of a person's spiritual experience, as it relates to moral and ethical living, is based on the lordship of Christ with the Bible providing both strength and guidance. As Peter put it, "Long for the pure milk of the word, that by it you may grow" (1 Peter 2:2). This emphasis is seen in Graham's stress on Bible study for those who make decisions for Christ in his crusades.

Indeed, Billy Graham gets quite specific on morality and the place of God's Word in relation to such issues. As a case in point, he takes up the evil of drunkenness. He writes,

> The Bible is not silent about any force which threatens the souls of men. It lashes out at any and all of Satan's tricks and devices, and it is very clear on this denunciation of drunkenness. The Bible said, "Woe to the crown of pride, to the drunkards of Ephraim . . ." The Bible again says, "Woe unto him that giveth his neighbour drink, that puttest thy bottle to him and makest him drunken also." "And take heed to yourselves lest at any time your hearts be overcharged with surfeiting and drunkenness." Again the Bible says, "Let us walk honestly, as in the day; not in rioting and drunkenness." "Woe unto them that rise up early in the morning, that may follow strong drinks; that continue until night." Again the Bible says, "Do not be drunk on wine, wherein is excess."[30]

And what Graham says about the morality of abusing alcohol and the use of Scriptures, he applies to other specific ethical issues. He fully believes that God's decrees in the Bible are *moral absolutes*. He says, "According to the Bible, morals are not relative—they are absolute and unchangeable. There is nothing in the Bible that would lead us to believe that God has ever lowered His standards."[31] In all Christian experience, the Holy Spirit, through the Scriptures, becomes the believer's Guide and strength.

THE SPIRIT INSTRUCTS

Evangelist Billy Graham fully recognizes the importance of the Holy Spirit's creating understanding when reading Scripture. For him the Holy Spirit not only stands as the One who inspired the Word of God, but also as the One who instructs believers in its truth, its ethical principles, in all aspects of theology, and in living the Christian life. Graham says, "The moment we receive Christ, God gives us a key for understanding the Bible so that we can unlock and understand the message of God to us. The Holy Spirit becomes our teacher. The Holy Spirit helps us to interpret the message. He applies it to our hearts. The Bible is an infallible guide for life."[32] In this way the Bible comes alive to the seeking reader. The Spirit of God instructs him or her in morals and doctrine. In this way the truth of God can be grasped.

BILLY GRAHAM'S USE OF THE BIBLE IN EVANGELISM

The first point to address in relation to the evangelistic preaching and ministry of Billy Graham centers in his confidence in the *power* of biblical truth. Of the Bible he says, "It has power like a sharp, two-edged sword."[33] Further, he points out, "It is the textbook of revelation."[34] The Bible is the essential source of the good news of God's salvation for us.

Billy Graham and his team of helpers also strive to use the Bible in a proper ethical manner in their evangelization. Rich Marshall, crusade leader and director of follow-up for Graham's crusades, says, "We never use the Scriptures as a hammer. We use it authoritatively, but not to 'fight' people."[35] In a spirit of humility, Graham gladly acknowledges that God's Spirit has used him significantly because of his proper use of, and the place he gives to, the Bible. He says, "I have found that when I present the simple message of the Gospel of Jesus Christ with authority and simplicity, quoting the word of God, He takes that message and drives it supernaturally into the human heart. It is a supernatural message, a supernatural authority, a supernatural power, by the Holy Spirit."[36]

Billy Graham has preached the gospel message on every continent and in multiple nations. Through it all he has become fully convinced that the gospel of Christ as found in the Bible is a message of power and relevance for any generation or culture, or wherever people may be found. In the hands of the Holy Spirit, the Bible has the power to change and transform lives. He says, "I know one thing [about the Bible]: It contains a mysterious power to direct all kinds and conditions of people into changed lives, and helps to keep them changed."[37] He gives personal testimony to this fact, saying, "I have found that the Scriptures have become a flame that has melted away unbelief in the hearts of people and moved them to decide for Christ. The Word has become a hammer breaking up stony hearts and shaping them into the likeness of God."[38]

Graham is quick to state that if the church ever turns from the simple proclamation of the gospel of Jesus Christ as found in the pages of the Bible, it will stand in opposition to the Holy Spirit. The Bible must have primacy in the preaching of Christ. The evangelist says,

> I believe effective preaching must be biblical preaching whether it is the exposition of a single word in the Bible, text, or chapter. The Word is what the Spirit uses. So the important element is, the Word of God proclaimed. . . . When we preach or teach the Scriptures we open the door for the Holy Spirit to do his work. God has not promised to bless oratory or clever preaching. He has promised to bless his word. He has said that it will not return unto him "empty."[39]

In discussing his use of the Scriptures, Graham says, "I do not quote [verses] . . . to uphold my views. I try to take my position on the basis of what the Bible teaches."[40] He has not moved from this stance in any significant way throughout his years of ministry. For Billy Graham, the Bible always speaks to all peoples; therefore, he uses it to the full. It has been estimated that Graham quotes up to forty or fifty Bible verses in each sermon.[41]

THE RELEVANCY OF SCRIPTURE TO ALL CULTURES

Billy Graham is not locked into using the Bible in evangelism in a way that makes it irrelevant to modern culture and its problems. He has been described as preaching with the Bible in one hand and a newspaper in the other, stating that the Bible is more up to date than the morning newspaper.[42] At the same time, Graham stresses this fact concerning the gospel: "I do not have to make the Gospel relevant; it is always relevant in any part of the world . . . [and] I must get the whole Gospel in [every] sermon."[43] What he strives to make relevant to the culture where he preaches is his introduction and illustrations. But the core gospel message is always the same. Indeed, he holds tenaciously to the gospel truth: "The Bible shows the timelessness of God's eternal truths."[44]

Baptist evangelist Larry Walker has said of Billy Graham, "He has an amazing 'cross-over' ability with different societies. He becomes 'all things to all men' to win them."[45] Perhaps this is one of the reasons for Graham's popularity. He strives to be aware and relevant to people where they are in life and share the message of Christ with them. In his crusades even the music has changed as different musical modes appeal to changing societies and generations. For example, on Saturday night in each crusade since the 1980s, he has conducted a "youth night." The stadium or hall where the crusade was being held resounded with gospel rock music as young people by the tens of thousands attended, and many made decisions for Christ. Teenagers jumped and waved their hands as the message of the gospel was presented in music form. But when the evangelist entered the pulpit, a quiet hush fell over the mass of young people. Indeed, the success of Graham's continuing ministry to teenagers, even though he is now in his eighties and suffering with Parkinson's disease, is nothing short of phenomenal. The response of teenagers is due to the simple gospel message made alive and relevant to contemporary culture. Billy Graham actually sees a higher percentage of decisions today than at any other given period in his ministry.

THE BIBLE AND GROWTH IN GRACE

Graham believes that the Bible has power to accomplish God's purpose in deepening and broadening the spiritual lives of believers. The Bible becomes a primary resource for spiritual maturity and strength, especially in difficult times. The evangelist lists involvement in God's Word as a major element in what he calls "Your Spiritual Survival Kit." He states, "We need to read and memorize Scripture."[46] For new converts, Graham stresses a regimen of Bible reading, prayer, and fellowship. He is convinced that the Bible has the answer to every problem, for both the new believer and those more mature in their faith. Because it is God's Word, it appeals to *all* believers at all levels of spiritual maturity.

Given this, Graham makes sure his preaching and instructing are Bible-based and practical. Virtually all of his illustrations are drawn from the Old and New Testaments. He stresses, in the words of the Psalmist: "How can a young man keep his way pure? By keeping it according to Thy word. . . . Thy word I have treasured in my heart, that I may not sin against Thee" (Psalm 119:9–11).

THE CRITICS

Of course not everyone agrees with Graham's view on the Bible. He has his share of critics. A former chaplain of St. Andrews College said, "Graham encourages biblical ignorance by believing in a docetic Christ, clay-made man, a floating zoo, an amphibious-footed Jesus, a son of God who demonstrated his divinity as a homebrew artist . . . and topped it off with an ascension that looks like a Cape Kennedy blastoff."[47] Such sharp criticism echoes of old-school liberalism.

There are also those who would like to label Billy Graham as being out of touch with the times. Nonetheless, multitudes around the world are still influenced by his teaching. As one observer has said, "In a way never witnessed before, the world continues to be the parish of this evangelist."[48]

BILLY GRAHAM'S ASSUMPTIONS

By way of summing up, it must never be forgotten that Billy Graham is first and foremost an evangelist. Moreover, he is a conservative evangelical evangelist. Therefore, there are certain presuppositions that he brings to his understanding, interpretation, and use of the Bible. First, he recognizes that the final authority concerning the truth of God does not rest in him, but in the Holy Scriptures. He believes in the moving of the Holy Spirit to bring that truth home to the human heart and mind. Thus he places the Bible at the core of his message. Graham agrees completely with the principle Martin Luther expressed when the Reformer wrote, "He who undertakes anything without the divine Word will labor in vain."[49] Such assumptions have shaped the evangelist's interpretation and preaching of the Bible.

As Graham travels the world, he brings these basic convictions to bear on his hearers. He preaches the Christ found in the Bible wherever he is, be it the White House or the bush country of interior Africa.

We can confidently conclude that Billy Graham is a biblicist in the historical, evangelical sense of the word. His entire world-view is Bible-based. In his book *World Aflame*, he states, "In this book, my thesis is based on the biblical philosophy of man and of history."[50] He also says, "We are called to live under the authority of Jesus Christ and the authority of the Scriptures."[51] Not only that, he has been faithful to his convictions through many decades of evangelistic ministry. Indeed, he has grown and matured in his approach, realizing more and more over the years the importance of being faithful to the Word of God in all of life and ministry.

Professor Robert Ferm contends that Billy Graham's approach to Bible-centered evangelism is historic evangelism. He says, "This is the first-century Gospel as preached by the apostles."[52] And it might also be added, preached by faithful evangelicals for two thousand years.

9

Boldness

❦

"We have and now declare war on spiritual apathy . . . and moral evil."

—BILLY GRAHAM

In the late 1940s Billy Graham was holding a citywide campaign in Augusta, Georgia. One night during the crusade a wild party started up in the hotel room next to the rooms where Billy Graham and Grady Wilson were staying. The music and shouting awoke Grady Wilson from a deep sleep. He went into the adjoining room to see if Billy was also bothered by the sound coming through the wall. Sure enough, Billy Graham was wide awake and worried that he would not be fresh for his preaching assignment the following day. The noise continued unabated until Graham decided he should ask the people in the next room to quiet down. He threw on his bathrobe and walked along the hallway to the offending room, where he knocked on the door. A man opened the door. "What do you want?" he asked with slurred speech.

"I want to speak to this crowd," said Billy Graham, stepping inside. He opened his mouth to ask the crowd to settle down so that other patrons in the hotel could get some sleep, but as he looked around at them, he had another idea. This was too good an opportunity to miss! "I'm a minister of the gospel," he said.

Silence fell over the rowdy crowd. Billy went on, "I'm holding a revival campaign in this town. Some of you may have read about it in the paper."

Suddenly a spirit of conviction came on the group. Many people put down their bottles and glasses and looked down at the floor. Billy Graham knew he had to speak out, even though many people were drunk and could easily turn against him. "I know God is ashamed of you," he began.

How would the crowd respond? He didn't have to wait long to find out. Men and women began to confess their sin. One partygoer was a deacon and Sunday school teacher in his church. "We know we shouldn't be doing this," he confessed.

Graham knew the group needed to hear his message, and so in his bathrobe in the middle of the unpopular task of breaking up a party, he preached an evangelistic sermon.

As a result of his boldness, several people responded to the message, and there was no more noise that night.

The Scriptural Meaning and Mandate for Boldness

The dictionary defines *boldness* as "possessing, showing, or requiring courage; audacious; fearless, spirited."[1] Joseph Thayer, in his Greek lexicon, defines the word as "freedom in speaking, unreservedness in speech; openly, frankly without concealment." Thayer goes on to give nuances of the word such as "free and fearless confidence, cheerful courage, boldness, assurance."[2] Paul wrote, "According to my earnest expectation and hope that in nothing I shall be ashamed, but with all boldness, as always, so now also Christ will be magnified in my body, whether by life or by death. For to me, to live is Christ, and to die is gain" (Philippians 1:20–21, NKJV).

In the context of evangelism, boldness in the effort to win people to faith in Christ is absolutely essential.

THE BASIS OF BOLDNESS

Several principles undergird the motivation and ability to be bold in evangelism. Initially, the courage to evangelize in all circumstances emerges out of God's Word. Believers are instructed in the Bible to be bold to believe, defend, and proclaim God's gospel. It may seem paradoxical to say that one has to be bold to defend what God has clearly revealed, but the truth of God is not always well received. For this reason Peter said, "Always [be] ready to make a defense to everyone who asks you to give an account for the hope that is in you" (1 Peter 3:15).

In some settings, resistance to the proclamation of the gospel flares to the point of persecution. To continue proclaiming under such circumstances requires a bold stand for the truth. In 1 Corinthians 2:14, Paul tells us, "A natural man does not accept the things of the Spirit of God." Human pride often rejects God's truth. Rebellion in the human heart— which constitutes the essence of sin—sometimes causes men and women to reject the gospel message to the point where they try to stamp out the bearer of that message. Thus it is not surprising to find persecution meted out to bearers of the gospel. We can see this at work in the story of the stoning of Stephen recorded in Acts 6–7. When Stephen delineated the history of God's revelation and applied this truth to the immediate situation, outrage erupted and Stephen was dragged out and stoned to death. The incident points out not only the depravity of the human heart, but the resistance that gospel proclamation arouses.

Yet precisely because of the depravity of human hearts, the message of the gospel must be preached. Christians must boldly stand and battle on. Indeed, some may pay a heavy price for their proclamation, but the Scriptures admonish believers to be courageous regardless of circumstances. Where does this boldness to proclaim the gospel come from?

THE SOURCE OF BOLDNESS

The Scriptures tell us that believers have access to the power of God, and that is the source of their boldness. The writer of Hebrews admonishes, "Let us then approach the throne of grace with confidence, so that we may receive mercy and find grace to help us in our time of need" (Hebrews 4:16, NIV). The call of God to evangelize is embraced because believers can boldly claim grace through Jesus Christ.

The church has been called to be bold; to go forth faithfully into the world and share God's truth. As our Lord said, "Be faithful unto death, and I will give you the crown of life" (Revelation 2:10).

Despite the fact that there will be opposition, we should not forget that few people remember the detractors of the bold evangelists of the past. The names of those who opposed Luther, Zwingli, and in more recent times Charles Finney, D. L. Moody, Billy Sunday, and others have long been forgotten. Who remembers those who threw the rotten eggs at John Wesley and George Whitefield as they preached? Who knows the name of the person who slung the last stone that blotted out the life of Stephen? The names of the people who stood against these giants of the faith have long been forgotten. However, the actions of those who have boldly shared the gospel through church history live on in our memories. God honors bold and faithful witnesses. "Those . . . will shine brightly . . . who lead the many to righteousness, like the stars forever and ever" (Daniel 12:3).

The weak, compromising person will never make a lasting impact for God or a significant contribution to a needy world. Only those who are bold will make a mark for God and the well-being of humanity.

Billy Graham is one of these bold people. There is no watering down of the gospel message with him. He does not "accommodate" himself to the particular situation where he finds himself. He boldly, unflinchingly declares the gospel.

Graham has often appeared on *Larry King Live*. When Larry King asks, as he inevitably does at some stage in the interview, "Is Jesus the *only* way?" Billy Graham always looks him in the eye and gives the same answer he always gives: "Yes." Regardless of how politically incorrect this view may be to many today, especially to those in the media, Billy Graham will not back away from it. He will not compromise. Two of the Graham children, Anne Graham Lotz and Franklin Graham, recently appeared on *Larry King Live*. Like their father, they took the same bold stance about the gospel. Boldness is infectious.

Nor does Billy Graham overly concern himself with what others think about the methods he uses to spread the gospel. When Stuart Hamblen, the West Coast radio personality (see chapter one), invited the evangelist to be a guest on his radio show, Graham confessed that he hesitated at first. He was concerned about what some in the church might think of his being on a program sponsored by a tobacco company. But as he considered the matter, boldness welled within him. He realized that by being a guest on the show he would have the opportunity to share the gospel with millions of listeners. He reasoned, "Hadn't Christ himself spent time with sinners? Hadn't he then been criticized by the religious leaders of his day for that very thing? Why should I not take the risk? I said yes!"[3]

POLITICS AND BOLDNESS

One of the boldest things that Billy Graham has ever done centers on his response to an invitation to speak in the Soviet Union. While President Reagan was busy declaring that communist country to be the "Evil Empire," Graham received an invitation to come to Moscow and speak at a peace conference. He realized that if he accepted the opportunity there would be those who would severely criticize him, including perhaps the president himself. Senator Mark Hatfield told him to expect such criticism. He said, "You will get the strongest criticism from the Christian right, because they will feel somehow that you're compromising with the devil." Criticism from the fundamentalist camp was hardly new to Billy Graham, but it always grieved him.

Graham prayed and anguished over what to do until finally he was convinced that God would honor his trip to the Soviet Union. Since 1959 he had been asking God to one day open the door for him to go behind the Iron Curtain to share the gospel. He also reasoned that speaking at the peace conference might give him an entrée for a later crusade. Still, controversy seemed inevitable, and sure enough it erupted when he announced his decision to go. Nevertheless, Graham said, "I knew it was going to be highly controversial so on the Sunday before I went, George Bush invited me to lunch at his home, because we had been friends for many years. And before the lunch, he said, 'You know, I don't think the Reagans have anybody here. . . . I think I'm going to call them and see if they'll come over.' He called, and President and Mrs. Reagan came."

Billy Graham faced a president he knew did not encourage relations with the Soviet Union. He cleared his throat and began, "Mr. President, I'm going, as you know, to Moscow to speak at a peace conference. I know your stand on this and you probably know mine."

"Oh," President Reagan replied, "don't worry about it. It will come out all right. I'm going to be praying for you."[4]

Billy Graham went to Moscow and did get to share the gospel behind the Iron Curtain. Admittedly this sharing was closely supervised and limited in scope, but it did open a door for him to have the Moscow crusade he had so longed for. By being bold enough to stand against the prevailing political and religious attitudes toward communism and the Soviet Union, Billy Graham was finally able to preach the gospel in a place few expected anyone would ever be allowed to do so.

COURAGE IN CONFLICTS

In May 1972, Billy Graham once again found himself in a situation where he had to ignore political realities in order to boldly proclaim the gospel. This time the setting was Northern Ireland. It was a particularly volatile time in Ireland, with distrust and hatred running high between Catholics and Protestants. Many people were astonished that Billy Graham would even consider a crusade under such conditions. Not only did they think such a crusade had little chance of success, they also pointed out that Graham would be putting himself in personal danger. Still, as the evangelist prayed he felt the crusade should go ahead, and so he visited Northern Ireland and the Republic of Ireland to set things up. While he was in Northern Ireland, the reality of what he was planning to do was brought home to him when a bomb exploded close by. Billy Graham rushed over to the site of the blast to offer help and comfort to a bus conductor whose wife had just been killed.

While in Belfast, Graham also preached at the Raven Hill

Presbyterian Church. He had preached in this church in 1946 during a tour of the country as a Youth for Christ evangelist. As Billy Graham rose to speak, the most prominent Protestant preacher in Northern Ireland at the time, Ian Paisley, was preaching a "counter sermon" in his church, severely condemning Graham because of his compromising attitude toward Roman Catholics. He said, "The church which has Billy Graham in its pulpit will have the curse of the Almighty upon it."[5] Two years before Graham's visit, Paisley had written a book entitled *Billy Graham and the Church of Rome: The Startling Exposure*. Paisley was negative toward everything Graham stood for. Nonetheless, the evangelist stood his ground.

During his time in Ireland, Billy Graham met with hundreds of Northern Ireland's political, religious, and popular leaders. He spoke at Queens University in Belfast, being invited by both the Roman Catholic and the Protestant chaplains of the school. He appeared on Ulster televisions several times as well as on the BBC.

In every meeting he held, Graham insisted that both Catholics and Protestants be present in equal proportions. It was "a requirement that brought together people who had never met or, if they knew each other at all, had certainly never sat down to eat or talk or pray with one another."[6] It certainly was not an easy time, but the bravery and courage Billy Graham manifested had an impact on Northern Ireland.

Later that same year, Graham would again put his life on the line when he was invited to proclaim the gospel in Nagaland, a state in northeastern India. The region was in turmoil; yet, paradoxically, Nagaland was recognized as one of the most Christian spots on earth. Early in November 1972, the Baptists of Nagaland celebrated one hundred years of ministry. They invited Graham to come for an evangelistic crusade and to speak during the celebration ceremonies. The evangelist accepted the invitation, but before he arrived, civil strife in Nagaland grew to such proportions that a number of people were killed in conflicts raging around the countryside. The situation became so tense that several of Graham's advisers told him to cancel the crusade. They feared that guerrillas might stage an uprising and kill many innocent people.

Billy Graham was in Bangkok at the time and decided to follow his advisers' counsel and cancel the crusade, although he did so very reluctantly. He had never before canceled a crusade for anything other than illness.

Meanwhile, back in Calcutta, Robert Conval, an Indian and fellow evangelist, was deeply disappointed at Graham's cancellation. "God can still do a miracle," Conval argued. He put in a call urging many people who were gathered at Kohima in Nagaland to pray that God would change Graham's mind and bring him to the crusade. The next morning, someone was knocking heavily on Billy Graham's door. It was a young American missionary to Nagaland. He looked at Graham and said, "I have come here as the servant of the Lord. You've got to go to Nagaland."[7] He then explained the whole situation and how the people were fervently praying for Billy. He challenged Graham's faith, reminding him that God had promised to protect his servants from danger.

To Billy Graham this was a sign from God. He himself had had a sleepless night and was praying earnestly that God would have His way in the affair. The answer had come, and Graham immediately gathered his team and set off for Nagaland. He later wrote in his diary, "Tears came to my eyes. I felt rebuked that I had even doubted about coming to these mountain people to minister the Gospel. I felt terribly unworthy."

He stayed in Komima, Nagaland, for four days, speaking in morning Bible sessions and in the late afternoon conducting typical evangelistic crusade services. Twenty different interpreters translated his messages into the regional dialects. Not everything was peaceful, however. During the Wednesday morning Bible class, where tens of thousands had gathered, gunfire was heard on the edge of the crowd close to the jungle. Panic was avoided as Graham urged the people to be calm. One man had been shot to death by a guerrilla. But the outcome of it all was a great encouragement to the Nagas and resulted in the salvation of many. Billy Graham's willingness to be bold for God saw him through to victory.

Billy Graham receives much criticism and at times outright aggression from the two extremes of the Christian spectrum, the extreme right and the extreme left. But regardless of where Graham finds himself, he holds his ground and fully declares the truth of Christ as he understands it. The most severe criticism he receives from the religious right centers on his openness to invite cooperation in his citywide crusades from all Christian groups, be they Catholics or so-called liberals. Some see this as compromising the gospel. Yet, Graham holds a deep conviction that if anyone is willing to cooperate, realizing he is going to preach the uncompromising, evangelical gospel, they are welcome to participate. As a result multitudes have come to faith in Jesus Christ.

Whether Billy Graham is being interviewed on television, at a press conference, or is simply sitting beside a person on an airplane, he always uses such situations as an opportunity to boldly share Christ with people.

WHY BOLDNESS IS SO IMPORTANT

The entire theology of the evangelistic enterprise can be summarized in three simple—yet profound—statements. These three declarations explain the motive for evangelism:

- The world and its people are lost, alienated from the "commonwealth of Israel" (Ephesians 2:12), and abide under the judgment of God. Because of the sin of Adam and Eve causing their expulsion from Eden, humankind cannot crash through the gates and regain paradise by their own efforts. This world is lost and stands in dire need of hearing the gospel.

- There is only one answer to the human dilemma. People may travel many avenues seeking restoration to the beautiful original state of creation, but all to no avail. The Bible says, "There is a way which seems right to a man, but its end is the way of death" (Proverbs 14:12). Although it may sound unduly exclusive, perhaps even arrogant to some, the Scriptures are clear: Jesus Christ is God's only way to restoration of fellowship with Himself. Jesus decisively declared, "I am the way, and the truth, and the life; no one comes to the Father, but through Me" (John 14:6).

- Since Jesus is God's answer to the dilemma that faces humankind, He uses His people to share this message abroad. The proclamation of the gospel has been committed to the church.

The needs of the world demand that we act boldly. People like Billy Graham lead the charge, fearlessly proclaiming the gospel around the world. This has been true through the ages of church history, and thus the evangelist has made his contribution to countless lives.

10

Godliness

cᗧ∞ᗝ

*"Godlikeness of character is the Christian's
proper heritage in this earthly walk."*

— BILLY GRAHAM

Billy Graham's early tutoring in godly Christian living came from his parents. Every Sunday the family would climb into their old car and drive five miles to the small Associate Reformed Presbyterian Church they attended. In 1933, Graham's mother came into a new experience of Christ and at the urging of her sister, Lil Barker, joined a Bible class. "The Lord has come in and lives in our hearts. I had never known that truth before," was how she described the experience.[1] Graham's father, Frank, was injured at the time, and after he recovered, the Lord spoke to him and his wife that they should dedicate themselves to more Bible study and prayer. They started reading devotional writings to their children and prayed together regularly in a family worship time.

His parents' newfound devotion to God occurred before young Billy Graham had experienced salvation. For him, religious life in the family was merely form without substance. Then came his conversion under the preaching of Mordecai Ham, a Baptist evangelist from

Kentucky. Graham's life was transformed. As he explained it, his life took a "180-degree turn." In his autobiography, the evangelist gives testimony to the radical change that occurred in his life.

> Before my conversion, I tended to be touchy, oversensitive, envious of others, and irritable. Now I deliberately try to be courteous and kind to everybody around me. I was experiencing what the apostle Paul described as: the old has gone, the new has come! (2 Corinthians 5:17). Mother especially, but other family members too, felt there was a difference. Most remarkable of all—to me at least—was the uncharacteristic enthusiasm I had for studies![2]

After Graham's salvation experience, he understood the importance of his parents' commitment to a holy lifestyle. He began to see the significance of prayer and Bible study. Furthermore, the desire to see others brought to faith in Christ began to grow in his heart. A foundation had been laid in his life and he set out on the road to personal godliness. After Graham's call to the ministry, this spiritual quest, both for himself and for his converts, deepened greatly. He grasped what Luke was saying in relation to the events surrounding the Day of Pentecost. The evangelist understood that godliness and evangelism are traveling companions on the road to spirituality. And for Graham and his team of helpers, this understanding had deep implications, which we will explore in this chapter.

BILLY GRAHAM'S "PROGRAM" FOR GODLINESS

Billy Graham holds that "God wants us to long for Him,"[3] and that such a longing lays the spiritual groundwork for godliness. After the foundation is laid in a person's life through conversion, then, the evangelist acknowledges, maturity centers in a continued absolute commitment to Jesus Christ as Lord. Such a commitment leads to a life of seeking God's kingdom first (Matthew 6:33). Graham expresses the principle this way: "In reality, Jesus Christ is the perfect fulfillment, example and demonstration of [godliness]."[4] The Lord Jesus becomes the challenge and example to all believers.

The Lord set the pattern for holy living when He cried out in the Garden of Gethsemane, "Not as I will, but as Thou wilt" (Matthew 26:39). Graham has said, "If we would find genuine happiness, we must begin where Jesus began."[5] In the absolute commitment of Jesus Christ to His heavenly Father, the challenge to holiness flows to all people of God. As Graham points out, "One must come to the end of 'self' before one can really begin to live."[6] Paul got to the heart of the issue in his letter to the Romans: "I urge you therefore, brethren, by the mercies of God, to present your bodies a living and holy sacrifice" (Romans 12:1). Obedience and righteous living constitute the crux of the matter. Graham makes it clear that God "puts reins upon our wayward souls that they may be directed into 'paths of righteousness.'"[7] This means a life of practicing the discipline of godliness based upon obedience to the Lord. But there are certain things that must be done to experience the kind of disciplined life that leads to personal holiness.

Billy Graham is forthright in laying down the principle that before purity of life can be experienced, all sin must be confessed and forsaken. He reminds us that we cannot cover up sin and think we have gotten away with it. God's searchlight, the Holy Spirit, sees into even the most shadowy corners of our soul. As a result we must be "sensitive to the presence of hidden sins . . . wrong motives, wrong attitudes, wrong habits, wrong relationships, wrong priorities. It may even be that . . . [we] will have to make restitution if [we] have stolen anything, or . . . may have to seek out someone and ask forgiveness for a wrong that [we] have committed. . . . Hold nothing back, as the songwriter says, 'give them all to Jesus.'"[8]

Graham also gives a word of encouragement: "You can confess your sins right now, bring them to God and say, 'Lord here they are.'" The Bible says, "If we confess our sins, He is faithful and righteous to forgive us our sins and to cleanse us from all unrighteousness" (1 John 1:9). God says that the one who "confesses and forsakes [sin] will find compassion" (Proverbs 28:13). Graham goes on, "It doesn't matter how ugly or dirty the sin is, you can bring it to God and call it by name and ask for forgiveness. God loves you and He will forgive you, He will cleanse you, He will wash away your sins. You can shout from the mountain-tops what God has done for you!"[9] Such confession opens the way to a godly life.

Bible Study

Billy Graham is also fully committed to faithful devotional reading of the Scriptures and to memorizing verses of the Bible. He says, "Every morning I read . . . the Bible without studying, just reading, just filling my soul." Indeed, being "in" the Word of God regularly in this manner enables the Holy Spirit to develop the "mind of Christ" in a person.

In an interview David Frost asked Billy Graham, "Do you, in simple human terms, ever get bored with the Bible?"[10] Graham's answer was emphatic. "Never," he replied.[11] Reading and studying the Bible is a central discipline to Billy Graham.

Prayer

Along with enthusiasm for the Scriptures, Billy Graham is committed to the absolute necessity of prayer for Christian godliness and maturity. When asked what he would do if he had to live his life over again, he invariably says he would "spend more time in study and more time in prayer."[12]

Graham points out that those who have turned the tide of history have turned it by means of prayer. In a message on prayer, the evangelist relates how King Hezekiah prayed and the entire army of the Assyrians was destroyed and the nation of Israel spared. He further points out that Elijah, a great man of prayer, lifted up his voice to God and fire from heaven fell and consumed the offering.[13]

Looking at the New Testament, Graham cites the Apostle Paul's dynamic prayer life. As a result of the apostles' fervent intercession, churches were born throughout Asia Minor and Europe. And down through the pages of history, Graham contends it was men and women of fervent prayer such as John Wesley, Jonathan Edwards, and others who accomplished great feats for Christ. "Time after time," the evangelist declares, "events have been changed because of prayer. If millions of us would avail ourselves of the privilege of prayer, we could go to our knees in believing prayer and change the course of events."[14]

Given this, Billy Graham urges all believers to "pray without ceasing" (1 Thessalonians 5:17). He declares, "This should be the motto of every follower of Jesus Christ. Never stop praying no matter how dark and hopeless it may seem."[15]

Again, as a practical matter, Graham urges the church to pray for those who do not know Jesus Christ. He stated that on one occasion, "I listened to a discussion of religious leaders on how to communicate the Gospel. Not once did I hear them mention prayer. And yet I know of scores of churches that win many converts each year by prayer alone. If there is a person in our acquaintance that needs Christ in his life, then we need to start praying for him."[16]

Indeed prayer has been an essential part of Graham's crusades since the Los Angeles crusade in 1949 when he invited Armin Guesswein to set up a prayer ministry. The more formal prayer preparation in his crusades started worldwide with Graham asking Millie Deinert to travel to England to prepare for an upcoming crusade with prayer. Through the years prayer preparation programs have grown tremendously. Now in the crusades both a chairman and chairwoman are selected to lead prayer ministries that intercede for God's power to fall on the crusade.

As a result of such prayer, Millie Deinert tells of women remarking to her, "We have learned to pray like never before." Graham's goal is to see revival take place because of the faithful prayer being offered up in both homes and churches.

Witnessing

Billy Graham sees another discipline involved in growing in godliness, that of sharing one's faith with the lost. As an evangelist it is not surprising that Graham should feel this way. As Cliff Barrows has said, "We were committed to witness from the beginning."[17] Not only does Graham preach to large crowds, he also consistently witnesses to individuals. This is in line with his admonition that "one faithful witness is worth a thousand mute professors of religion."[18]

Graham's daughter Anne Graham Lotz tells the story of one occasion when her parents were on a short vacation, staying in a beach home of some friends. Suddenly Billy disappeared. After an hour Ruth grew concerned and went to find him. Eventually she discovered him in the backyard with the gardener. Her husband had led the man to Christ. As Anne Graham Lotz points out, it is great to see thousands of people coming to Christ in a crusade, but her father is just as thrilled over leading one person to faith in Jesus Christ in the backyard.

Billy Graham sees this discipline of witnessing as vital and essential to a happy and prosperous life of godliness. He remembers very well the words of the Lord Jesus when He said, "You shall be My witnesses" (Acts 1:8).

As much as Billy Graham practices personal godliness, he understands that the success of the Billy Graham Evangelistic Association's ministry rests on the purity and dedication to Christ of *all* of the organization's members. As a result, over the years, he has worked hard to ensure that those who preach the light also walk in it.

GODLINESS FOR THE TEAM

From the outset, Billy Graham has been vigilant to combat the negative image that mass evangelists have acquired through the years. *Elmer Gantry*, the well-known novel by Sinclair Lewis, focused on scraps and pieces from the lives and ministries of various evangelists. Lewis put all these snippets together and personified them in his main character, Elmer Gantry. In so doing, he created a stereotype of evangelists as engaging in insincerity, exploitation, and fleecing of followers.

When Graham was conducting a crusade in Modesto, California, he and his associates became sensitive to what many people felt about evangelists. They determined that something had to be done in order to dispel any possible accusations that they were not operating on the basis of purity, integrity, and honesty.

Graham realized, however, that there are temptations those in ministry do face. He says, "It seems to me that an evangelist, and the clergy for that matter, especially faces temptations in three areas: pride, money, and morals."[19] In this context, he called George Beverly Shea, Grady Wilson, and Cliff Barrows to his hotel room several months before the start of the Los Angeles crusade in 1949. He said to these men, his closest advisers, "God has brought us to this point, maybe he is preparing us for something that we don't know. Let's try to recall all the things that have been a stumbling block and a hinge to evangelists in years past, and let's come back together in an hour and talk about it and pray about it and ask God to guard us from them."[20] The group left and then reassembled an hour later to look at the various pitfalls and possible problems that could lie ahead for them in the future.

The first issue they addressed was that of money. Evangelists were often accused of fleecing those who come to hear them speak. The second problem was that of personal purity. There has always been the innuendo that some involved in the Lord's work are guilty of sexual sins. As well, two more potential problems also surfaced: inflated publicity—making statements that are not true about the success of a campaign—and dealing with criticism from local pastors. The men determined there and then that they would be ethical and act with integrity in relation to all of these issues.

To aid in this, Billy Graham and his associates formulated for themselves an outline of simple rules that would keep them from "all appearance of evil" (1 Thessalonians 5:22, KJV). They drew up a document that included the following:

THE MODESTO MANIFESTO

1. **Honesty:** It was resolved that all communications to media and to the church would NOT be inflated or exaggerated. The size of crowds and number of inquirers would not be embellished for the sake of making the B.G.E.A. look better. . . .

2. **Integrity:** It was resolved that financial matters would be submitted to a board of directors for review and facilitation of expenditures. Every local crusade would maintain a policy of "open books" and publish a record of where and how monies were spent. . . .

3. **Purity:** It was resolved that members of the team would pay close attention to avoiding temptation—never being alone with another woman, remaining accountable to one another, etc. A practice of keeping wives informed of their activities on the road and helping them feel a part of any and all crusades they undertook would be encouraged.

4. **Humility:** (Encouragement and edification of ALL believers.) It was resolved that members of the team were never to speak badly of another Christian minister, regardless of his denominational affiliation or differing theological views and practices. The mission of evangelism included strengthening the body of Christ as well as building it![21]

Billy Graham has taken these commitments so seriously that, as Sterling Houston quotes him, the evangelist has said, "If ever I were to do anything dishonoring to Christ, I would rather He take me home to heaven before I did it."[22]

As Graham's ministry grew, the Modesto Manifesto grew in like manner. The principles embodied in the document have been applied in many new areas of service. Most recently, the principles of godliness contained in the Modesto Manifesto were embodied in a covenant released at the Amsterdam 2000 Conference for itinerate evangelists. The covenant reads:

A COVENANT FOR EVANGELISTS
AMSTERDAM 2000

As a company of evangelists called and gifted by God to share the good news of Jesus Christ throughout the world, we earnestly pledge ourselves to:

1. **Worship** the one true and living God. Father, Son and Holy Spirit (Deut. 6:4);

2. **Submit** to the Holy Scriptures, the infallible Word of God, as the basis for our life and message (II Tim. 3:16-17);

3. **Proclaim** the Gospel of Jesus Christ, God's Son and our Redeemer, the one and only Savior of the world (Acts 4:12);

4. **Seek** always to preach and minister in the power of the Holy Spirit (Acts 4:29-31);

5. **Live** a life of constant personal prayer, Bible study and devotion to God, and also be a part of a local fellowship of believers (James 4:10; Heb. 10:25);

6. **Pray** that all persons of all languages and cultures may have access to the Gospel and the Bible (Acts 1:8);

7. **Practice** purity in both singleness and marriage, caring for our family and bringing up our children in the nurture of the Lord (Eph. 5:25; 6:1-4);

8. **Walk** humbly before God and our fellow human beings, renouncing arrogance, pride and boastful self-promotion (Micah 6:8; Eph. 4:1-2);

9. **Maintain** financial integrity and accountability in all of our activities, so that the cause of Christ may not be discredited (I Tim. 6:10-11);

10. **Serve** the needy and oppressed, remembering the mercy and compassion of Jesus (James 2:14-17);

11. **Encourage** the discipling and nurturing ministry of local churches (Matt. 28:19-20);

12. **Work** together in unity with our brothers and sisters in Christ (John 17:23);

13. **Equip** others for the practice of evangelism, giving special care to involve new believers in the sharing of their faith (Eph. 4:11-13);

14. **Stand** in solidarity with our brothers and sisters in Christ who suffer persecution and even martyrdom for their faithful Gospel witness (II Cor. 1:8-11).

Knowing that apart from Jesus Christ we can do nothing, we make these pledges with prayerful reliance on His help. As we do so, we ask for the prayer and support of Christ's followers so that world evangelization may be advanced, the church built up and God glorified in ever-increasing measure.[23]

There is little doubt about the positive effectiveness of such efforts for godliness by the BGEA and other evangelists. Indeed, few would argue with the fact that no other evangelist has enjoyed such a reputation for integrity as Billy Graham. Yet negative criticisms continue to arise, such as the *Charlotte Observer*'s exposé of Billy Graham's so-called twenty-three-million-dollar "secret fund." This despite the fact that the fund was no secret at all. Nevertheless, the principles of the Modesto Manifesto have guided his ministry for many years, fostering a positive and wholesome image of himself and his associates among Christians and the general populace.

GODLINESS FOR NEW CONVERTS

Billy Graham also deeply desires to see those who come to Christ through his crusades and other ministries of the BGEA grow in godly Christian maturity. He has said, "Converts (or 'inquirers' as we call them) need encouragement and instruction. Evangelism is more than simply encouraging decisions for Christ. It is urging people to become disciples, followers of Jesus Christ."[24] He also points out, "Parents do not abandon a baby at birth, but nourish and protect the life of that child. So evangelists are to assume responsibility for those born into the family of God under their ministry."[25]

To aid in this endeavor, Graham trains counselors to deal personally with each individual who makes a decision during his crusades. The night a person makes a decision, their name and address are sent to a central location in the city where the crusade is being held. From there the information is forwarded immediately to a local church. The purpose of this is so the church can follow up on those who make commitments. On a night when many decisions are recorded, it is not unusual for the workers to be up until one o'clock in the morning processing the decision cards so that local churches will have the information as soon as possible. In order to make sure no one is left out by mistake, counselors are also required to make personal contact with each inquirer within forty-eight hours of their decision to follow Christ.

The BGEA also commits to send each inquirer a packet of helpful materials on how to begin their walk with the Lord. One set of materials is entitled *Living in Christ* and contains a copy of the Gospel of John with a section in it entitled "Words of Encouragement from Billy Graham." Instructions are also included on how to get the most from the Gospel of John. A number of Bible lessons and Scripture memorization cards are also included in the packet so the inquirer can grow into a life of discipleship. Four aspects or disciplines of living for Christ are presented under the following headings:

- The Bible is food for the spiritual life.
- Prayer is your lifeline to God.
- A Christian is to be Christ's witness.
- You can't be an effective Christian on your own. Get involved in a church.

Moreover, there are special guides and helps for children who make decisions for Christ. One booklet is entitled *Thank You Jesus; Discovery Book*, and another *Jesus Loves Me*. Following the general line of the adult programs and helps, these booklets are designed to get children started in their walk with Christ. The program is quite thorough. It helps the young "decision maker" to acquire a beginning understanding of living the Christian life.

Another book given to inquirers is entitled *30 Discipleship Exercises: the Pathway to Christian Maturity*. This is a Bible study book for small groups. The book contains thirty lessons dealing with such subjects as the Lordship of Christ, the Assurance of Salvation, Obedience to the Lord, How to Pray, How to Walk in Victory, the Place of the Church in the Believer's Life, Understanding the Fruits of the Spirit, Love, and God's Providential Care. Not only does this book help new converts, it also aids those who are recommitting their lives to Christ.

For at least one year after their decision is recorded, the Graham organization keeps in touch with those who accept salvation. Bible study groups are often organized in cities where a crusade has been held. Local pastors are contacted to see if they have followed up on the new converts. The pastors are also "followed up" on to see if they have continued contact with the new inquirers. The BGEA does all it can to see that those who make decisions for Christ are cared for and nurtured.

DO THE CONVERTS LAST?

All this emphasis on the follow-up of those who make decisions during a crusade raises the inevitable question: Do the converts last?

Through the years, a major criticism of mass evangelism has been that converts do not "stick." Billy Graham is well aware of the fact that when the Word goes forth, not everyone who hears the gospel message will be moved to the extent that they will end up as a fruit-bearing Christian. In an interview the evangelist was asked, "As you see people coming forward in your campaigns . . . to make their decision, what do you think when you see hundreds of people coming forward? What thoughts are going through your mind?" Graham's answer: "The 'Parable of the Sower' in which Jesus indicated there were four types of soil that the Word of God lands upon. A fourth of those will go on to grow in the grace and knowledge of Christ and become true disciples, but three fourths of those will not. For various reasons they will drop out. Maybe the pressure and allurements of the world, or maybe the materialism, or whatever it may be will wipe it all out. And Jesus spelled it out very carefully in the Gospels and I don't know that one could say that a fourth—he didn't say a fourth—but he had four different categories and I have always thought in any group that comes forward to make a commitment, if I preached the Gospel faithfully, a fourth of them will be there five years from now or ten years from now."[26]

Billy Graham is well aware of the reality that some of those who make decisions for Christ will fall away. Nevertheless, he does not take this situation casually. He does all that is within his power as an evangelist to mitigate the problem. The BGEA spends large sums of money giving help and guidance to the inquirers. Graham's deepest desire is to see discipleship and godliness emerge in the lives of those who make decisions in his crusades.

GODLY EVANGELISM

Billy Graham is a man of God. He genuinely wants godliness and integrity to shine through every phase of his personal life and work. Once, in an interview, he was asked what he would like the first line of his obituary to read. He answered, "He was faithful and that he had integrity. I would like to be considered a person who loved God with all my heart, mind and soul."[27] This attitude explains why there is such a positive spin-off from the life and ministry of Billy Graham.

The Bible says, "Righteousness exalts a nation, but sin is a disgrace to any people" (Proverbs 14:34). This being true, it may be right there that Billy Graham has made one of his greatest contributions. When just "one sinner repents," there is not only rejoicing in heaven, but many on earth do the same. The godly are the "light of the world" and the "salt of the earth." The more "light" and "salt," the better the world. The influence of Billy Graham on society and culture because of the millions who have been converted under his ministry and now live changed lives is significant. True, the crime rate and immorality still climb, but one wonders what it would be like if the evangelist had not led so many to Christ and into a life of godliness.

Not only that, Billy Graham has become a role model for many. This can be seen from three perspectives. First, Graham has set a high standard for other evangelists, pastors, and preachers. Church leaders, with few exceptions, hold him in high regard and emulate his life and commitment to the cause of Christ. Second, Graham has been a challenge to the spirituality of a multitude of true believers. The church of Jesus Christ looks to him as an example of godly living and faithful service to his Lord. Finally, Graham, because of his godliness, has been something of a challenge to the many who have not yet come to faith in Jesus Christ. It is difficult to ignore such a man of God. When he speaks, people listen, even if they may disagree. And he gently leads those who do listen with an open mind out of the "world" and into the kingdom of God.

Many years ago, in a city about to be destroyed, Abraham prayed that the destruction be diverted. God said, "I will not destroy it on account of the ten" godly men (Genesis 18:32). If only ten godly people are in the city, God will preserve the whole city. Society is far more dependent on godly believers than they ever realize. Therein, Billy Graham, a man utterly committed to leading everyone he comes in contact with to faith in Christ and a life of godliness, makes his mark. Biblical evangelism emanates godliness and holiness.

11

Revival

❦

"Revival is essential."

— BILLY GRAHAM

Almost immediately after the close of the Los Angeles crusade in 1949, Billy Graham and his associates traveled to the Boston area. On the first Saturday night there a rally was held in a large hall. It occurred amid much criticism from certain church circles. No one was sure how the criticism would affect attendance at the meeting, but when Billy Graham stood to preach the hall was filled to overflowing. The following afternoon a rally was planned for 3 P.M. An hour and a half before the meeting was set to begin, the hall was jam-packed. Fire marshals closed the doors and many Christians stood outside praying for what was happening inside. It was a mighty time, and many inquirers came forward when Graham gave the invitation to accept Christ.

The fledgling team of evangelists quickly realized that the hall was much too small for the number of people God was drawing to their meetings. So they rented Symphony Hall, calculating that it would surely meet their needs. It did not. The next night it, too, was filled to capacity, and so Billy Graham moved to the Opera House. Once again, the team had underestimated the groundswell of interest, and finally Boston Gardens opened its doors and the largest crowd ever assembled in that venue gathered to hear the evangelist preach.

During this time in Boston, multitudes were converted from every walk of life—newspaper reporters, people from bars, and many more. It was a true touch of God's reviving hand in the part of America that had given birth to the First Great Awakening.

And then there was London with the Harringay crusade. We have mentioned this crusade several times in this book, but we will take another look at it from the perspective of revival.

THE HARRINGAY CRUSADE

As a pattern in all revivals, initially a sense of need arises. In 1954 Great Britain had come through World War II battered and bruised. There was a feeling of futility in the minds of many Englishmen. Strangely, in the nation that during the Victorian era was known for its church attendance and Christian approach to life, churches now remained largely empty on Sundays. A pervasive secularism reigned in the land.

In this setting, Billy Graham was invited to London to conduct a crusade. Graham began preparation by bringing together as many people as possible for prayer, the key instrument of assault on the spiritual vacuum in any country. Many believers sensed the need and gave themselves to fervent intercession. An air of expectancy began to grow as Billy Graham boarded the ship and set sail for England. Again, as is often the case when revival seems near, he met much opposition and resistance. Liberal theologians were hard on the attack. One critic wrote of the evangelist, "His theology is fifty years behind contemporary scholarship."[1] At the other end of the religious spectrum, strict "Calvinists" objected to Graham's use of the invitation to come and receive salvation. As well, there was a lingering streak of anti-Americanism among British people, making Graham's job of connecting with his audience all the more difficult.

Rather than be discouraged, Billy Graham saw in these dynamics the harbinger of revival, and upon his arrival in London he preached the gospel with power. Soon the signs of true awakening began to manifest themselves. The number of converts began to grow exponentially. Harringay Arena was packed for each meeting, as people flocked to hear the Word of God and to find new life in Christ. That is always one of the clear marks of revival. Spiritual awakening and evangelism are partners. And in London in 1954, revival was on the way. It was even heard in the streets.

As Christians left the arena after a meeting at Harringay they would burst into singing. During this time it was not unusual to go down into one of London's underground stations and hear a hymn being sung or to climb aboard a bus and find that the passengers were singing Christian songs at the tops of their voices. Such behavior was unheard of and unprecedented in Great Britain and soon newspapers, radio, and television were covering each day's events. The church in England was mightily moved as a result.

BILLY GRAHAM SPEAKS ON REVIVAL

Billy Graham is quick to acknowledge that if evangelism is to be effective in reaching the multitudes for Christ, it rests solely in the hands of the Holy Spirit using God's people as His agents. But when the church fails in its task, or becomes spiritually "unhealthy," it falls to men like Graham to appeal for a true reviving move of God upon Christian believers. Thus, in his crusades, the evangelist appeals for revival and awakening among the people of God. In a sermon entitled *America's Lost Frontier*, published in 1962, he lays down this dictum: "What do we need? I say tonight at the outset of this crusade, we need a great national spiritual awakening. We need a revival from God. We need to hear from the heavens. We need to come apart and listen to God. Or, I tell you here tonight, we're in for judgment."[2] In *Storm Warning* Graham sounds a similar alarm: "Without a sudden and massive worldwide revival of God's people and a return to the morality and the values set down in the Word of God, the earth is already under the condemnation of God, and its judgment will be swift, unavoidable, and total."[3]

This theme has been sounded throughout the history of evangelism, and Graham lends his voice to the chorus that has gone before. Clearly the evangelist sees true spiritual revival as the only hope for societies and countries. He states, "Western culture and its fruits had its foundations in the Bible, the Word of God, and in the revivals of the seventeenth and eighteenth centuries."[4] Here he is referring to the work of men like George Whitefield and John and Charles Wesley.

John Wesley labored tirelessly, preaching for over fifty years. In true revival spirit, he was virtually obsessed with reaching people for Christ. It was an amazing feat by any standard to travel over a quarter of a million miles before the advent of the railroad. Wherever Wesley went he preached. In the course of his life he preached some 42,400 sermons, which averages out to be more than two sermons a day. We catch a glimpse of John Wesley's determination and stamina in one of his journal entries:

> **March 17, 1752:** At the Foundry. How pleasing it would be to flesh and blood to remain at this little quiet place, where at length to weather the storm! Nay, I am not to consult my own ease but the advancing of the kingdom of God. Ten thousand cares are no more weight to my mind . . . than ten thousand hairs on my head.[5]

Billy Graham has the same kind of drive to preach. He is quick, though, to point out that evangelism and revival are not synonymous.

EVANGELISM AND REVIVAL

Revival is concerned with the renewal of God's people; evangelism is concerned with those who have never known Christ. But the two are ultimately connected. When God's people are truly revived and renewed spiritually, it results in a new vision for a lost world and a new commitment to reach out to those who do not belong to Christ. Evangelism is the fruit of revival.[6]

The evangelist is aware of the difference between, yet interdependence of, revival and evangelism. He summarizes it by saying, "In preparation of evangelism, *revival is essential.*"[7] The two unite to influence the world for Christ.

When Graham was preparing for his Toronto crusade in 1955, he listed five purposes for the event: "(1) To stir the city out of religious indifference; (2) To arouse hundreds to commit their lives to Christ as Lord and Master; (3) *To bring a spiritual revival to the churches and church members;* (4) To see a definite moral and spiritual as well as a social impact left in the community; and (5) To exalt not Billy Graham, but the 'Lord and Savior, Jesus Christ who died on the cross for our sins.'"[8]

Perhaps Billy Graham's awareness of the need for worldwide revival is best expressed in a sermon he delivered in London.

> I would call you back to the God of Wesley and Whitefield. I would call you back to the God that your fathers and mothers worshiped. And I would call you back to the God that made Britain the greatest nation that the world has ever known. I would call you back to the principles that govern British life, spiritually and morally. I would call you back to home life that once we knew on these islands, and once we knew in the United States and Canada.[9]

Obviously, what Graham is calling the nations to experience is a return to God. And simply put, that constitutes the essence of revival. It is something that Billy Graham yearns to have continue in a city long after he and his team have left.

In 1997 in San Francisco, the evangelist addressed a crowd of thousands saying, "I hope when this crusade is over, we won't let the spirit that has developed die, and that we will see a great spiritual awakening." As American society continues to deteriorate with crime, corruption, violence, secularism, and immorality, the need for revival asserts itself more and more. In the face of this reality, Billy Graham cries out for a great revival to come that "would purge America of the rats and termites that are subversively endeavoring to weaken the defense of this nation from within."[10]

Expounding on the need for revival, Graham wrote a small book entitled *Revival in Our Time*. In this book he says, "We need a Holy Ghost, heaven-sent revival!"[11] He then quotes 2 Chronicles 7:14: "If my people, which are called by my name, shall humble themselves, and pray, and seek my face, and turn from their wicked ways; then will I hear from heaven, and will forgive their sin, and will heal their land" (KJV). He brings it all together by saying, "I believe that God is true to His Word, and that He must rain righteousness upon us if we meet His conditions."[12] Graham appears to understand well the nature and need of true revival for a degenerate society.

The anticipation of renewal and revival follow many of Graham's crusades. In the Rio de Janeiro, Brazil, crusade in 1974, one of the leading pastors in the city, Dr. Nilson Fanini, was reported as saying, "Dr. Graham's coming could have a catalytic effect in initiating the revival he longs to see."[13] And concerning the early crusade in Boston, mentioned above, one observer evaluated Graham's influence and contribution with these words: "If what followed fell short of the great awakening, short of Jonathan Edwards and George Whitefield, it did cause dry bones to rattle in normally sedate New England to the degree revival came, it sparked a commensurate measure of evangelism."[14]

THE WORLD'S NEED

Billy Graham also feels the concern and need for revival far beyond the confines of Western society. He clearly longs for revival wherever he goes in the world. In the Japanese crusade of 1994, he said, "We revel in the joy and renewal He is bringing to this land. Yet we know this is only the beginning: the church in Japan is now being awakened—the full harvest is yet to be gathered."[15] One of the most thrilling experiences for the evangelist, as he acknowledges, was to see the revival spirit throughout South Korea. At a gathering in Seoul, over one million people came together to hear Graham preach the Word of God.

While Billy Graham is the first to admit that his crusades do not always bring change, or even cause a ripple in a city, he continues to believe that any godly input to a geographical area produces at least some fruit. In an interview with David Frost, Graham said that it was his hope that wherever he goes he could "get millions talking and discussing—even arguing—religion. In other words, cause a religious stir. In the book of Acts, wherever the apostles went, there was a 'stirring.' It is better than apathy."[16] Indeed, this phenomenon often occurs during Graham's crusades, contributing toward revival.

The main point is, however, that Billy Graham has a grasp of what constitutes revival, and its importance, particularly in a spiritually deteriorating culture. And he longs to see revival in the profound historical, biblical sense. Furthermore, it would seem correct to say that his crusades (some more than others) have seen a touch of revival and have certainly "revived" many an apathetic believer. In Graham's early days his desire was to ignite the whole world to see a great awakening. Now in his older years, he is content to let God be God, knowing he did what he could to spark and foster spiritual awakening. He has always carried a sense of inadequacy for the task, but as he himself says in this regard, "I have done what I could."[17]

GOD'S SOVEREIGNTY IN REVIVAL

What, then, is Billy Graham's understanding of the way revival comes to people? Most important, he understands that revival emerges from the sovereign grace of God. God sends revival, and He does it as He pleases in His own way and timing. Graham would agree completely with Jonathan Edwards, God's spokesman in America's First Great Awakening, who said, "[Revival's] beginnings have not been of man's power or device and its being carried on depends not on our strength or wisdom."[18] Revival comes, Edwards contends, as God wishes. Yet our Lord uses humans as His instruments. And what constitutes this human element in a spiritual awakening? God moves in answer to the prayers of His people.

PRAYER BRINGS REVIVAL

Billy Graham fully recognizes that revival, in the purest sense, comes through persistent prayer along with the faithful declaration of the Word of God. He points out,

John Wesley prayed, and revival came to England, sparing that nation the horrors of the French Revolution. Jonathan Edwards prayed, the revival spread throughout the colonies. History has been changed time after time because of prayer. I tell you, history could be altered and changed again if people went to their knees in believing prayer.[19]

This appeal to prayer goes out to the entire church, but pastors, preachers, evangelists, and leaders should especially give heed. Graham in his *Biblical Standard for Evangelists* appeals for revival prayer. He also gives a succinct definition of what happens in a real revival. He says,

The . . . appeal in this final affirmation is for "the Body of Christ" to join us in prayer and work . . . for revival. The greatest need for God's people today is a true spiritual revival—a fresh outpouring of the Holy Spirit on the Church, a profound experience and turning from sin, and a deepening commitment to God's will in every aspect of life.[20]

Prayer, the Word, and the sovereignty of God always weave the pattern of real revival. As the church begins to sense the need of an awakening and engages in fervent prayer, the sovereign God is at work. Thus Graham makes much of the necessity for prayer, and prays for real revival himself. Melvin Graham, Billy's brother, has said, "Billy prays for revival more than anything else."[21]

One of the evangelist's earliest experiences of revival praying occurred some six months before the Los Angeles crusade in 1949. During an all-night prayer meeting at a Youth for Christ gathering at Winona Lake Conference Center in Indiana, Graham stood up at 3 A.M. and read Joel 3:14: "Multitudes, multitudes in the valley of decision: for the day of the LORD is near in the valley of decision" (KJV). In that meeting God fell mightily upon those gathered and they experienced a true touch of personal revival. From such encounters with the Holy Spirit Graham declares, "Understanding the consequence of sin and arrogance, I believe it should be the duty of every Christian to pray for repentance and revival in the land. We must do the work of believers, as Paul instructed, we must also seek the face of God as never before. I believe it is time we led the world to pray."[22]

Graham applauds prayer movements such as the National Day of Prayer, which Shirley Dobson and Vonette Bright organized in the spring of 1992. The evangelist called it "a remarkable event." More than twenty-five-thousand communities across America engaged in prayer vigils on the steps of their city and town hall buildings— Washington, D.C., being no exception. Tens of thousands met to pray for the revival of the Christian faith in the land. Graham said, "I believe this is the kind of commitment we must make in order to turn things around."[23]

The prayer movement swept the country. In Spokane, Washington, more than 180 teenagers gathered to pray for solutions to the problem of drugs, violence, and promiscuity in their schools. In Atlanta, Georgia, church members met on the steps of the state capitol to pray. In Texas 2,500 teenagers met for a concert of prayer in a coliseum.

President Bush officially decreed it the National Day of Prayer, and as Graham describes, the day was "a wonderful outpouring of God's Spirit." He went on to say, "This is precisely the kind of fervor and dedication it will take on a nationwide scale to bring about the change and revival in our land." Graham clearly recognizes prayer as essential. God sovereignly moves in response to prevailing intercession.

Billy Graham clearly longs to be used by the Holy Spirit to spawn another Great Awakening. He has attempted to light the fire of revival wherever he has gone. Graham cries out as a prophet, "Yes we need to be saved—saved from ourselves. . . . Hosea the prophet urged the people of his day, 'Sow to yourselves in righteousness, reap in mercy, break up your fallow ground; for it is time to seek the Lord till He come and rain righteousness upon you' (Hosea 10:12)."[24] Every generation needs a prophet who will cry out for revival. Billy Graham has been that prophet for several generations, and in that he stands in the historical, biblical, evangelical spirit.

12

A Worldwide Ministry

⌒∞⌒

"Let's put our arms around the world and love them."

— BILLY GRAHAM

In 1990, after completing a mission in Hong Kong, Billy Graham was in conversation with Henry Holly, a team member assigned to international work. The evangelist asked him, "Where can we go next?"

Henry Holly replied, "Well, you have practically been everywhere in the world, except for one place. I often pray for this country myself, because God has given me a love for the region."

"What place are you talking about?" asked Billy Graham, his interest piqued.

"North Korea," responded Henry Holly.

The two men continued to talk, and Billy Graham began to catch a vision for preaching in one of the most unreachable countries on earth. But how? It would not be easy. North Korea was under the control of the strictest of communist regimes. It seemed unlikely that the authorities there would welcome the world's most well-known Christian evangelist. Still, Graham could not get North Korea out of his thoughts. He began to make inquiries about how to get there. Through various contacts, such as Steven Linton, a scholar at the Columbia University Center for Korean Research, the evangelist was put in touch with Ho Jon, North Korean Ambassador to the United Nations.

Negotiations went on for a year until finally an official invitation was extended for Billy Graham to visit North Korea. The invitation came from the Korean Protestant Federation, which represented the nation's several thousand Protestants.

Graham wasted no time in heading to Asia. He spent a few days in Tokyo recovering from jet lag before flying on to Pyongyang with several members of his team. They arrived in the North Korean capital on March 31, 1992, and were immediately escorted into a reception room at the airport for a formal greeting. The welcoming committee was composed of a delegation of Christians representing the Protestant and Catholic churches, along with the chairman of the Korean Protestant Federation, Kang Yong Sop.

Billy Graham addressed the group with these words: "I do not come as an emissary of my government or my nation, but as a citizen of the Kingdom of God. As Christ's ambassador, I have come first of all to visit the Christian community—to have fellowship with my brothers and sisters in Christ, to pray and to worship with them, and to preach the gospel of Jesus Christ in your churches."[1]

The trip to North Korea came at the height of that country's isolation from the West, and it was a personal triumph for Billy Graham. But where did a man born and raised in a small town in the southern United States get the vision and the determination to proclaim the gospel literally around the world?

The answer lies primarily in the Great Commission Jesus delivered to His disciples shortly before His ascension. To the disciples He said, "Go therefore and make disciples of all the nations, baptizing them in the name of the Father and the Son and the Holy Spirit, teaching them to observe all that I commanded you; and lo, I am with you always, even to the end of the age" (Matthew 28:19–20).

Moreover, the Bible tells us that if Christians fail to take the gospel to all the world, the message will not be heard. Indeed today, millions, if not billions, of people know little or nothing about the glorious Good News of Christ. It remains our joy and responsibility as Christians to take that message to these people. As Paul said:

> There is no distinction between Jew and Greek; for the same Lord is Lord of all, abounding in riches for all who call upon Him; for "Whoever will call upon the name of the Lord will be saved." How then shall they call upon Him in whom they have not believed? And how shall they believe in Him whom they have not heard? And how shall they hear without a preacher? And how shall they preach unless they are sent? Just as it is written, "How beautiful are the feet of those who bring glad tidings of good things!" (Romans 10:12–15)

There hangs in Billy Graham's small office in Montreat, North Carolina, a relief map of the world with Jesus' words printed prominently on it: "And this gospel of the kingdom shall be preached in the whole world for a witness to all the nations, and then the end shall come" (Matthew 24:14). From the beginning of his ministry, Graham has seen his calling as not just to the United States or the Western world, but to the whole world. He laments, "The sad thing is that now, almost 2,000 years after [Christ's] birth, many of the earth's people have not heard the Good News and, consequently, do not know the joy of his salvation."[2]

NEW VENTURES

Billy Graham is not the first to catch the vision of bringing the gospel to the whole world. So, too, did William Carey, known as the "father of modern missions." Carey was born in 1761 and grew up in a poor village in the Midlands of England. He was converted at seventeen and immediately began to marry his love of world geography (or what was known of it then) with his passion to see others come to Christ. In 1792 Carey published his significant book *Enquiry*, which soon became the manifesto for modern missionaries. At the time of its publication, *Enquiry* was the most comprehensive gathering of information on the world and its people ever compiled.

William Carey eventually went to India as England's first Baptist missionary. He remained there until his death in 1834. In India he established the Serampore Mission, a Christian community that had an impact on all of India. Carey translated many Christian and secular works, and he fought to bring an end to the practice of *sati*, the burning alive of a widow on her husband's funeral pyre. He also influenced young British civil servants to deal with the Indian people in a just and culturally sensitive way. No other missionary in history achieved what William Carey achieved. He conceived of world missions and then led the way to show how Christians could influence whole nations.

Yet Billy Graham can make his own claim. He has proclaimed the gospel to more people in more countries than any other person in history. Of course he has been aided in this by new developments in technology, especially in the second half of the twentieth century. For example, in March 1995, through the use of satellite technology, Billy Graham was able to broadcast from San Juan, Puerto Rico, to the entire world a series of crusade messages. Graham had previously conducted satellite crusades in the Far East, Africa, and Germany, but never simultaneously to a worldwide audience. Apart from the technology, the venture involved unprecedented cooperation from numerous sources around the globe. The results were amazing. Uplinks went to 185 countries, and it is estimated that ten million people a night heard Billy Graham preach the gospel. Over two million people registered decisions for Christ as a result.

The next year, 1996, Graham telecast a single program entitled "Starting Over." It went to two-hundred countries, was translated into forty-eight languages, and reached a potential 2.5 billion people.

Such efforts demand extensive preparation. First, the broadcasts have to be targeted to specific and strategic areas. Crusade services have to be recorded and then edited and translated into various languages and fed by satellite to the nations of the world. Second, because Billy feels it is vital that people who respond are integrated into the Christian community, Christian workers have to be trained in all of the downlink sites throughout the world. Moreover, workers also need to be enlisted for publicizing and staging the event in each country. But most important of all, volunteers have to be lined up to be responsible for spiritual training, counseling, and maintaining the follow-up program for those who commit themselves to Christ.

So why would Billy Graham take the time and the money to undertake such a mammoth project? It was not some isolated incident designed to showcase or promote his ministry. Instead, it was an outworking of the commitment to world evangelization that the evangelist has tried to exemplify for over fifty years.

Graham's growing global awareness had its inception in the spring of 1946 when Youth for Christ became an international organization. Charles Templeton, Tori Johnson, singer Stratton Shufelt, and Billy Graham undertook a forty-six-day tour of Great Britain and the European continent. Graham returned to Britain later that same year for a six-month tour. During this tour he spoke at 360 meetings and had extended campaigns in Manchester, Birmingham, Belfast, and London. During this time a world consciousness and concern was implanted in his heart.

The evangelist's world concern grew throughout the following years. And then the great London Harringay crusade, discussed previously, took place. In the triumph of this crusade, Billy Graham determined to do his best to fulfill the words of Christ when He said, "Preach the gospel to all creation" (Mark 16:15). It was at that time that he received the vision of becoming a world evangelist.

Immediately after the Harringay crusade, Graham and his small group of helpers engaged in a whirlwind tour of European cities. Because of the tremendous impact of the gospel on London during the Harringay crusade, every city the team visited hired the largest stadium for Graham to preach in. The response was overwhelming. Crowds overflowed every venue to hear the Good News preached. In Stockholm, for example, 65,000 crammed into the Skansen Arena for the largest evangelistic meeting ever held in Sweden. In Copenhagen, 15,000 people gathered in pouring rain in the city square as Billy Graham stood to declare Christ. The attendance in Amsterdam reached 40,000. As well,

Graham held a four-day crusade in Paris. It was the first time in the history of modern France that all the Protestant churches rallied behind a major evangelistic effort. The next year Graham picked up the challenge of preaching the gospel in the Far East.

THE IMPACT ON WORLD EVANGELIZATION

A detailed account of all Graham's crusades around the globe would fill many volumes. He has virtually spoken to the entire world. And it is not just the crusades in themselves. As a former associate of Graham's puts it, a five-day crusade with Billy Graham in the pulpit is just the tip of the Billy Graham Evangelistic Association iceberg.

From its incorporation in Minnesota in 1950, the BGEA has grown into a multifaceted ministry that could easily compete for a distinction once bestowed upon the British Empire: The sun never sets on the BGEA. People on every continent of the planet are touched by Billy Graham's work around the clock through the many aspects of the ministry:

- A man listens to the *Hour of Decision* in China.

- A woman reads a Graham book in Brazil.

- A young person sees a Graham movie in South Africa.

- A grandmother receives her subscription to *Decision* magazine in Australia.

- A Russian worker finds a tract written in his language.

- A family in Rwanda receives humanitarian aid.

- An inquirer gets counseling at a BGEA-associated crusade in India.

- A student group visits the museum at the Billy Graham Center in Illinois.

- A child watches a Graham home video in London.

Graham's influence is felt in almost every nation.

Berlin

Not only did Billy Graham follow the ideology of William Carey in relation to missions, he also carried in his heart a lesser-known dream of the "father of modern missions." In 1812 William Carey had what he called a "pleasing dream." The dream was to gather together believers from around the world for a great conference in Cape Town, South Africa. There they would discuss the furtherance of the gospel worldwide.

In 1966 Billy Graham facilitated the Berlin Conference on Evangelization, the first gathering of its sort. People came together from many parts of the world and from various Christian groups to hammer out a viable evangelical theology. The theme of the conference read: "One Race, One Gospel, One Task." Indeed, the conference was well received, though it did have one weakness. It was predominantly Western in its makeup. The BGEA set about designing a way to correct this imbalance, and the concept behind the Lausanne Conference was born.

The Lausanne Conference

In August 1974, a reporter for *Time* magazine wrote this:

> Millions of Christians still take the Commission of Christ literally, still believe that one of their foremost tasks is to preach the gospel to the unbaptized. . . . Last week, in the lakeshore resort of Lausanne, Switzerland, that belief found a formidable form, possibly the widest-ranging meeting of Christians ever held. Brought together largely through the efforts of Reverend Billy Graham, some twenty-four hundred Protestant evangelical leaders from 150 countries ended a ten day international Congress on World Evangelization that served notice of the vigor of conservative, resolutely biblical, fervently mission minded Christianity.[3]

Twenty-four-hundred representatives from evangelical circles around the world gathered for one of the most significant meetings of the twentieth century. The inspiration and challenge of those days highly motivated the attendees to fulfill the Great Commission within

their generations. Seminars on virtually every aspect of world evangelization were provided at the congress. No one in attendance could say
they were not helped to engage in the Great Commission in some way.
The conference was a milestone, and of it Maurice Rowlandson says,
"Looking back [on Lausanne] almost twenty years later, it is clear that
Lausanne became a watershed for evangelicals. . . . The growth of the
influence of the evangelical wing [of the church] can be largely traced
back to that congress."[4]

Amsterdam '83 and '86

The success of the Lausanne Congress on World Evangelization
spurred Billy Graham in the 1980s to sponsor two significant conferences in Amsterdam, the Netherlands. The two conferences were
specifically geared toward itinerant evangelists. The first took place in
1983, and the second in 1986. Graham, who had subsidized the Berlin
and Laussane Conferences, now had an even more ambitious financial
goal. Because these itinerant evangelists did not have the larger organizations supporting them that the previous delegates had often had,
Graham decided he would raise all the money needed to gather these
people from all over the world.

Many stories emerged during these conferences that were fascinating—even touching. Franklin Graham, Billy's son, and director of the
relief ministry Samaritan's Purse, assembled a large store of clothing,
books, and other amenities for the many less-privileged delegates. These
evangelists not only went away better equipped to fulfill their ministry, but
also decently dressed and with helpful materials to aid in their evangelizing. It was an enriching time for all the delegates, whether from an affluent society or from a poverty-stricken country. A great impetus to world
evangelization permeated the entire atmosphere of these conferences.

Amsterdam 2000

Billy Graham once again called evangelists from around the
world to gather in 2000. As reported, they assembled "for one simple
purpose. . . . They came from the great cities of the world: Buenos

Aires, London, Los Angeles, Moscow, Nairobi, Narjing, and Sidney. They came from villages so small that the names don't appear on most maps. They came — 10,732 of them from 209 countries and territories around the world. They came together to focus on one simple purpose: to find new and more effective ways to proclaim the Gospel throughout the world."[5] In capsule form, that was Amsterdam 2000, a nine-day conference for evangelists and evangelism leaders.

The rational for this venture centered in strengthening evangelists, providing challenges and practical helps to strengthen the local church and to further the kingdom of God in bringing glory to Jesus Christ.

The theme of Amsterdam 2000 reads: "Proclaiming Peace and Hope for the New Millennium." This theme struck a responsive chord among the attendees as they listened to such outstanding speakers as John Stott, Ravi Zacharias, Steven Olford, Luis Palau, the Archbishop of Canterbury, Anne Graham Lotz, Franklin Graham, Billy Kim, Charles Colson, and others. The conference also provided attendees with more than two hundred workshops to choose from. Moreover, the unity and fellowship experienced across the church spectrum and from around the world were overwhelming. Unfortunately, Billy Graham could not attend the conference himself due to illness, but he addressed the gathering via satellite. In his words of welcome he stated, "This conference could be the catalyst for the most productive advance of the gospel ever. . . . You and I are poised to see from Amsterdam 2000 an enormous increase in the harvest."

Indeed, several positive steps were taken at the conference. The early statement of faith of the BGEA was presented as the guiding document for the event. The document reads:

The Statement of Faith for the Billy Graham Evangelistic Association Serves as the basic theological framework for the Amsterdam 2000 Conference of Preaching Evangelists. The Billy Graham Evangelistic Association believes . . .

The Bible to be the infallible Word of God, that it is His holy and inspired Word, and that it is of supreme and final authority.

In one God, eternally existing in three persons—Father, Son, and Holy Spirit.

Jesus Christ was conceived by the Holy Spirit, born of the Virgin Mary. He led a sinless life, took on Himself all our sins, died and rose again, and is seated at the right hand of the Father as our mediator and advocate.

That all men everywhere are lost and face the judgment of God, and need to come to a saving knowledge of Jesus Christ through His shed blood on the cross.

That Christ rose from the dead and is coming soon.

In holy Christian living, and that we must have concern for the hurts and social needs of our fellowmen.

We must dedicate ourselves anew to the service of our Lord and to His authority over our lives.

In using every modern means of communication available to us to spread the Gospel of Jesus Christ throughout the world.

Again Franklin Graham was there with food, clothing, books, and other helps from Samaritan's Purse. The travel, lodging, and food for attendees (except those from North America and Western Europe) were provided by the Graham organization. For the first time in their lives, many Third World itinerant evangelists found themselves in the company of like-minded people. Bonds between Africans and Fijians, Filipinos and Czechs were made that are now blossoming into life-long commitments to pray for and encourage one another. It was a moving and life-changing experience for many. People returned home with renewed vigor and information on how to reach the people around them more effectively with the gospel.

While Billy Graham was unable to be there physically, his presence was sensed, and the thousands of evangelists expressed gratitude to him for facilitating the event.

Worldwide Covenants

Following the Lausanne Conference, a continuation committee was organized, which has continued to work for many years. The committee was designed essentially to foster world evangelization. The Lausanne Continuation Committee holds meetings in local areas around the world. For example, a series of meetings in Singapore in 1977 and 1978, supported by Billy Graham, gave rise to a new awareness for evangelism in that part of the world. Strategic issues and strategies and theological papers were produced that brought the evangelical world together in a unique way. As one expressed it,

> In these myriad extensions of what has come to be called the Spirit of Lausanne, the Lausanne covenant has played a major unifying role again, particularly in the third world, where it provided a formal basis on which Baptists, Mennonites, Methodists, Pentecostals, and others, including evangelical members of the WCC-affiliated denominations, could agree to work together. It's a coalescence of the spirit of evangelism as exemplified by Billy Graham. . . . The international bulletin of mission research has asserted that the covenant may now be the broadest umbrella in the world under which professing Christians can be gathered to pray and strategize for the salvation of their cities.[6]

Furthermore, regional conferences for itinerant evangelists have emerged out of the various meetings. For example, in 1994 Billy Graham sponsored a large gathering of evangelists from North America. The event was held in Louisville, Kentucky, and named the North American Conference of Itinerant Evangelists (NACIE). From such conferences have come some excellent publications, such as *A Biblical Standard for Evangelists* (Amsterdam, 1983) and *Biblical Affirmations for Evangelists* (NACIE, 1994).

BILLY GRAHAM'S SUCCESS IN WORLD EVANGELIZATION

Billy Graham's "success" has come in many guises. As pointed out earlier, Graham has been on the world's list of most admired men for many years. Presidents have called him in for prayer and counsel. Newspapers give him and his crusades front-page coverage; and he is in constant demand as a guest on television talk shows. But this in itself does not equate to success in the final analysis, at least in relation to kingdom endeavors. So what constitutes success in God's kingdom? It is certainly not mere numbers of attendees at a crusade rally, or even the number of decisions recorded. The best definition of success in the kingdom is found in the Scriptures where Jesus says that when one lost sheep is brought into the fold, "he rejoices over it more than over the ninety-nine which have not gone astray" (Matthew 18:13). Seeing people truly saved from eternal damnation matters most. If genuine conversions serve as the final criteria for success in the task, it seems fair to say that Billy Graham has been most successful in his evangelistic endeavor. Testimonies of transformed lives abound as a result of Graham's ministry.

It is interesting to note that while multitudes have made genuine decisions for Christ through Billy Graham's worldwide crusade ministry, percentagewise the largest number of these decisions have been made *outside* North America and Western Europe where the gospel is reasonably well known.

Billy Graham believes any "success" in world evangelization centers in the fact that he is willing and able to adapt to the culture where he preaches. He is always well informed on the culture, history, and social dynamics of the country where he is ministering. He also reads a number of international newspapers and magazines each day to keep himself current on world events.

As an evangelist, Billy Graham truly has had an impact on the world. Of course there are those who think he has spent too much time overseas, but Graham disagrees with them. Concerning his decisions about where to hold his crusades, whether in America or in another country, he has said, "The Lord gave a right balance."[7]

In this regard one biographer has said, "By 1956 Billy Graham no longer was merely an American preacher. What he said, or did, or was could make for good or ill across the world."[8]

Billy Graham's world consciousness and influence began early in his ministry. No doubt Graham's studies in anthropology at Wheaton

College planted some early seeds of world concern and gave him insight into the true nature of humanity. He recognized that by the creative hand of God we are all of one family; the gospel, therefore, must be proclaimed to all in that bond of oneness. He could not divorce himself from any people or group because we are all one in Adam, and all need desperately to be brought by redemption into the "last Adam," the Lord Jesus Christ (1 Corinthians 15:45). Throughout his life, Billy Graham has made this the focus of his ministry, and the world has heard him gladly.

13

The Church

⸎

*"Jesus delivered to the church its immediate,
compelling commission . . . evangelization."*

— BILLY GRAHAM

George Beverly Shea tells the story of a pastor who strongly opposed one of Billy Graham's crusades. But despite the pastor's opposition, many in his congregation were attending crusade meetings and being helped and encouraged in their faith. Yet the pastor, who was on the liberal side theologically, could find few good things to say about Billy Graham.

Toward the end of the crusade, Graham called the pastor and asked him to come to one of the meetings and sit on the platform with him. Taken aback, the pastor politely asked the evangelist if he played golf. Graham answered in the affirmative, and the two men quickly arranged to spend a few hours together on the golf course. As a result the pastor's attitude began to soften, and the following night he attended the crusade meeting. He sat on the platform with other dignitaries, and Billy Graham invited him to lead the vast audience in prayer.

Because of this experience, the pastor's life and ministry were transformed. The next Sunday he stood before his congregation and said, "I have never given an invitation to receive Christ in the fifteen years I have been your pastor, but I am giving one now." And several people came forward. Indeed, the pastor was so changed he became a pastor-evangelist, going about sharing the gospel message with any and all who wanted to hear it. In the course of events, the pastor's church was likewise transformed, and that is of prime importance. The church is critical in all evangelism.

In regard to the vital role of the church, Billy Graham says, "Of all the many groups in which humans have collected themselves, of all the tribes, clans, organizations, and societies throughout history, none has been so powerful, so far-reaching, or more universal than the Church."[1]

Graham, of course, would be the first to say that when we stand before God, the question concerning salvation will not be what church we have been attending, but what we have done with Jesus Christ. Responding to Him is the prime issue. Nonetheless, Graham holds the church in high esteem. He makes a serious effort to enlist and involve the church in all he undertakes as an evangelist. Ralph Bell, an associate evangelist with Graham, readily admits, "Our work could not go on without the church support. Billy Graham and the Team see themselves as servants of the church."[2] In like manner, Sterling Houston, crusade director for the BGEA, says, "The BGEA must function in ways that honor, serve and build up the church or we are not biblical."[3]

While Billy Graham heartily agrees with such statements, what is his understanding of the church? What makes up his doctrinal position concerning the "Bride of Christ"?

VIEW OF THE CHURCH

Concerning the life of the church, Graham has made a number of definitive statements in his book *Billy Graham Answers Your Questions*. He writes:

Being a member of Christ's church involves more than an outward attachment. . . . Church membership, in the true sense, is being a real part of a company of people who have staked their all on the belief that all that Jesus said was true. . . . A member of Christ's church is one who has made Christ central in his life.[4]

Billy Graham understands the church in a twofold manner. First, the church in its universal aspect, and second, the church as a local body of believers. On the local level he brings things together saying that the church is the family of believers (Ephesians 2:19).[5] And what is true of the church in its local aspect is likewise true on the universal level. The church in every sense stands as the great family of believers. Graham declares that the church, "on the local limited scale, like the universal Church, is the body of Christ." He bases this statement on Ephesians 1:22–23 where Paul writes, "And He put all things in subjection under His feet, and gave Him as head over all things to the church, which is His body, the fulness of Him who fills all in all." Billy Graham goes on from there to delineate in more detail his doctrine of the church from this twofold perspective.

The Church Universal

Billy Graham sees the church as composed of the entire body of believers, as he puts it, from the Day of Pentecost until the return of Christ when God's people will be resurrected. Admittance to the church in this broad sense comes about through hearing the gospel and responding positively to its message through repentance and faith. In this regard Graham says, "Those who are counted part of this one, true, universal Church of God are those who have repented of their sins, sought God's pardon, and accepted the Lord Jesus Christ as their personal Savior."[6]

Graham sees no delay in membership into the church universal through a process of indoctrination, catechism, or any restriction that a local church may enact relative to receiving its members. He stresses, "You become a member of this church, the universal church, the moment you become a believer."[7]

It is the evangelist's conviction that the church universal—and the local church for that matter—is not the result of human work or organizational effort. He says, "The Church is the only institution organized by Christ. . . . The Church is the result of Christ's death and resurrection." In a word, "Jesus Christ Himself founded the church."[8] Furthermore, when a person becomes a "member" of the universal church, obligations are immediately forthcoming. In Graham's *Peace with God*, he says to those who respond to the gospel,

> Now that you have accepted Christ as your Savior and put your trust and confidence in Him, you have already become a member of the great universal Church. You are a member of the household of faith. You are a part of the body of Christ. Now you are called upon to obey Christ, and if you obey Christ, you will follow His example of joining with others in the worship of God.[9]

Graham then emphasizes, "It is to the Church and its Christ that you owe allegiance."[10]

All of this implies that the church, in both aspects of its manifestations, rests upon Jesus Christ as the chief cornerstone, and He is thus the Head in the fullest sense of the word. Graham states,

> [Jesus Christ] is the great cornerstone upon which the Church is built. He is the foundation of all Christian experience, and the Church is founded upon Him. . . . Jesus proclaimed Himself to be the founder of the Church, the builder of the Church, and the Church belongs to Him alone. He has promised to live with, and in, all those who are members of this Church. Here is not only an organization but an organism that is completely unlike anything else that the world has ever known: God Himself living with, and in, ordinary men and women who are members of His Church.[11]

The Local Church

Billy Graham believes that membership in a Christ-centered local church is vitally important because the local church is a group of people joined together for worship, fellowship, and instruction. Membership in a local church, he says, will in turn strengthen a person's walk with God and make it possible to have a more positive and effective testimony for Christ.

However, Graham cautions that membership in a local church does not save a person. He goes on to declare, "Nowhere in the Bible do we find teaching that we are saved by uniting with a church."[12] Yet at the same time, he wants it to be fully understood that those who are saved should definitely identify themselves with a local body of believers. He says, "Christ loved the church and gave Himself for it. If our Lord loved it enough to die for it; then we should respect it enough to support and attend it."[13] He goes on, "Christians have always required a living relationship with such assemblies."[14]

The foundational purpose for the gathering of God's people together in corporate life centers in worship. Graham says, "In church we come together with the believers to worship God."[15] He emphasizes again that "the purpose of this Christian society called the 'Church' is, first: to glorify God by our worship. We do not go to church just to hear a sermon. We go to church to worship God."[16] Graham stresses that the church is for fellowship and that fellowship must be in mutual harmony and with the glorifying of God in worship.

Graham also states that as the church gathers for worship, members also "come together to learn more about God and His word."[17] He elaborates this thought by urging believers to "seek to live each day for Christ," and then goes on to say, "An important part of that is growing in your relationship to God by having fellowship with other believers in hearing His word taught, which is why the Church is important."[18]

The evangelist sees it as important that "the Church is for the strengthening of faith."[19] The Scriptures declare the fact that "faith comes from hearing, and hearing by the word of Christ" (Romans 10:17). As believers come together in fellowship and hear the Word of God, their faith is strengthened and encouraged. The faithful proclamation of the essential truths of Jesus Christ in the context of church worship deeply moves hearers and strengthens their faith and commitment to the Lord Jesus.

According to Billy Graham, the church is also "a medium of service. We are saved to serve. There are a thousand and one tasks to be done for Christ. This work can best be accomplished through the fellowship of a local church. A virile Christianity has never existed apart from the church. The church is the organization of Christ on earth."[20] Graham develops this theme by declaring, "I am convinced that the cluster of believers . . . these brothers and sisters in Christ where you join to pray and study, give and witness, is the basic unit through which God is working to redeem the world."[21]

BEING BUILT UP IN THE FAITH

Moreover, the church exists not only for the purpose of bringing people to faith in Christ, but also for building up believers in the faith. As Graham says, "I believe the changing of people's hearts is the primary mission of the Church."[22] And this means not only evangelization, but also seeing Christians come to maturation in their relationship with the Lord. Graham states, "The Church has a very specific assignment, and only the church provides the nurture for spiritual growth."[23]

Being in a defined geographical, cultural location, a local church can reach out in ways that bring glory to God and the alleviation of problems and pain for multitudes of people. Graham places strong emphasis on the importance of the church in this aspect of ministry. He says, "Jesus stated that his true followers would be those who cared for the hungry and others in need (Matthew 25:31-46). The Bible also says, 'If a brother or sister is without clothing and in need of daily food, and one of you says to them, "Go in peace, be warmed and be filled," and yet you do not give them what is necessary for their body, what use is that?' (James 2:15-16)."[24]

Graham also urges that "the Church should be the means of channeling your funds for Christian work."[25] Through faithful stewardship to their church, God's people can do much to help needy people and situations.

ORGANIZATIONAL PRINCIPLES

How does Billy Graham view the order and structure of the local church? He insists that the church must maintain a strong leadership structure with the pastor in the primary role. He says, "The Bible tells us that we should submit to those who have such responsibility 'they keep watch over you as men who must give an account. Obey them so their work will be a joy, not a burden, for that would be of no advantage to you' (Hebrews 13:17)."[26] However, he does not elucidate a complex church administrative structure. He simply sees the local church as being led by pastors who teach, preach, and minister God's Word as Christ's "undershepherds." The evangelist leaves the details of structure up to the local churches with their varying doctrinal and denominational views.

DENOMINATIONS

Billy Graham points out first that most of the major denominations, when it comes to evangelism, exhibit a gracious spirit of cooperation. When evangelism is the focus, the denominations do not condemn each other for deviating from the other's system of church structure and government. In the final analysis, Graham believes that most of the major denominations have basically the same Christian doctrines. He says, "I have found that non-essentials separate people more often than essentials. In reading the history of denominations, it is interesting to note that . . . divisions have always resulted from somewhat minor differences. . . . I made up my mind to fellowship with all those who love Jesus Christ with all their heart, and are seeking to serve Him."[27]

The evangelist confesses, "I have sometimes been criticized for doing this, but I would rather lose a few friends than the blessing and favor of my Lord."[28] In that same spirit, he also feels he must "submit" to the church. Citing the Apostle Paul's spirit in this regard he states, "Scripture indicates that first he earned the confidence of the church by his submission to it and his service to it."[29]

Graham also emphasizes the fact that the Bible says that Christ loves the Church and therefore "I must love it too. I must pray for it, defend it, work in it, pay my tithes and offerings to it, help to advance it, promote holiness in it, and make it the functional and witnessing body our Lord meant it to be."[30] In this regard, Graham is a faithful Southern Baptist and a supporting member of the First Baptist Church of Dallas, Texas. Yet he also says, "I feel that I belong to all the churches. I am equally at home in an Anglican or Baptist church or a Brethren assembly."[31]

CRITICISMS

As could be expected, when Billy Graham holds a crusade in a community, the bulk of the criticism arises from churches and pastors. One recurrent criticism of Graham is expressed by Charles Dullea, who while basically positive about Graham, feels, "[Billy Graham] leaves some doctrines unaffirmed, saying nothing about the sacraments and little about the Church."[32] There may be some substance to this criticism, but Billy Graham would be the first to acknowledge that he does not hold a crusade to elucidate all the doctrines of the Christian faith. He does not see himself as a theologian or as someone come to indoctrinate his listeners in a full-orbed biblical theology. As an evangelist, he preaches only the doctrinal elements necessary to proclaiming the gospel and calling people to repentance and faith.

Perhaps Graham should say more, but such issues can often be divisive among believers, and an evangelistic crusade is not a time to precipitate divisions. Thus he restricts himself to preaching the basic content of the gospel. But he certainly does all he can do to integrate inquirers into a local church of their choice. They can then adhere to the doctrines of that particular church. Graham feels that his ministry centers in preaching the gospel while the process of bringing new Christians to maturity in Christ is the basic responsibility of the local church. This has been historically true of many evangelists. In America, Charles G. Finney, D. L. Moody, Billy Sunday, and many other mass evangelists have taken this approach.

Others have criticized Billy Graham because he does not hold his crusades in church buildings. Leaning on historical precedents, Graham answers his critics with these words, "In almost every generation God has raised up evangelists, who have often had to pursue their calling outside the structured church."[33] Furthermore, there is the problem of finding a church building big enough to hold tens of thousands of people. Not only that, many unbelievers feel far more comfortable in a stadium than in a church building. It took some time, but John Wesley, the Anglican priest, eventually learned this lesson and took to the open fields to preach to the lost.

A PRACTICAL HELP

As just a single example among many that could be cited, one of the most practical contributions Billy Graham has made to the church centers in the Schools of Evangelism the BGEA sponsors. These conferences are designed to help pastors become more informed and adept at developing effective outreach in their congregations. Billy Graham feels that these schools may be making the most profound contributions to evangelization of any of the work he or the entire BGEA undertakes.

The Schools of Evangelism began quite early in the history of the BGEA when Lowell Berry, a concerned and dedicated layman, financially underwrote the enterprise. For several years the conferences were held in conjunction with the crusades. The conference program would be held during the day, then the attendees would attend the crusade meeting at night. This approach was used around the world. In recent years, however, Schools of Evangelism have been held in different venues at various times. They are something of a smaller version of the conferences for evangelists held in Amsterdam. The schools have been well received and instrumental in equipping churches around the globe to do the work of evangelism.

Although there are always rumblings of criticism, it seems fair to say that the local church has by and large profited considerably from the efforts of Billy Graham. Of further significance is the fact that in those places where Billy Graham has held crusades, he has helped to foster an atmosphere of openness and receptivity to the gospel message that often did not exist prior to his arrival. Rare is the community that fails to be positively affected with the gospel of Jesus Christ when Billy Graham holds a crusade. Through his crusades Billy Graham changes lives, and those lives influence churches and communities at large. Therein he has made a most significant contribution, and the history of evangelical evangelism gives this a resounding affirmation.

14

The Lasting Legacy

❦

"There's too much Billy Graham here."

— BILLY GRAHAM

When Billy Graham reads this book, he is likely to raise a ruckus. This is the man who modestly said, upon first touring the Billy Graham Center at Wheaton College, "There's too much Billy Graham here." He won't sit quietly and allow himself to be compared with the great men of the Bible and church history.

Nonetheless, this comment by the Reverend Maurice Wood, Bishop of Norwich and member of Britain's House of Lords, expresses the thoughts of many:

> I believe that in each generation God raises up certain people he can trust with success. I would put Billy in line with the Wesleys and St. Augustine. Toss Francis in, if you like. He's in that league, anyway. And what's extraordinary is that he doesn't seem to know it. But he is the most spiritually productive servant of God in our time.[1]

No other person in history has preached to so many—more than two billion people at crusades, by radio, TV, and satellite broadcasts—

proclaiming the simple message of salvation in Christ, personally lived out in a transparent and honest fashion.

His open, self-effacing demeanor is undoubtedly a key component in his astonishing ability to put people from all walks and stations of life, from all cultures and religions, immediately at ease in his presence. It enables him to draw vastly differing people together to work toward a common goal, proclaiming the gospel of Jesus Christ to the whole world.

In this concluding chapter, we will examine, albeit in a cursory way, several aspects of the effect Billy Graham has had on the world he has traveled and on the evangelical movement he has represented. We will focus on the views of several people who have had varying connections with his ministry and whose opinions on Graham's legacy and his ultimate impact on culture and on evangelicalism differ and yet converge.

How is the world different as a result of this singular life? Three recurring themes emerge in analyzing the results of Graham's ministry in the life of the individual, the church, and the world: First, his example of integrity and single-mindedness has enhanced the credibility of Christian evangelism; second, his inclusive approach has created unity among diverse groups in sharing the simple message of the gospel; and third, the replication of his ministry through training and evangelism conferences has multiplied his effectiveness into the future.

Some of the incidents recorded in this final summary have been touched upon previously, but a recounting is in order here. Further, it will put the evangelist in the sweep of evangelical evangelism and assure him a proper place in that setting, thus giving him historical authenticity.

Undoubtedly, as has been mentioned, the most profound effect is the change in the lives of countless thousands of individuals who will spend eternity with Christ having heard the message through this man. Those believers, in turn, have influenced and changed their families, workplaces, churches, communities, and nations, as they became new people in Christ. This result is impossible to measure, but it is extremely significant as salt and light pour into the world.

Erwin W. Lutzer, senior pastor of Moody Church in Chicago, has seen the effect of Graham's reputation on individuals. He described his experience in witnessing to airline passengers when he travels: "A person will often ask me what I really believe, thinking I seem to be a bit of a fanatic. I say, 'Have you ever heard of Billy Graham? I basically believe what Billy Graham does.' Immediately the individual nods his head and feels comfortable because of Billy's model of integrity and his work with various denominations."[2]

As a youngster growing up on an isolated Canadian farm, Lutzer was fascinated with Graham. Elvis Presley was the rage for his generation of teenagers, but Lutzer's teenage hero was Billy Graham. From about age ten onward, he bought any materials he could find about Graham, like a picture book Lutzer memorized. He practiced Graham's preaching style and listened to the *Hour of Decision* radio program several times each Sunday as it aired on different stations. He wanted to become a preacher, and he followed Graham's example.

A MODEL OF INTEGRITY AND SINGLE-MINDEDNESS

The pattern for future evangelists established by Graham stresses the need for both personal integrity and a constant focus on the primary task God has called each one to do. The high standards he and the team have held are manifested in several of Graham's well-known traits, including his humility, teachability, genuineness, dedication, and gracious response to criticism. As an organization, the BGEA has worked hard to safeguard its moral integrity in finances and personal conduct.

Humility

Graham's legendary humility didn't keep him from thinking big as an eager young evangelist. W. T. Watson, founder and president of Florida Bible Institute where Graham attended, said, "Billy always wanted to do something big. He didn't know exactly what yet, but he couldn't wait just to do something big, whatever it was."[3]

Nor are humility and self-promotion mutually exclusive. In the early days of his preaching, he paid a sign painter $2.10 to make a banner saying, "Hear Billy Graham" when he preached at a little mission church. He often distributed handmade fliers proclaiming, "Dynamic Youthful Evangelist Billy Graham," "A Great Gospel Preacher at 21" and "Billy Graham, One of America's Outstanding Young Evangelists—Dynamic Messages You Will Never Forget."[4] He knew how to get people's attention and then focus it on Jesus Christ.

As Watson said, Graham dreamed big. From the beginning, he worked hard to accomplish great things for God. One might think that huge, successful crusades and worldwide fame just happened to fall on Graham's ministry. But in reality, he has consistently applied an energy level and a work ethic that would exhaust most people.

It would be easy to get puffed up with self-importance when one is on the Most Admired list year after year, when throngs of people come out to hear one preach, and when U.S. presidents and other world leaders seek one out. But on Billy Graham Day in his hometown of Charlotte, North Carolina, in 1971, when President Nixon and his wife, Pat, presented a plaque in Graham's honor, he said, "It's too much for a country boy. I'm turning it all over to the One to whom it belongs—to the Lord. He's the one who made it possible."[5]

When asked to speak at the Amsterdam 1986 conference, he said, "Look, I don't want to dominate this. This is not a Billy Graham show."[6] Likewise, photographer Russ Busby, who has traveled the world with Graham documenting his ministry, said, "The biggest asset Billy has is his honest humility."[7]

Teachability

Graham's teachable spirit is another oft-noted asset demonstrated by his willingness to learn. He has continued to refocus his views as he experiences the world and its hurting people. An observer at the Lausanne Congress on World Evangelization in 1974 said, "I became convinced that Dr. Graham actually felt that he had much yet to learn and that he needed the counsel and help of other Christians."[8] In Billy's own words, "I am a man who is still in process."[9]

Lon Allison, Director of the Billy Graham Center at Wheaton College, believes that one of Graham's greatest strengths is in being eminently teachable, which comes out of true humility, a characteristic mentioned over and over by people describing him. Allison sees the evangelist's life as a picture of who God is in total. In Graham's early ministry, he emphasized judgment, and more recently, God's love. Allison says, "God is a God of justice and he demands right living from his followers. But on the other side is his mercy, absolute love and beneficence, and Billy's life has moved across these two poles."[10]

Genuineness

Besides being humble and teachable, Graham is real. While he tends to over-praise his friends and associates (he cannot be "out-complimented"[11]), he is sincere. It would seem, from all the studying and research done on this man by many people, that Graham is "of a piece." He is what he seems to be inside and out, at home and at work, in the daylight and in the dark of night, in crowds or alone. This transparent genuineness attracts people and allows them to believe what he says. He doesn't just say it; he lives it as well. In a day when people long for leaders they can trust, who say what they mean and mean what they say, such a man stands out.

He stands out because he has always emphasized the importance of the believer's personal walk with Christ, both for himself and others. Not only does he spend hours alone with God in Bible study and prayer, he also exhorts crusade and telephone counselors, team members, itinerant evangelists, and crusade attendees to seek God in a personal way. One focus at the Amsterdam 2000 conference was the "inner life of the evangelist."

Dedication

Graham has managed to remain focused on his true calling in his dedication to evangelism. He said repeatedly that he only wants to preach the gospel, and he has done just that. John O. Yarbrough, vice president for evangelization of the North American Mission Board of the Southern Baptist Convention, noted Graham's commitment to his main task of preaching the gospel of Christ without getting sidetracked on a political or social agenda. "D. L. Moody and [Charles] Finney built colleges, [John] Wesley established a denomination, and Billy Sunday got sidetracked into prohibition, but Graham has stayed true to his call of evangelism throughout his life," Yarbrough said.[12]

These additional efforts of evangelists are valuable also, but Graham's single-minded devotion to just one thing has yielded rich results.

Response to Criticism

Another component of Graham's example of integrity is the way he has handled criticism. He responds graciously to all criticism, even that which is bitter and negative. He takes legitimate criticism to heart, and he learns and grows from it, again demonstrating his teachable spirit.

Perhaps the hardest to bear is criticism from fellow believers. Savonarola was actually martyred by his own church. And some of Graham's sharpest attacks have come from within the church. He was criticized by Bob Jones and others on the right for mixing and mingling with denominations that did not share all the doctrines of evangelicalism.

On the other hand, liberals criticized him for preaching a simplistic message that neglected realities such as social injustice. He was condemned for not doing enough to end segregation; conversely, he was condemned for requiring integration at crusades. Liberals said he should have convinced Nixon to stop the bombing and end the Vietnam War. Conservatives said he should not have gone to the Soviet Union to preach and possibly play into the manipulative hands of the communists.

But while examples abound of courageous actions Graham took on controversial issues, even more striking is the way he has responded to faultfinding. With rare exceptions, he has chosen not to respond to attacks. It is tempting to set the record straight when maligned, but his approach was simply to acknowledge the often hurtful remarks in a loving note, stating that he would consider the views represented and pray for the person holding them. It is noteworthy that many of his critics have been transformed to admirers and close friends over the years.

In addition to responding gently, Graham used legitimate criticism as an impetus to change and improve himself and his ministry. Going all the way back to the lesson learned from his first meeting with Harry Truman, he has grown from merited criticism. Graham and his associates Cliff Barrows, Grady Wilson, and Gerald Beavan met with Truman in 1950 and concluded the meeting with prayer. As they left the White House, reporters asked about the meeting, and Graham cheerfully related what they had talked about. The four men provided a photo opportunity as they knelt on the White House lawn to thank God for the meeting with the president, and the resulting photograph along with Graham's candid remarks annoyed Truman. Graham never made that mistake again. His subsequent conversations with officials were kept confidential.

Another example of learning from criticism is a change in Graham since the days of his close relationship with and support of Richard Nixon. During his presidency, Nixon regularly asked Graham's advice, and the two were personal friends. Graham believed in Nixon's integrity and faith well into the Watergate scandal. Graham urged him to admit his mistakes and was devastated by media excerpts from the White House transcripts that revealed a man much different from the friend he had known. Graham was widely criticized for allowing Nixon to use him for political gain. Although he never agreed that Nixon had used him, since Watergate Graham has maintained a lower profile with high-profile politicians.

When criticized for appearing to use emotional pressure to bring people forward at crusades, Graham actually changed his methods. He stopped speaking after the invitation and bowed to pray silently during the singing of "Just As I Am."

In 1982, Baptists in Moscow, unaware that Graham had been working privately for the release of imprisoned pastors, were disappointed that he had not spoken out more forcefully against religious suppression.[13] When he returned to the Soviet Union in 1984, he was prepared to speak boldly, but privately. Graham spoke with Boris Ponomarev, chief of international affairs for the Communist Party Central Committee and a member of the Politburo. Ponomarev responded with a forty-five-minute monologue on Soviet foreign policy aimed at Ronald Reagan. Graham then explained to him the importance of religion in America and said that before the two nations could be friends, Soviet leaders would have to improve the conditions for religious people. He said, "A major reason the American public does not support closer ties with the Soviet Union is because of what is perceived as religious discrimination and even oppression, especially of [Christians] and Jews."[14] Ponomarev later expressed appreciation for what Graham had said and indicated that the advice had been taken seriously by the Soviet leaders.

Graham and the team have worked steadfastly to honor God with their conduct, both public and private. Without integrity, even tireless effort will fail. In emphasizing openness, willingness for scrutiny, and the importance of a constant, close, and humble walk with God, Graham has focused his heart properly. In examining his written and spoken words, as well as his deeds, the truth of Proverbs 23:7 emerges: "For as he thinks within himself, so he is."

SAFEGUARDING MORALITY

As part of its determination to maintain integrity, the BGEA constructed numerous safeguards to protect the team from siren calls of immorality in any form. In 1948, Graham and his new team took action to avoid the frequent criticisms of evangelists in the areas of finances, moral integrity, antichurch attitudes and lack of follow-up with those who made decisions.[15] They implemented measures to prevent even an appearance of evil, including "external mechanisms to insure one's virtue."[16]

One facet of this effort is that the BGEA has paid Graham a salary comparable to that received by the pastor of a large church since the early 1950s. He has no personal involvement in the freewill offerings taken at crusades.

Graham also took steps to protect donors who wanted to give annuities, a widely used method of charitable contributions. He insisted that none of the donated principal be used as long as the donor was alive, so that in a worst-case scenario, if the ministry were to go bankrupt, no donor would be hurt financially.[17] Many organizations put 40 percent or 50 percent of annuity donations directly into working funds, assuming the remainder will earn sufficient income to cover interest payments to donors. But the BGEA took a conservative and safe approach.

In 1979, Graham played a pivotal role in founding the Evangelical Council for Financial Accountability (ECFA) "to enunciate, maintain and manifest a code of financial accountability and reporting which is consistent with enlightened and responsible Christian faith and practice."[18] The organization's example of being open to scrutiny has raised the level of accountability and fiscal diligence in many ministries.

The team has also taken extraordinary steps to avoid even accidental situations that could appear questionable. Graham never goes into a hotel room alone until it is verified to be empty, and he never rides alone in a car with a woman outside his family. The open-door policy in the BGEA offices makes secretaries and team members readily observable at work.

Graham has gone to great lengths to work with churches for his crusades and to encourage active individual participation in the local church. A typical crusade involves from 500 to 1,200 area churches representing 70 to 90 different denominations and groups. These churches provide thousands of volunteers, including 10,000 people who pray in advance for a crusade, 5,000 counselors trained to help inquirers, a choir of 4,000, and 1,000 ushers.[19] Pastors who have never met before work together and build relationships in the months before a crusade.

Since the 1949 Los Angeles crusade, Dawson Trotman, founder and head of the Navigators, and later Charlie Riggs and Tom Phillips, have trained counselors through a "Life and Witness" instruction class comprised of four two-hour sessions to equip counselors to answer questions and meet the needs of inquirers. Counselors also pray with the seekers, help them connect with churches, and give them literature on how to establish a personal walk with God.

The team also has determined to be conservative and to avoid exaggeration when reporting numbers of attendees and inquirers at crusades. This measure has increased the trustworthiness and credibility of the BGEA even as society as a whole has seemed to become less trustworthy and less trusting.

In the second half of the twentieth century and into the new millennium, Graham has faced challenges unknown to the historical evangelists cited in this book. With the affluence of America, the speed of communications and travel, and with a globe shrunken by technology, temptations unheard of in the past snapped at the heels of Graham and his team. The safeguards taken were necessary and have proved effective as the team tried to be proactive in heading off trouble before it arrived. Of course, even these efforts could not ward off all criticism and negative reactions to Graham's ministry, nor could all mistakes be avoided. But by and large, the precautions and rigorous standards have paid off with a reputation of honesty and uprightness.

A Unifying Force

One of Graham's strengths is bringing people together in a spirit of unity, whether they are of different nationalities, races, cultures, or churches. The results of this joining of hands are far-reaching and include what many believe is revival in the church.

Reviving the Church

Billy Graham modestly said that he thinks that two or three times during his crusades there may have been "almost a revival." But Elmer Towns, author of *The Ten Greatest Revivals Ever*, written with Douglas Porter, ranks the World War II Revival, from 1935 to 1950, number six on his list, and Graham's Los Angeles and subsequent crusades of the time period figure into it prominently. Towns and Porter define an evangelical revival as, an extraordinary work of God in which Christians repent of their sins as they become intensely aware of His presence and His extraordinary works, and they manifest a positive response to God in renewed obedience to the known will of God, resulting in both a deepening of their individual and corporate experience with God and an increased concern to win others to Christ.[20]

These authors believe that revival, or a special outpouring of God on His people, has various expressions, and that usually revival breaks out in many places around the world at one time. They link the revival springing from the Los Angeles crusade with the ministry of Duncan Campbell in the Lewis Awakening in Scotland during that period.

Graham's belief in instantaneous conversion, as opposed to the idea of planting a seed that will grow and develop gradually over time, brings home the urgency of the moment and the need to make an immediate decision for Christ. But in keeping with New Testament and church history revivals, Graham does not emphasize the "feeling" of spiritual excitement or intensity, but rather the importance of walking daily with God and bearing fruit for Him. The decision for Christ is just the beginning of a lifelong commitment and relationship.

The evangelist has stated, time and again, that the only hope for the world is reconciliation to God through His Son, which brings revival to the human heart. He believes that the personal revival of a sold-out surrender to Christ, as he had as a young man, occurs in individuals when they yield to Him. John Wesley's life-changing personal revival occurred one night in Britain when he heard a reading of Luther's comments on Romans and knew the assurance of his own salvation.

And Wesley and Graham have more in common. Both preached for fifty years and labored tirelessly. Both men prayed hours each day, and prayer is the catalyst for revival. They sought revival from the Lord. As Hosea 10:12 says, "Break up your fallow ground, for it is time to seek the LORD until He comes to rain righteousness on you."

While numbers do not necessarily indicate revival, numbers can sometimes be one indication of an outpouring of God's spirit. When one thinks of the thousands who have responded to God, for example, in Korea and in Hong Kong at Graham crusades, and the subsequent renewal and growth in local churches there, it is reasonable to believe that those campaigns brought a measure of true revival. Graham, who believes that revival is preparation for evangelism, spoke to more than one million people in Seoul in 1973, and 100 million in Hong Kong in 1990.[21] Both areas have been marked by enormous growth and effective ministry by the church since then.

Racial Reconciliation

It seems natural that one aspect of revival would also be reconciliation among racial groups. Graham's middle-of-the-road evangelicalism has broken new ground on diversity and inclusiveness, although he was criticized from both sides for doing either not enough or too much in the area of race relations.

Beginning in the early 1950s, Graham preached that Jesus was neither white nor black, and that He probably had brown skin. But he was criticized for not taking a firmer position against segregation when he preached to segregated audiences in the South. He opposed racial discrimination, but he believed the answer was a relationship with Christ that would transform believers' hearts and bring an end to inequality. He favored a gradual integration rather than forcing it all at once. While confrontation and opposing authority were abhorrent to him, Graham moved incrementally toward bold action on the issue. While he may not have moved fast enough for some, his record speaks for itself:

- In 1953, more than ten years before enactment of the Civil Rights Act of 1964, he refused to conduct a segregated crusade in Chattanooga, Tennessee, and personally removed the ropes dividing seating between Blacks and Whites.[22]
- In 1958, his crusade was the first nonsegregated mass meeting in South Carolina.

- In 1960, his crusade was the first integrated public meeting in what are known today as Zambia and Zimbabwe, formerly Northern and Southern Rhodesia in Africa.

- In 1973, his crusade was the first fully integrated public meeting in South Africa.

Inclusiveness

In addition to racial reconciliation, Graham has worked for a sense of inclusiveness that embraces denominations with doctrinal differences. As a result, Christians have found unity in coming together to preach the simple message of Christ. Groups that had fought or ignored one another have seen that they could accomplish more together in a synergistic effort than they could on their own. By emphasizing what they had in common, Graham has enlarged the army of workers for the harvest.

John Yarbrough explained Graham's contribution to this ecumenical development:

> He brought credibility to the church which helped open the door for the gospel around the world. And he didn't try to get people to leave their doctrine in a drawer or forsake their denominational heritage. He simply asked people to join together to share the simple gospel without compromising doctrinal distinctives.[23]

"His greatest legacy may be his ability, unchallenged in history, to bring all sides together," Allison has said. "He bridges the broad dimensions of evangelicalism and draws everybody together."

But salvos were again launched from both sides against Graham during the 1950s when he began to widen the scope of his ministry to include Roman Catholics and mainline denominations. Jesuit scholar Gustave Weigel accused him of being intellectually light in his messages during the 1957 New York crusade, and John E. Kelly of the National Catholic Welfare Council expressed admiration for Graham and his efforts, but forbade Catholics to listen to Graham or attend crusade services because he taught heretical doctrine.

Fundamentalists were infuriated when Graham preached at liberal seminaries and invited liberal theologians to sit on crusade platforms. They also opposed the Revised Standard Version, first published in 1952, which Graham supported because he thought it made the Bible easier to read and understand.

In 1955 in Scotland, Graham said, "I am neither a fundamentalist nor a modernist. . . . The ecumenical movement has broadened my viewpoint and I recognize now that God has his people in all churches."[24]

In his book *Cooperative Evangelism*, BGEA researcher Robert O. Ferm said, "All great evangelists cooperated with a wide range of churchmen in order to fulfill the Great Commission to preach the Gospel to all humankind."[25] In describing his vision for the newly formed *Christianity Today* magazine in 1955, Graham said the magazine would "plant the evangelical flag in the middle of the road, taking a conservative theological position but a definite liberal approach to social problems. . . . Fundamentalism has failed miserably with the big stick approach; now it is time to take the big love approach."[26]

Graham's efforts also crystallized extreme positions on both the left and right. As he took the middle ground, separatists on the right hardened their positions, and liberals rejected his stance against universalism. While he unified and expanded the evangelical outreach, the results included a clear delineation and polarization on either side. Great evangelists through the ages have also desired a unity that would override denominational differences. St. Francis ministered to people without regard to their faith. Richard Baxter strove for unity despite differences, and of course Paul emphasized that "there is neither Jew nor Greek, there is neither slave nor free man, there is neither male nor female; for you are all one in Christ Jesus" (Galations 3:28).

Humanitarian Efforts

Graham's ever-increasing burden for the world's needy and hurting people has led to large-scale humanitarian efforts. Jesus, too, focused on the message of the gospel and the needs of people. As St. Francis was moved to dedicate his life to serving the poor and needy in a holistic ministry, Graham has been struck by the pain and suffering of humankind as he has traveled the world. He has helped to highlight the church's responsibility in responding to both physical and spiritual needs. He has said,

> As Christians we have a responsibility toward the poor, the oppressed, the downtrodden, and the many innocent people around the world who are caught in wars, natural disasters, and situations beyond their control.[27]

> We cannot, and we must not, isolate ourselves from the world in which we live and the problems it faces. . .The Gospel of Christ has no meaning unless it's applied to our fellow man who hurts and is in need. That's our neighbor, and Jesus said we're to love our neighbor as ourselves.[28]

The BGEA Love in Action committees at work in each crusade city collect and distribute food and clothing to those in need in the community. Its World Emergency Relief Fund gives hundreds of thousands of dollars to disaster victims annually for food, shelter, medical, and other needs. And Samaritan's Purse, headed by Franklin Graham, provides millions of dollars in relief to stricken areas of the world each year as well as building homes and orphanages.

A World Christian

These worldwide ministries and Graham's open-arms policy have earned him a reputation as a world Christian able to transcend nationalities. Jim and Gretchen Riedel work with the Navigators in discipleship ministry, and Jim is head of the crusade telephone ministry at the Billy Graham Center at Wheaton College. They served as missionaries in Australia for four years, and the experience changed their view of Billy Graham. "When Australians talked about him, they did not think of him as an American," Gretchen said. "He was like one of them, not like someone from another culture. He truly is a world Christian."[29]

He is global, and yet he is also American. He has had personal relationships with all the U.S. presidents from Harry Truman to George W. Bush. In his 1999 book *A Charge to Keep,* Bush said,

Actually, the seeds of my [spiritual] decision had been planted the year before, by the Reverend Billy Graham. He visited my family for a summer weekend in Maine. I saw him preach at the small summer church, St. Ann's by the Sea. We all had lunch on the patio overlooking the ocean. One evening my dad asked Billy to answer questions from a big group of family gathered for the weekend. He sat by the fire and talked. And what he said sparked a change in my heart. I don't remember the exact words. It was more the power of his example.

The Lord was so clearly reflected in his gentle and loving demeanor. The next day we walked and talked at Walker's Point, and I knew I was in the presence of a great man. He was like a magnet; I felt drawn to seek something different. He didn't lecture or admonish; he shared warmth and concern. Billy Graham didn't make you feel guilty; he made you feel loved. Over the course of that weekend, Reverend Graham planted a mustard seed in my soul, a seed that grew over the next year. He led me to the path, and I began walking. And it was the beginning of a change in my life.[30]

Graham has also had an impact on other nations. Lon Allison believes that Graham has given the Western world its most appropriate picture of biblical or evangelical Christianity as he has moved during the last twenty years from the role of evangelist to that of world statesman, giving his commentary on world events tremendous weight. His views and advice are sought out in times of disaster like the Oklahoma federal building bombing or the Columbine school shootings. He is endlessly interviewed by media personalities like Larry King. And with his decades of experience in dealing with world leaders, he is respected at the highest levels of government and politics. "He has rightly interpreted the world and has emphasized taking a higher moral ground on issues," Allison said.

A scholar from a leading Chinese university studying at the Wheaton College Graduate School told Allison that Graham's early trips to China paved the way for Nixon's historic visits later. While that was not the purpose of Graham's visits, his presence in China in the early 1960s began to convince Chinese intellectuals that Westerners might be nonthreatening.

He has participated in many historic occasions, including a commemoration of the removal of the Berlin Wall. In 1990, he preached on the steps of the reunified government Reichstag building in the center of Berlin near the Brandenburg Gate linking East and West Berlin. A guest of both West and East German churches, Graham rejoiced that the wall was down, but he said, "There is no hope for the future of Europe, America, or any other part of the world outside of the Gospel of Christ."[31] Thirty years earlier in 1960 before the wall was built, he had preached in the same spot in a tent in front of the Reichstag building during a tour of West Berlin, with heavy opposition from the East German government and press.

Graham has been the first to preach the gospel in many places in the world. The first time he preached in a communist country was in Yugoslavia in 1967, and he has preached in many others since then, including speaking fifty times in four cities in the Soviet Union during his 1984 trip.

This list of world leaders Graham has known seems endless. And he has used his contacts to help resolve delicate international predicaments. For example, the lengthy negotiations conducted by Graham and his team helped obtain the release of the six Soviet Pentecostal dissidents in 1983. And his visits to American troops in Korea and Vietnam brought hope from home. Undoubtedly, his close-up view of war contributed to his desire to work for peace throughout the world.

World Peace

Graham told an audience in a Baptist church in Moscow in 1982 that he had experienced three conversions in his lifetime: "his first acknowledgment of Christ as his Lord and Savior, his determination to work for a racially just society, and more recently, his commitment to work for world peace for the rest of his life."[32] His visit to Auschwitz in 1978 had solidified his desire to strive for peace and reconciliation. In 1982, despite severe criticism and warnings that he would be used and manipulated by the communist government, Graham attended the Soviet Peace Conference in Moscow.

He has always opposed communism and unilateral disarmament,

believing that military defenses are necessary. But since the 1980s, he has come out strongly in favor of eliminating and destroying nuclear weapons, reminding his hearers that permanent peace will only come with Christ's kingdom.

Graham's developing views are yet another example of his willingness to learn, to continue to think through issues, and to grow into new positions. But his commitment to Christ, the Bible, and the simple gospel message has not changed.

Many believe that Graham's crusades and relationship building in iron curtain countries helped pave the way for the collapse of communism. Richard Nixon credited him with helping accomplish the peaceful liberation of Eastern Europe and breakthroughs in the Soviet Union as well.[33]

Engaging Culture

Graham has challenged the late twentieth-century church to enter and confront our culture with the message of Christ. Stephen Olford, founder of the Center for Biblical Preaching in Memphis and noted in chapter two for his strong influence on Graham's early ministry, believes that Graham's preaching has affected culture in ways not always recognized.

He vividly recalls the 1954 Harringay crusade, one of Graham's most significant ever, in his view. "He was opposed by the press, politicians and many religious leaders," he said. "He broke right through all those barriers with his humility, brokenness, and winsomeness. The first cultural impact was God-awareness. God became news. That continues to impact culture today."

Olford believes that Graham has also restored the concept of moral absolutes. After a crusade, many people become refocused on the Bible and right living. He said, "When he preached on the Ten Commandments in New York City in 1957, the whole atmosphere began to change, and people began talking about debts they needed to pay and immorality issues in their lives as never before."

Graham also regained the respectability and acceptability of the evangelist. Olford said, "Long before the televangelist scandals in this country, the evangelist was the most despised man in the Christian religion, looked down upon by the Anglican Church and other religious leaders. But today even Billy's enemies call him 'Mr. Clean.'"[34]

Graham has credited belief in the Bible along with the revivals of the seventeenth, eighteenth, and nineteenth centuries as having a strong influence on Western culture. And he has constantly warned that culture will not improve without personal commitments to God. Many believe that Graham may have at least slowed the flood of secularization in the U.S. since World II. But it is impossible to say how much farther down the slippery slope to being a post-Christian society the country would be now without his influence.

Separate But Not Separated

The term "New Evangelicalism" was coined in the mid-1950s by Pastor Harold John Ockenga of the Park Street Church in Boston and reflected the new direction Graham and others were taking. It connoted a conservative Christianity that differed from old-line fundamentalism in several important ways. New Evangelicals believed the basic doctrines of fundamentalism, but desired a new approach to evangelism. They also favored coming together, rather than staying separate from groups and denominations with minor theological differences.

Looking back, this change in direction can be seen as a move made from strength and confidence in God. No longer would evangelicals be controlled by the fear of being tainted by differences. It's impossible to be salt in the world without entering it. The movement's adherence to God's Word and true doctrine permitted believers to remain in mainline denominations if they so desired, with the benefit of counteracting liberalism's doctrinal differences. It also allowed for an ecumenical approach to fulfilling the Great Commission.

The goal was to proclaim the gospel while thoroughly examining long-held positions by applying rigorous standards of scholarship. *Christianity Today* became a serious Christian magazine in which the hard questions were asked, debated, and answered. Evangelicals would approach, enter, and confront culture with the challenge of the gospel, being careful not to lose the message in an attempt to be culturally relevant.

After a flurry of attacks by fundamentalists Bob Jones and Carl McIntire, Graham resigned from the *Sword of the Lord* magazine board in 1957, signaling his break with fundamentalism's separatist policies. His new approach has included updating crusade music, drama, and testimonies over the years in order to be relevant to modern culture. But the content and urgency of Graham's message have not changed.

A MAN OF THE FUTURE

Graham's ministry has always been characterized by a willingness to do new things in new ways. His concern for the future has resulted in the training of thousands of evangelists to take the gospel into the uttermost parts of the world.

Innovation

The list of "firsts" for Billy Graham proves him to be an innovator. From removing segregation ropes at the Chattanooga crusade to requiring that 10 percent of worldwide evangelism conference attendees be women despite the common evangelical practice of denying women public leadership roles, he was clearly ahead of his time.

Likewise, by focusing on shared beliefs with Roman Catholics and various Protestant denominations, he bridged centuries-old chasms and replaced division with unity.

Graham also innovated in his methods to communicate the gospel. In addition to writing more than twenty books, Graham spearheaded the establishment of *Christianity Today, Decision* magazine, World Wide Pictures to produce evangelistic films, World Wide Publications to produce books, the *Hour of Decision* radio program, the "My Answer" syndicated newspaper column, the National Prayer Breakfast in Washington, D.C., The Cove evangelistic training center outside of Asheville, North Carolina, and hundreds of international schools of evangelism, conferences on evangelism, and major relief agencies.

Graham has touched the whole world. Besides traveling to eighty-four countries, he preached to the entire world by satellite communications in 1995. Elmer Towns, dean of the school of religion at Liberty University and a teacher in the Billy Graham Advanced School of Evangelism, has said, "Billy Graham has done things that have not previously been done. He was one of the first to use secular media to propagate the Gospel through radio, TV and newspaper. He used media not just to announce crusades, but to actually spread the message."[35]

Graham has made full use of newspaper coverage, radio and television interviews, and now the Internet to share the gospel, understanding the ability of publicity to generate public interest. In the 1950s, crusade reporting led to increased media coverage of religion, including the establishment of regular religion sections in *Time* and *Newsweek* and in many daily newspapers. Graham has always been willing to try new means, methods, and technologies to reach people in as many ways as possible. Even the BGEA team, basically intact for fifty years, has been enormously innovative in its approach to structuring and conducting crusades and other evangelistic outreaches and training.

Evangelism Conferences

Perhaps one of the most enduring effects of the ministry will grow from the extensive training sessions conducted by the BGEA over the years. The Berlin Congress in 1966 was attended by 1,200 evangelists, theologians, scholars, and other church leaders from 104 nations. By 1974, 2,400 people were invited to the Lausanne Congress in Switzerland. With an eye on the years ahead, Graham asked that 60 percent of the Lausanne participants be under forty-five years of age with only 10 percent of the invitations going to elder statesmen over age sixty-five.[36] It was at Lausanne that the concept of getting the gospel message to the world's unreached people groups emerged.[37]

Another emphasis at Lausanne was the need for greater cultural sensitivity when presenting the gospel to other cultures. Plenary speakers also expressed a renewed concern for social responsibility and action by evangelicals.

In 1983, Graham's vision since 1954 "to reach the little guys out in the bushes"[38] was realized when 3,900 itinerant evangelists were invited to the nine-day Amsterdam instructional conference, with 70 percent coming from developing nations. Many of the attendees had never been outside of their own countries before. By the time of the 1986 Amsterdam conference, 48,000 applications were received, and 8,200 evangelists were invited, 75 percent from "Two-Thirds World countries" (often called Third World even though they comprise two-thirds of the world's population). Attendees represented 173 countries.

In 1988, 26 "mini-Amsterdams"[39] were held in Latin America, and 6,000 evangelists who worked in both North and South America gathered in Los Angeles. Dozens of these smaller conferences have been held around the world since then.

By the year 2000, technological advances had accomplished what had seemed impossible: continued connection and follow-up with the more than 10,000 widely scattered evangelists who attended Amsterdam 2000. Lon Allison attended the conference and said, "We were surprised to find that 71 percent of the participants have access to email, even though three-fourths of the attendees are from the Two-Thirds World. This astonishing development makes ongoing contact and mentoring possible after the conference."[40]

In 1974 Marie Little spent a year in Lausanne with her husband, Paul, preparing for the first Lausanne conference. On loan to the BGEA from Inter-Varsity Christian Fellowship, Paul Little (now deceased) served as program director of the conference, and Marie recruited interpreters for French, German, and Spanish translations. She appreciated the insight expressed in an October 2000 *Christianity Today* editorial about the influence of the Lausanne and Amsterdam conferences: "Grassroots evangelicals have learned to recognize worldviews and to tailor their witness to the presuppositions of the people they meet."[41] Graham's way of linking the presuppositions of people with their need for God has offered hope in the midst of postmodernism.

Jim and Gretchen Riedel got a firsthand view as they served as stewards at Amsterdam 2000. Conferees came from 210 countries—more than in the United Nations. Plenary sessions were translated into thirty languages available through radio headphones. "A little taste of heaven" is the way Gretchen described the experience of singing with 10,000 people in 240 different languages. "All those people praising God together in many different languages. I picture heaven just like that," she said.

One building the size of three football fields seated the more than 10,000 attendees, who stayed at sixty different hotels and at the Jaarbeurs Conference Center forty-five minutes away at Utrecht, which housed 7,000 people. Stewards literally fed the 5,000—actually 10,732—in three seatings each day of the nine-day conference. There were no drinking fountains, so stewards distributed thousands of bottles of water every day. Stewards provided participants with bag lunches and boxed breakfasts, and served sit-down dinners including linen tablecloths.

The BGEA had determined that financial need would not prevent attendance, consistent with the policy for previous conferences. Two-thirds of the attendees received a subsidy from the BGEA, some up to 95 percent of the cost. While some of the participants were full-time evangelists, many also worked at a second job to pay family bills. Five staffed medical clinics offered services to conferees, and both financial and personal counseling were also available at no charge. Ministry exhibitors set up booths to highlight missions agencies, youth ministries, and schools involved in evangelism. Samaritan's Purse provided shopping tickets to each attendee for ten items, including clothing and other supplies.

The dedication of the BGEA staff was matched by the dedication of those who attended. One man from Africa walked for four days to get to the small plane to take him to the city where he could board a flight to Amsterdam. After the conference, he walked back home for four days as well.

The Amsterdam 2000 committee had spent five years preparing for the conference, gathering current and future evangelists from the entire globe. The conference's goal was that the participants would return home to evangelize every nook and cranny of the entire world, taking the message of God's love to people everywhere. Participants broke into smaller national groups for interactive workshops, seminars, and strategy meetings. Church leaders from the many countries were also invited to network with the evangelists.

"BGEA leadership wanted to make it less North American and more international, so many of the speakers were from Africa, China, Russia, Korea and South America," Jim Reidel said. Billy Graham had planned to attend the conference, but due to illness, he only appeared on the last night of the conference via satellite from the Mayo Clinic in Rochester, Minnesota, with Ruth, who had surprised Billy when she arrived in Rochester on the day of the telecast. With their usual cultural sensitivity, the couple merely touched their foreheads together because they knew that kissing might have offended some people at the conference.

Elmer Towns ranks the Amsterdam conferences as Graham's greatest legacy. The training provided at the conferences includes sermon composition, fundraising, effective use of films and videotapes, giving an invitation, and crusade organization. Brazilian pastor Nilson Fanini summarized the far-reaching effects of the evangelism conferences when he attended the 1986 Amsterdam conference: "There will be just one Billy Graham in church history. You would need a thousand evangelists to do his job. And I believe that is what the Holy Spirit is going to have: a thousand Billy Grahams in Africa, a thousand Billy Grahams in Asia, a thousand Billy Grahams in South America."[42] Surely the multiplication of this evangelistic ministry through efforts like the training conferences will continue to have an impact on the world in the years ahead.

THE INDELIBLE MARK

In reviewing Graham's ministry, can we conclude that it has left its mark by combining the twelve historical principles outlined in this book? A review of the twelve principles depicts a historic evangelism as:

- Empowered by the Holy Spirit
- Preaching a full and true gospel

- Evidencing the centrality of Christ
- Trusting in God's sovereignty
- Addressing human needs with a whole gospel
- Acquainted with suffering
- Based on the Bible
- Demonstrating boldness
- Striving for godliness
- Desiring revival
- Worldwide in focus
- Church-centered

A review makes it clear that when measured by these historical and biblical principles Billy Graham's ministry is clearly authentic.

The Holy Spirit

"Without the Holy Spirit, the work would die," says Graham. "The Holy Spirit in contextualizing the gospel is what makes it come alive to people."[43] Graham sees the Spirit of God at the very core of the entire enterprise of evangelism, and he recognizes his utter dependence upon His work to bring the gospel home to the human heart.

The Full and True Gospel

Few if any would argue that Billy Graham fails to declare the historic, evangelical gospel. As he stated, "I feel the *whole* context (of the *kerygma*) must be in every sermon."[44] Moreover, it has surely become obvious that as an evangelist Billy Graham feels called to his task. Remembering Paul's word that the gospel is the "power of God unto salvation" (Romans 1:16, KJV), Graham has brought many to faith in Jesus Christ. That constitutes a tremendous contribution to the individual and to the very structure of current culture.

The Sovereignty of God

Again, Billy Graham's essential theology concerning the attributes of God puts him in the notable historic line of giants of the faith like Augustine, Calvin, Luther, Whitefield, Spurgeon, and a host of others, not to mention many contemporaries. In a personal interview, Billy said,

> I believe God has prepared the hearts of certain people in every audience I speak to. I never think about the results. I know there are people that God has prepared their hearts, and in that sense they are chosen by God. I have total relaxation, I just know something is going to happen that God has planned.[45]

Further, as he has said, "I have sensed the sovereignty of God in my life, ministry, in all."[46] That's sovereignty; and few would deny that ministry predicated on that biblical historic principle makes a positive contribution to the well-being of many.

Christology

It is clear that Graham holds to an evangelical view of the Person of Jesus Christ. He places Christ first and foremost in all he undertakes in evangelism. "[Jesus Christ] is the centrality of evangelism and all else."[47] That quite well covers the issue, and Jesus made it clear that when He is exalted He will draw people to Himself and transform lives.

Holistic Ministry

Graham has excelled, at least in comparison with many evangelists, in maintaining a balance between social ministry and evangelism. Yet many of his efforts are unknown. For example, few people know how much money and effort Graham put into rescuing Jewish people from the Soviet Union in communist days. Graham succeeded in getting many out of the hands of the Soviets. And such stories can be multiplied over and over again. He does care for the total person regardless of his focus on evangelism. He has inspired the evangelical world to bring social action and evangelism back together again.

Suffering

It goes without saying that Billy Graham has paid a price for his ministry of evangelism. What commends the evangelist so highly in this regard centers in his reaction to the slings and arrows that have been hurled his way. He responds in prayer, not retaliation. In fact, it is rare for him to even attempt to defend himself. He lets his record speak for itself and recognizes that success will not arise from argument but from a humble spirit. Such an approach to suffering for the Savior is certainly biblical and Christlike. It becomes a source of inspiration, help, and encouragement to those who do suffer for Christ.

The Bible

Billy Graham's well-known phrase, "The Bible Says," has become the hallmark of his preaching, writing, witnessing, and all communication. Actually, his time-honored phrase says it all: He truly does believe the Bible, preach the Bible, and live the Bible. His encounter with God and the Scriptures at Forest Homes in 1949 settled that issue once and for all. And who could argue that such an approach is not historic evangelicalism? Again, Graham falls in line and in step with that army of God's faithful ministers. Further, the pure communication of Holy Scriptures always makes its contribution, and that on a broad scale.

Boldness

Fifty-plus years of evangelism, never compromising the message, enduring a thousand temptations to "cut corners," staying strong in every conceivable situation he found himself in—all this speaks to the boldness of the evangelist. Of course, he has not been perfect and at times has been seriously misunderstood. But he has stood, and that constitutes boldness in the finest tradition of the gospel. As a consequence he has touched many lives and strengthened the church to stand in the time of conflict.

Godliness

It is well to recall a statement of Anne Graham Lotz, Billy's daughter. She describes her father as "sweetness and gentleness when under pressure."[48] And she knows him well. When under pressure one's genuine godliness is best revealed. To say that Billy Graham has been under pressure on countless occasions is an understatement. But in it all, his integrity, Christian spirit, and commitment to God's will have been evident. This no doubt accounts for the fact that he is admired around the world and has been so for decades. Moreover, it has surely become clear that Graham has a deep desire not only for personal holiness, but for all those on the team and for everyone who makes a decision in the context of his ministry. And not to sound too repetitive, but that also is historical evangelical evangelism. Moreover, when the church actually practices being the "salt of the earth," society is greatly blessed. Therein Graham has made one of his greatest contributions in demonstrating and challenging God's people to that high level of godly living and service.

Revival

The question is often raised: Do the crusades of Billy Graham actually produce revival? Some affirm they do; others disagree. Perhaps a word from the evangelist will help here. In a personal interview he said, "I think when one person surrenders their life as best they can . . . that is revival in that person. And that happens all the time."[49] Such seems essentially true. But Graham also goes beyond that principle and expands the vision. His brother Melvin stated that Billy prayed for revival in the broad, sweeping sense more than anything else. In that spirit, Billy Graham pointed out that in the early days of crusade work his theme song was "Send a Great Revival." It would appear he has a heart for revival, be it on a personal basis or in the broad, historic sense of a widespread move of the Holy Spirit. And he recognizes it all rests in the sovereignty of God. Along with his fellow historic evangelicals, he longs to see just that take place again. Any contribution toward real revival is a contribution indeed. America—the world—desperately needs to experience a true spiritual awakening.

Worldwide Ministry

The worldwide consciousness that clearly grips Graham's heart began during his first visit to Europe, but the vision of the Great Commission saw a profound deepening the first time he went to Korea and Japan. He said that experience was "the first time I saw the mission field."[50] Since those days, Billy's world consciousness, and commitment, has become legendary. The fact that he has served in over eighty countries, the barriers he has crossed, and the multitudes reached in every conceivable context has become an inspiration and contribution to virtually the whole church of Jesus Christ. Billy Graham is indeed, a *world* evangelist. It must grieve him now that his travel has to be restricted because of health. But the entire evangelical world owes him a debt of gratitude for his historic contribution to the kingdom of God and to the many nations and societies he has touched.

The Church

There is little doubt that Charles Spurgeon, the great pastor-evangelist, would smile on Billy Graham's approach to couching his evangelistic ministry in the setting of the local church. When asked if he needed the church in his evangelistic ministry he strongly replied, "Absolutely." This fact becomes evident in several areas; he always goes to a city only at the invitation of the churches; he always enlists the many workers, such as the counselors, from the churches; he does all he can to get the inquirers into a church. Billy as churchman well realizes that "Christ also loved the church and gave Himself up for her" (Ephesians 5:25). That, too, is biblical, historical evangelism.

THE BIG PICTURE

In conclusion, Billy Graham's ministry has been shown to be in keeping with the twelve principles evident in historical evangelism. It would seem that God has rolled all of these characteristics into the ministry of one man and his team so that the whole world could hear God's message. And with his vision for training future evangelists, the impact of Graham's life's work will grow into the future. Most agree that crusades, which Franklin is updating to the name *festivals*, will continue to be a part of evangelism.

Billy Graham is considered a father figure to all evangelists. He has set the standard of leadership. The church is broader, stronger, and bolder because of him. And light has been shed around the world by his clear presentation of Christ and the lives changed by commitment to Him.

Russ Busby, Graham's photographer since 1956, has said, "I believe the only way to explain Billy's success is simply that God chose Billy Graham to represent Him at this particular time in history. Billy is one in a long line of God's servants, as we can all be in our own way if we listen to and obey Him."[51] Graham has tried to imitate Jesus. No one can do so perfectly, but he has tried to do it well.

When visitors step into the colloquially named "Rapture Room" at the Billy Graham Center at Wheaton College, they are surrounded by blue sky and white clouds, and they hear Handel's *Messiah*. On the wall as they exit the area is a verse from Revelation 21:4: "for the old order of things has passed away" (NIV). History moves ahead, noting certain individuals and movements who leave their marks. Billy Graham has changed the old order of things in terms of how evangelism is done in the beginning of the twenty-first century. He has made sure every available means is used to proclaim Christ to the nations. His ministry lines up with historical, evangelical evangelism, and yet it embraces the future when history will converge in the glorious return of the Christ he has faithfully preached.

Part of Graham's legacy is that he takes nothing for granted in proclaiming Christ to all audiences. In that sense he "preaches to the choir," rather than assuming that everyone in a church, a Christian college, or any other group is fully committed to Christ. Therefore, it would be in keeping with his practice to end this book with an invitation Graham has given again and again:

> Surrender your life to the Lord Jesus Christ. Let him come into your heart and change you. He can give you a new dimension of living. He will help you achieve your goals as you seek his guidance. God knows what is best for us. The Bible says, "Whoever believes in the Son has eternal life"(John 3:16). I pray that you will make this important decision today.[52]

Appendix A

༄

BOOKS & BOOKLETS BY BILLY GRAHAM

America's Hour of Decision. Wheaton, IL: Van Kampen Press, 1951.

Angels: God's Secret Agents. Nashville: Word Books, 1975.

Answers to Life's Problems. Nashville: Word Books, 1988.

Approaching Hoofbeats. Nashville: Word Books, 1983.

The Bible Says. Minneapolis: World Wide Publications, 1988.

A Biblical Standard for Evangelists. Minneapolis: World Wide Publications, 1984.

Billy Graham Answers Your Questions. Minneapolis: World Wide Publications, n.d.

Billy Graham Talks to Teenagers. Grand Rapids, MI: Zondervan, 1958.

Calling Youth to Christ. Grand Rapids, MI: Zondervan, 1947.

The Challenge. New York: Doubleday, 1969.

The Chance of a Life Time. Grand Rapids, MI: Zondervan, 1952.

Death and the Life After. Nashville: Word Books, 1995.

The Holy Spirit. Nashville: Word Books, 1978.

Hope for the Troubled Heart. Nashville: Word Books, 1991.

How to Be Born Again. Nashville: Word Books, 1977.

The Jesus Generation. Grand Rapids, MI: Zondervan, 1971.

Just As I Am: The Autobiography of Billy Graham. San Francisco: HarperCollins, 1997.

My Answer. New York: Doubleday, 1960.

Peace with God. Nashville: Word Books, 1963.

Revival in Our Time. Wheaton, IL: Van Kampen Press, 1950.

The Secret of Happiness. Nashville: Word Books, 1955.

The Seven Deadly Sins. Grand Rapids, MI: Zondervan, 1955.

Storm Warning. Nashville: Word Books, 1992.

Till Armageddon. Nashville: Word Books, 1981.

Unto the Hills. Nashville: Word Books, 1986.

World Aflame. New York: Doubleday, 1965.

Appendix B

⚜

The Lausanne Covenant[1]

INTRODUCTION

We members of the Church of Jesus Christ, from more than 150 nations, participants in the International Congress on World Evangelization at Lausanne, praise God for His great salvation and rejoice in the fellowship He has given us with Himself and with each other. We are deeply stirred by what God is doing in our day, moved to penitence by our failures and challenged by the unfinished task of evangelization. We believe the gospel is God's good news for the whole world, and we are determined by His grace to obey Christ's commission to proclaim it to all mankind and to make disciples of every nation. We desire, therefore, to affirm our faith and our resolve, and to make public our covenant.

1. The Purpose of God

We affirm our belief in the one eternal God, Creator and Lord of the world, Father, Son and Holy Spirit, who governs all things according to the purpose of His will. He has been calling out from the world a people for Himself, and sending His people back into the world to be His servants and His witnesses, for the extension of His Kingdom, the building up of Christ's body, and the glory of His name. We confess with shame that we have often denied our calling and failed in our mission, by becoming conformed to the world or by withdrawing from it. Yet we rejoice that even when borne by earthen vessels the gospel is still a precious treasure. To the task of making that treasure known in the power of the Holy Spirit we desire to dedicate ourselves anew (Isa. 40:28; Matt. 28:19; Eph. 1:11; Acts 15:14; John 17:6,18; Eph. 4:12; 1 Cor. 5:10; Rom. 12:2; 2 Cor. 4:7).

2. The Authority and Power of the Bible

We affirm the divine inspiration, truthfulness and authority of both the Old and New Testament Scriptures in their entirety as the only written word of God, without error in all that it affirms, and the only infallible rule of faith and practice. We also affirm the power of God's word to accomplish His purpose of salvation. The message of the Bible is addressed to all mankind. For God's revelation in Christ and in Scriptures is unchangeable. Through it the Holy Spirit still speaks today. He illumines the minds of God's people in every culture to perceive its truth freshly through their own eyes and thus discloses to the whole church ever more of the many-colored wisdom of God (2 Tim. 3:16; 2 Pet. 1:21; John 10:35; Isa. 55:11; 1 Cor. 1:21; Rom. 1:16; Matt. 5:17-18; Jude 3; Eph. 1:17-18; 3:10,18).

3. The Uniqueness and Universality of Christ

We *affirm* that there is only one Saviour and only one gospel, although there is a wide diversity of evangelistic approaches. We recognize that all men have some knowledge of God through His general revelation in nature. But we deny that this can save, for men suppress the truth by their unrighteousness. We also reject as derogatory to Christ and the gospel every kind of syncretism and dialogue which implies that Christ speaks equally through all religions and ideologies.

Jesus Christ, being Himself the only God-man, who gave Himself as the only ransom for sinners, is the only mediator between God and man. There is no other name by which we must be saved. All men are perishing because of sin, but God loves all men not wishing that any should perish but that all should repent. Yet those who reject Christ repudiate the joy of salvation and condemn themselves to eternal separation from God. To proclaim Jesus as "the Saviour of the world" is not to affirm that all men are either automatically or ultimately saved, still less to affirm that all religions offer salvation in Christ. Rather it is to proclaim God's love for a world of sinners and to invite all men to respond to Him as Saviour and Lord in the wholehearted personal commitment of repentance and that Jesus Christ has been exalted above every other name; we long for the day when every knee shall bow to Him and every tongue shall confess Him Lord (Gal. 1:6-9; Rom. 1:18-32; 1 Tim. 2:5-6; Acts 4:12; John 3:16-19; 2 Pet. 3:9; 2 Thess. 1:7-9; John 4:42; Matt. 11:28; Eph. 1:20-21; Phil. 2:9-11).

4. The Nature of Evangelism

To evangelize is to spread the good news that Jesus Christ died for our sins and was raised from the dead according to the Scriptures, and that as the reigning Lord He now offers the forgiveness of sins and the liberating gift of the Spirit to all who repent and believe. Our Christian presence in the world is indispensable to evangelism, and so is that kind of dialogue whose purpose is to listen sensitively in order to understand. But evangelism itself is the proclamation of the historical, biblical Christ as Saviour and Lord, with a view to persuading people to come to Him personally and so be reconciled to God. In issuing the gospel invitation we have no liberty to conceal the cost of discipleship. Jesus still calls all who would follow Him to deny themselves, take up their cross, and identify themselves with this new community. The results of evangelism include obedience to Christ, incorporation into His church and responsible service in the world (1 Cor. 15:3-4; Acts 2:32-39; John 20:21; 1 Cor. 1:23; 2 Cor. 4:5; 5:11,20; Luke 14:25-33; Mark 8:34; Acts 2:40,47; Mark 10:43-45).

5. Christian Social Responsibility

We affirm that God is both the Creator and the Judge of all men. We therefore should share His concern for justice and reconciliation through human society and for the liberation of men from every kind of oppression. Because mankind is made in the image of God, every person, regardless of race, religion, color, culture, class, sex or age, has an intrinsic dignity because of which he should be respected and served, not exploited. Here too we express penitence both for our neglect and for having sometimes regarded evangelism and social concern as mutually exclusive. Although reconciliation with man is not reconciliation with God, nor is social action evangelism, nor is political liberation salvation, nevertheless we affirm that evangelism and socio-political involvement are both part of our Christian duty. For both are necessary expressions of our doctrines of God and man, our love of our neighbour and our obedience to Jesus Christ. The message of salvation implies also a message of judgment upon every form of alienation, oppression and discrimination, and we should not be afraid to denounce evil and injustice wherever they exist. When people receive Christ they are born again into His kingdom and must seek not only to exhibit but also to spread its righteousness in the midst of an unrighteous world. The salvation we claim should be transforming us in the totality of our personal and social responsibilities. Faith without works is dead (Acts 17:26,31; Gen. 18:25; Isa. 1:17; Ps. 45:7; Gen. 1:26-27; Jas. 3:9; Lev. 19:18; Luke 6:27,35; Jas. 2:14-26; John 3:3,5; Matt. 5:20; 6:33; 2 Cor. 3:18; Jas. 2:20).

6. The Church and Evangelism

We affirm that Christ sends His redeemed people into the world as the Father sent Him, and that this calls for a similar deep and costly penetration of the world. We need to break out of our ecclesiastical ghettos and permeate non-Christian society. In the church's mission of sacrificial service, evangelism is primary. World evangelization requires the whole church to take the whole gospel to the whole world. The church is at the very center of God's cosmic purpose and is His appointed means of spreading the gospel. But a church which preaches the cross must itself be marked by the cross. It becomes a stumbling block to evangelism when it betrays the gospel or lacks a living faith in God, a genuine love for people, or scrupulous honesty in all things including promotion and finance. The church is the community of God's people rather than an institution, and must not be identified with any particular culture, social and political system, or human ideology (John 17:18; 20:21; Matt. 28:19-20; Acts 1:8; 20:27; Eph. 1:9-10; 3:9-11; Gal. 6:14,17; 2 Cor. 6:3-4; 2 Tim. 2:19-21; Phil. 1:27).

7. Cooperation in Evangelism

We affirm that the church's visible unity in truth is God's purpose. Evangelism also summons us to unity, because our oneness strengthens our witness, just as our disunity undermines our gospel of reconciliation. We recognize, however, that organizational unity may take many forms and does not necessarily forward evangelism. Yet we who share the same biblical faith should be closely united in fellowship, work and witness. We confess that our testimony has sometimes been marred by sinful individualism and needless duplication. We pledge ourselves to seek a deeper unity in truth, worship, holiness and mission. We urge the development of regional and functional cooperation for the furtherance of the church's mission, for strategic planning, for mutual encouragement, and for the sharing of resources and experience (John 17:21,23: Eph. 4:3-4; John 13:35; Phil. 1:27; John 17:11-23).

8. Churches in Evangelistic Partnership

We rejoice that a new missionary era has dawned. The dominant role of Western missions is fast disappearing. God is raising up from the younger churches a great new resource for world evangelization, and is thus demonstrating that the responsibility to evangelize belongs to the whole body of Christ. All churches should therefore be asking God and themselves what they should be doing both to reach their own area and to send missionaries to other parts of the world. A re-evaluation of our missionary responsibility and role should be continuous. Thus a growing partnership of churches will develop, and the universal character of Christ's church will be more clearly exhibited. We also thank God for agencies which labour in Bible translation, theological education, missions, church renewal and other specialist fields. They too should engage in constant self-examination to evaluate their effectiveness as part of the church's mission (Rom. 1:8; Phil. 1:5; 4:15; Acts 13:1-3; 1 Thess. 1:6-8).

9. The Urgency of the Evangelistic Task

More than 2,700 million people, which is more than two-thirds of mankind, have yet to be evangelized. We are ashamed that so many have been neglected; it is a standing rebuke to us and to the whole church. There is now, however, in many parts of the world an unprecedented receptivity to the Lord Jesus Christ. We are convinced that this is the time for churches and parachurch agencies to pray earnestly for the salvation of the unreached and to launch new efforts to achieve world evangelization. A reduction of foreign missionaries and money in an evangelized country may sometimes be necessary to facilitate the national church's growth in self-reliance and to release resources for unevangelized areas. Missionaries should flow ever more freely from and to all six continents in a spirit of humble service. The goal should be, by all available means and at the earliest possible time, that every person will have the opportunity to hear, understand, and receive the good news. We cannot hope to attain this goal without sacrifice. All of us are shocked by the poverty of millions and disturbed by the injustices which cause it. Those of us who live in affluent circumstances accept our duty to develop a simple life-style in order to contribute more generously to both relief and evangelism (John 9:4; Matt. 9:35-38; Rom. 9:1-3; 1 Cor. 9:19-23; Mark 16:15; Isa. 58:6-7; Jas. 1:27; 2:1-9; Matt. 25:31-46; Acts 2:44-45; 4:34-35).

10. Evangelism and Culture

The development of strategies for world evangelization call for imaginative pioneering methods. Under God, the result will be the rise of churches deeply rooted in Christ and closely related to their culture. Culture must always be tested and judged by Scripture. Because man is God's creature, some of his culture is rich in beauty and goodness. Because he has fallen, all of it is tainted with sin and some of it is demonic. The gospel does not presuppose the superiority of any culture to another, but evaluates all cultures according to its own criteria of truth and righteousness and insists on moral absolutes in every culture. Missions have all too frequently exported with the gospel an alien culture, and churches have sometimes been in bondage to culture rather than to the Scripture. Christ's evangelists must humbly seek to empty themselves of all but their personal authenticity in order to become the servants of others, and churches must seek to transform and enrich culture, all for the glory of God (Mark 7:8-9,13; Gen. 4:21-22; 1 Cor. 9:19-23; Phil. 2:5-7; 2 Cor. 4:5).

11. Education and Leadership

We confess that we have sometimes pursued church growth at the expense of church depth, and divorced evangelism from Christian nurture. We also acknowledge that some of our missions have been too slow to equip and encourage national leaders to assume their rightful responsibilities. Yet we are committed to indigenous principles, and long that every church will have national leaders who manifest a Christian style of leadership in terms not of domination but of service. We recognize that there is a great need to improve theological education, especially for church leaders. In every nation and culture, there should be an effective training programme for pastors and laymen in doctrine, discipleship, evangelism, nurture and service. Such training programmes should not rely on any stereotyped methodology but should be developed by creative local initiatives according to biblical standards (Col. 1:27-28; Acts 14:23; Titus 1:5,9; Mark 10:42-45; Eph. 4:11-12).

12. Spiritual Conflict

We believe that we are engaged in constant spiritual warfare with the principalities and powers of evil, who are seeking to overthrow the church and frustrate its task of world evangelization. We know our need to equip ourselves with God's armor and to fight this battle with the spiritual weapons of truth and prayer. For we detect the activity of our enemy, not only in false ideologies outside the church, but also inside it in false gospels which twist Scripture and put man in the place of God. We need both watchfulness and discernment to safeguard the biblical gospel. We acknowledge that we ourselves are not immune to worldliness of thought and action, that is, to a surrender to secularism. For example, although careful studies of church growth, both numerical and spiritual, are right and valuable, we have sometimes neglected them. At other times, desirous to ensure a response to the gospel, we have compromised our message, manipulated our hearts through pressure techniques, and become unduly preoccupied with statistics or even dishonest in our use of them. All this is worldly. The church must be in the world; the world must not be in the church (Eph. 6:12; 2 Cor. 4:3-4; Eph. 6:11; 13:18; 2 Cor. 19:35; 1 John 2:18-24; 4:18; Gal. 1:6-9; 2 Cor. 2:17; 4:22; John 17:15).

13. Freedom and Persecution

It is the God-appointed duty of every government to secure conditions of peace, justice and liberty in which the church may obey God, serve the Lord Christ, and preach the gospel without interference. We therefore pray for the leaders of the nations and call upon them to guarantee freedom of thought and conscience, and freedom of practice and propagate religion in accordance with the will of God and set forth in the Universal Declaration of Human Rights. We also express our deep concern for all who have been unjustly imprisoned, and especially for our brethren who are suffering for their testimony of the Lord Jesus. We promise to pray and work for their freedom. At the same time we refuse to be intimidated by their fate. God helping us, we too will seek to stand against injustice and to remain faithful to the gospel, whatever the cost. We do not forget the warnings of Jesus that persecution is inevitable (1 Tim. 1:1-4; Acts 4:19; 5:29; Cal. 3:24; Heb. 13:1-3; Luke 4:18; Gal. 5:11; 6:12; Matt. 5:10-12; John 15:18-21).

14. The Power of the Holy Spirit

We believe in the power of the Holy Spirit. The Father sent His Spirit to bear witness to His Son; without His witness ours is futile. Conviction of sin, faith in Christ, new birth and Christian growth are all His work. Further, the Holy Spirit is a missionary spirit; thus evangelism should arise spontaneously from a Spirit-filled church. A church that is not a missionary church is contradicting itself and quenching the Spirit. Worldwide evangelization will become a realistic possibility only when the Spirit renews the church in truth and wisdom, faith, holiness, love and power. We therefore call upon all Christians to pray for such a visitation of the sovereign Spirit of God that all His fruit may appear in all His people and that all His gifts may enrich the body of Christ. Only then will the whole church become a fit instrument in His hands, that the whole earth may hear His voice (1 Cor. 2:4; John 15:26-27; 16:8-11; 1 Cor. 12:1; John 8:6-8; 2 Cor. 3:18; John 7:37-39; 1 Thess. 5:19; Acts 1:8; Pss. 85:4-7; 67:1-3; Gal. 5:22-23; 1 Cor. 12:4-31; Rom. 12:3-8).

15. The Return of Christ

We believe that Jesus Christ will return personally and visibly in power and glory, to consummate His salvation and His judgment. This promise of His coming is a further spur to our evangelism, for we remember His words that the gospel must first be preached to all nations. We believe that the interim period between Christ's ascension and return is to be filled with the mission of the people of God, who have no liberty to stop before the End. We also remember His warning that false Christs and false prophets will arise as precursors of the final Antichrist. We therefore reject as a proud, self-confident dream the notion that man can ever build a utopia on earth. Our Christian confidence is that God will perfect His kingdom, and we look forward with eager anticipation to that day, and to the new heaven and earth in which righteousness will dwell, and God will reign forever. Meanwhile, we rededicate ourselves to the service of Christ and of men in joyful submission to His authority over the whole of our lives

(Mark 14:62; Heb. 9:28; Mark 13:10; Acts 1:8-11; Matt. 28:20; Mark 13:21-23; John 2:18; 4:1-3; Luke 12:32; Rev. 21:1-5; 2 Pet. 3:13; Matt. 28:18).

Conclusion

Therefore, in the light of this our faith and our resolve, we enter into a solemn covenant with God and with each other, to pray, to plan and to work together for the evangelization of the whole world. We call upon others to join us. May God help us by His grace and for His glory to be faithful to this our covenant! Amen, Alleluia!

Appendix C

❧

The Manila Manifesto [1]

Calling the whole church to take the whole gospel to the whole world.

In July of 1989, Lausanne II met in Manila, the Philippines. The "Manila Manifesto" was written and adopted by the conference. It shows the development of thought and emphasis relative to world evangelization since the formulation of the Lausanne Covenant of 1974. It is as follows:

INTRODUCTION

In July 1974 the International Congress on World Evangelization was held in Lausanne, Switzerland, and issued the Lausanne Covenant. Now in July 1989, over 3,000 of us from about 170 countries have met in Manila for the same purpose, and have issued the Manila Manifesto. We are grateful for the welcome we have received from our Filipino brothers and sisters.

During the 15 years which have elapsed between the two congresses some smaller consultations have been held on topics like Gospel and

Culture, Evangelism and Social Responsibility, Simple Life-style, the Holy Spirit, and Conversion. These meetings and their reports have helped to develop the thinking of the Lausanne movement.

A "manifesto" is defined as a public declaration of convictions, intentions and motives. The Manila Manifesto takes up the two congress themes, "Proclaim Christ until He comes" and "Calling the Whole Church to take the Whole Gospel to the Whole World." Its first part is a series of 21 succinct affirmations. Its second part elaborates these in 12 sections, which are commended to churches, alongside the Lausanne Covenant, for study and action.

Twenty-One Affirmations

1. We affirm our continuing commitment to the Lausanne Covenant as the basis of our cooperation in the Lausanne movement.

2. We affirm that in the Scriptures of the Old and New Testaments God has given us an authoritative disclosure of his character and will, his redemptive acts and their meaning, and his mandate for mission.

3. We affirm that the biblical gospel is God's enduring message to our world, and we determine to defend, proclaim and embody it.

4. We affirm that human beings, though created in the image of God, are sinful and guilty, and lost without Christ, and that this truth is a necessary preliminary to the gospel.

5. We affirm that the Jesus of history and the Christ of glory are the same person, and that this Jesus Christ is absolutely unique, for He alone is God incarnate, our sin-bearer, the conqueror of death and the coming judge.

6. We affirm that on the cross Jesus Christ took our place, bore our sins and died our death; and that for this reason alone God freely forgives those who are brought to repentance and faith.

7. We affirm that other religions and ideologies are not alternative paths to God, and that human spirituality, if unredeemed by Christ, leads not to God but to judgment, for Christ is the only way.

8. We affirm that we must demonstrate God's love visibly by caring for those who are deprived of justice, dignity, food and shelter.

9. We affirm that the proclamation of God's kingdom of justice and peace demands the denunciation of all injustice and oppression, both personal and structural; we will not shrink from this prophetic witness.

10. We affirm that the Holy Spirit's witness to Christ is indispensable to evangelism, and that without his supernatural work neither new birth nor new life is possible.

11. We affirm that spiritual warfare demands spiritual weapons, and that we must both preach the word in the power of the Spirit, and pray constantly that we may enter into Christ's victory over the principalities and powers of evil.

12. We affirm that God has committed to the whole church and every member of it the task of making Christ known throughout the world; we long to see all lay and ordained persons mobilized and trained for this task.

13. We affirm that we who claim to be members of the Body of Christ must transcend within our fellowship the barriers of race, gender and class.

14. We affirm that the gifts of the Spirit are distributed to all God's people, women and men, and that their partnership in evangelization must be welcomed for the common good.

15. We affirm that we who proclaim the gospel must exemplify it in a life of holiness and love; otherwise our testimony loses its credibility.

16. We affirm that every Christian congregation must turn itself outward to its local community in evangelistic witness and compassionate service.

17. We affirm the urgent need for churches, mission agencies and other Christian organizations to cooperate in evangelism and social action, repudiating competition and avoiding duplication.

18. We affirm our duty to study the society in which we live, in order to understand its structures, values and needs, and so develop an appropriate strategy of mission.

19. We affirm that world evangelization is urgent and that the reaching of unreached peoples is possible. So we resolve during the last decade of the twentieth century to give ourselves to these tasks with fresh determination.

20. We affirm our solidarity with those who suffer for the gospel, and will seek to prepare ourselves for the same possibility. We will also work for religious and political freedom everywhere.

21. We affirm that God is calling the whole church to take the whole gospel to the whole world. So we determine to proclaim it faithfully, urgently and sacrificially, until he comes.

A. The Whole Gospel

The gospel is the good news of God's salvation from the powers of evil, the establishment of His eternal kingdom and His final victory over everything which defies His purpose. In His love God purposed to do this before the world began and effected His liberating plan over sin, death and judgment through the death of our Lord Jesus Christ. It is Christ who makes us free, and unites us in his redeemed fellowship.

1. Our Human Predicament

We are committed to preaching the whole gospel, that is, the biblical gospel in its fulness. In order to do so, we have to understand why human beings need it.

Men and women have an intrinsic dignity and worth, because they were created in God's likeness to know, love and serve Him. But now through sin every part of their humanness has been distorted. Human beings have become self-centered, self-serving rebels, who do not love God or their neighbor as they should. In consequence, they are alienated both from their Creator and from the rest of His creation, which is the basic cause of the pain, disorientation and loneliness which so many people suffer today. Sin also frequently erupts in antisocial behavior, in violent exploitation of others, and in a depletion of the earth's resources of which God has made men and women his stewards. Humanity is guilty, without excuse, and on the broad road which leads to destruction.

Although God's image in human beings has been corrupted, they are still capable of loving relationships, noble deeds and beautiful art. Yet even the finest human achievement is fatally flawed and cannot possibly fit anybody to enter God's presence. Men and women are also spiritual beings, but spiritual practices and self-help techniques can at the most alleviate felt needs; they cannot address the solemn realities of sin, guilt and judgment. Neither human religion, nor human righteousness, nor socio-political programs can save people. Self-salvation of every kind is impossible. Left to themselves, human beings are lost forever.

So we repudiate false gospels which deny human sin, divine judgment, the deity and incarnation of Jesus Christ, and the necessity of the cross and the resurrection. We also reject half-gospels, which minimize sin and confuse God's grace with human self-effort. We confess that we ourselves have sometimes trivialized the gospel. But we determine in our evangelism to remember God's radical diagnosis and his equally radical remedy.

2. Good News for Today

We rejoice that the living God did not abandon us to our lostness and despair. In His love He came after us in Jesus Christ to rescue and remake us. So the good news focuses on the historic person of Jesus, who came proclaiming the kingdom of God and living a life of humble service, who died for us, becoming sin and a curse in our place, and whom God vindicated by raising Him from the dead. To those who repent and believe in Christ God grants a share in the new creation. He gives us new life, which includes the forgiveness of our sins and the indwelling, transforming power of his Spirit. He welcomes us into His new community, which consists of people of all races, nations and cultures. And He promises that one day we will enter His new world, in which evil will be abolished, nature will be redeemed, and God will reign for ever.

This good news must be boldly proclaimed, wherever possible, in church and public hall, on radio and television, and in the open air, because it is God's power for salvation and we are under obligation to make it known. In our preaching we must faithfully declare the truth which God has revealed in the Bible and struggle to relate it to our own context.

We also affirm that apologetics, namely "the defense and confirmation of the gospel" (Phil. 1:7), is integral to the biblical understanding of mission and essential for effective witness in the modern world. Paul "reasoned" with people out of the Scriptures, with a view to "persuading" them of the truth of the gospel. So must we. In fact, all Christians should be ready to give a reason for the hope that is in them (1 Pet. 3:15).

We have again been confronted with Luke's emphasis that the gospel is good news for the poor (Luke 4:18, 6:20, 7:22) and have asked ourselves what this means to the majority of the world's population who are destitute, suffering or oppressed. We have been reminded that the law, the prophets and the wisdom books, and the teaching and ministry of Jesus, all stress God's concern for the materially poor and our consequent duty to defend and care for them. Scripture also refers to the spiritually poor who look to God alone for mercy. The gospel comes as good news to both. The spiritually poor, who, whatever their economic circumstances, humble themselves before God, receive by faith the free gift of salvation. There is no other way for anybody to enter the Kingdom of God. The materially poor and powerless find in addition a new dignity as God's children, and the love of brothers and sisters who will struggle with them for their liberation from everything which demeans or oppresses them.

We repent of any neglect of God's truth in Scripture and determine both to proclaim and to defend it. We also repent where we have been indifferent to the plight of the poor, and where we have shown preference for the rich, and we determine to follow Jesus in preaching good news to all people by both word and deed.

3. The Uniqueness of Jesus Christ

We are called to proclaim Christ in an increasingly pluralistic world. There is a resurgence of old faiths and a rise of new ones. In the first century too there were "many 'gods' and many 'lords'" (1 Cor. 8:5). Yet the apostles boldly affirmed the uniqueness, indispensability and centrality of Christ. We must do the same.

Because men and women are made in God's image and see in the creation traces of its Creator, the religions which have arisen do sometimes contain elements of truth and beauty. They are not, however, alternative gospels. Because human beings are sinful, and because "the whole world is under the control of the evil one" (1 Jn. 5:19), even religious people are in need of Christ's redemption. We, therefore, have no warrant for saying that salvation can be found outside Christ or apart from an explicit acceptance of his work through faith.

It is sometimes held that in virtue of God's covenant with Abraham, Jewish people do not need to acknowledge Jesus as their Messiah. We affirm that they need him as much as anyone else, that it would be a form of anti-Semitism, as well as being disloyal to Christ, to depart from the New Testament pattern of taking the gospel to "the Jew first." We therefore reject the thesis that Jews have their own covenant which renders faith in Jesus unnecessary.

What unites us is our common convictions about Jesus Christ. We confess him as the eternal Son of God who became fully human while remaining fully divine, who was our substitute on the cross, bearing our sins and dying our death, exchanging His righteousness for our unrighteousness, who rose victorious in a transformed body, and who will return in glory to judge the world. He alone is the incarnate Son, the Saviour, the Lord and the Judge, and He alone, with the Father and the Spirit, is worthy of the worship, faith and obedience of all people. There is only one gospel because there is only one Christ, who because of his death and resurrection is himself the only way of salvation. We therefore reject both the relativism which regards all religions and spiritualities as equally valid approaches to God, and the syncretism which tries to mix faith in Christ with other faiths.

Moreover, since God has exalted Jesus to the highest place, in order that everybody should acknowledge him, this also is our desire. Compelled by Christ's love, we must obey Christ's Great Commission and love his lost sheep, but we are especially motivated by "jealousy" for his holy name, and we long to see him receive the honor and glory which are due to him.

In the past we have sometimes been guilty of adopting towards adherents of other faiths attitudes of ignorance, arrogance, disrespect and even hostility. We repent of this. We nevertheless are determined to bear a positive and uncompromising witness to the uniqueness of our Lord, in his life, death and resurrection, in all aspects of our evangelistic work including inter-faith dialogue.

4. The Gospel and Social Responsibility

The authentic gospel must become visible in the transformed lives of men and women. As we proclaim the love of God we must be involved in loving service, and as we preach the Kingdom of God we must be committed to its demands of justice and peace.

Evangelism is primary because our chief concern is with the gospel, that all people may have the opportunity to accept Jesus Christ as Lord and Savior. Yet Jesus not only proclaimed the Kingdom of God, he also demonstrated its arrival by works of mercy and power. We are called today to a similar integration of words and deeds. In a spirit of humility we are to preach and teach, minister to the sick, feed the hungry, care for prisoners, help the disadvantaged and handicapped, and deliver the oppressed. While we acknowledge the diversity of spiritual gifts, callings and contexts, we also affirm that good news and good works are inseparable.

The proclamation of God's kingdom necessarily demands the prophetic denunciation of all that is incompatible with it. Among the evils we deplore are destructive violence, including institutionalized violence, political corruption, all forms of exploitation of people and of the earth, the undermining of the family, abortion on demand, the drug traffic, and the abuse of human rights. In our concern for the poor, we are distressed by the burden of debt in the twothirds world. We are also outraged by the inhuman conditions in which millions live, who bear God's image as we do.

Our continuing commitment to social action is not a confusion of the Kingdom of God with a Christianized society. It is, rather, a recognition that the biblical gospel has inescapable social implications. True mission should always be incarnational. It necessitates entering humbly into other people's worlds, identifying with their social reality, their sorrow and suffering, and their struggles for justice against oppressive powers. This cannot be done without personal sacrifices.

We repent that the narrowness of our concerns and vision has often kept us from proclaiming the lordship of Jesus Christ over all of life, private and public, local and global. We determine to obey his command to seek 'first the kingdom of God, and his righteousness' (Mt. 6:33).

B. The Whole Church

The whole gospel has to be proclaimed by the whole church. All the people of God are called to share in the evangelistic task. Yet without the Holy Spirit of God all their endeavors will be fruitless.

5. God the Evangelist

The Scriptures declare that God himself is the chief evangelist. For the Spirit of God is the Spirit of truth, love, holiness and power, and evangelism is impossible without him. It is he who anoints the messenger, confirms the word, prepares the hearer, convicts the sinful, enlightens the blind, gives life to the dead, enables us to repent and believe, unites us to the Body of Christ, assures us that we are God's children, leads us into Christlike character and service, and sends us out in our turn to be Christ's witnesses. In all this the Holy Spirit's main preoccupation is to glorify Jesus Christ by showing him to us and forming him in us.

All evangelism involves spiritual warfare with the principalities and powers of evil, in which only spiritual weapons can prevail, especially the Word and the Spirit, with prayer. We therefore call on all Christian people to be diligent in their prayers both for the renewal of the church and for the evangelization of the world.

Every true conversion involves a power encounter, in which the superior authority of Jesus Christ is demonstrated. There is no greater miracle than this, in which the believer is set free from the bondage of Satan and sin, fear and futility, darkness and death.

Although the miracles of Jesus were special, being signs of his Messiahship and anticipations of his perfect kingdom when all nature will be subject to him, we have no liberty to place limits on the power of the living Creator today. We reject both the skepticism which denies miracles and the presumption which demands them, both the timidity which shrinks from the fullness of the Spirit and the triumphalism which shrinks from the weakness in which Christ's power is made perfect.

We repent of all self-confident attempts either to evangelize in our own strength or to dictate to the Holy Spirit. We determine in future not to "grieve" or "quench" the Spirit, but rather to spread the good news "with power, with the Holy Spirit and with deep conviction" (1 Thess. 1:5).

6. The Human Witnesses

God the evangelist gives his people the privilege of being his "fellow workers" (2 Cor. 6:1). For, although we cannot witness without him, he normally chooses to witness through us. He calls only some to be evangelists, missionaries or pastors, but he calls his whole church and every member of it to be his witnesses.

The privileged task of pastors and teachers is to lead God's people (*laos*) into maturity (Col. 1:28) and to equip them for ministry (Eph. 4:11-12). Pastors are not to monopolize ministries, but rather to multiply them, by encouraging others to use their gifts and by training disciples to make disciples. The domination of the laity by the clergy has been a great evil in the history of the church. It robs both laity and clergy of their God-intended roles, causes clergy breakdowns, weakens the church and hinders the spread of the gospel. More than that, it is fundamentally unbiblical. We therefore, who have for centuries insisted on "the priesthood of all believers" now also insist on the ministry of all believers.

We gratefully recognize that children and young people enrich the church's worship and outreach by their enthusiasm and faith. We need to train them in discipleship and evangelism, so that they may reach their own generation for Christ.

God created men and women as equal bearers of his image (Gen. 1:26-27), accepts them equally in Christ (Gal. 3:28) and poured out His Spirit on all flesh, sons and daughters alike (Acts 2:17-18). In addition, because the Holy Spirit distributes his gifts to women as well as to men, they must be given opportunities to exercise their gifts. We celebrate their distinguished record in the history of missions and are convinced that God calls women to similar roles today. Even though we are not fully agreed what forms their leadership should take, we do agree about the partnership in world evangelization which God intends men and women to enjoy. Suitable training must therefore be made available to both.

Lay witness takes place, by women and men, not only through the local church (see Section 8), but through friendships, in the home and at work. Even those who are homeless or unemployed share in the calling to be witnesses.

Our first responsibility is to witness to those who are already our friends, relatives, neighbors, and colleagues. Home evangelism is also natural, both for married and for single people. Not only should a Christian home commend God's standards of marriage, sex and family, and provide a haven of love and peace to people who are hurting, but neighbors who would not enter a church usually feel comfortable in a home, even when the gospel is discussed.

Another context for lay witness is the workplace, for it is here that most Christians spend half their waking hours, and work is a divine calling. Christians can commend Christ by word of mouth, by their consistent industry, honesty and thoughtfulness, by their concern for justice in the workplace, and especially if others can see from the quality of their daily work that it is done to the glory of God.

We repent of our share in discouraging the ministry of the laity, especially of women and young people. We determine in future to encourage all Christ's followers to take their place, rightfully and naturally, as his witnesses. For true evangelism comes from the overflow of a heart in love with Christ. That is why it belongs to all his people without exception.

7. The Integrity of the Witnesses

Nothing commends the gospel more eloquently than a transformed life, and nothing brings it into disrepute so much as personal inconsistency. We are charged to behave in a manner that is worthy of the gospel of Christ, and even to 'adorn' it, enhancing its beauty by holy lives. For the watching world rightly seeks evidence to substantiate the claims which Christ's disciples make for him. A strong evidence is our integrity.

Our proclamation that Christ died to bring us to God appeals to people who are spiritually thirsty, but they will not believe us if we give no evidence of knowing the living God ourselves, or if our public worship lacks reality and relevance.

Our message that Christ reconciles alienated people to each other rings true only if we are seen to love and forgive one another, to serve others in humility, and to reach out beyond our own community in compassionate, costly ministry to the needy.

Our challenge to others to deny themselves, take up their cross and follow Christ will be plausible only if we ourselves have evidently died to selfish ambition, dishonesty and covetousness, and are living a life of simplicity, contentment and generosity.

We deplore the failures in Christian consistency which we see in both Christians and churches: material greed, professional pride and rivalry, competition in Christian service, jealousy of younger leaders, missionary paternalism, the lack of mutual accountability, the loss of Christian standards of sexuality, and racial, social and sexual discrimination. All this is worldliness, allowing the prevailing culture to subvert the church instead of the church challenging and changing the culture. We are deeply ashamed of the times when, both as individuals and in our Christian communities, we have affirmed Christ in word and denied him in deed. Our inconsistency deprives our witness of credibility. We acknowledge our continuing struggles and failures. But we also determine by God's grace to develop integrity in ourselves and in the church.

8. The Local Church

Every Christian congregation is a local expression of the Body of Christ and has the same responsibilities. It is both "a holy priesthood" to offer God the spiritual sacrifices of worship and "a holy nation" to spread abroad his excellences in witness (1 Pet. 2:5,9). The church is thus both a worshipping and a witnessing community, gathered and scattered, called and sent. Worship and witness are inseparable.

We believe that the local church bears a primary responsibility for the spread of the gospel. Scripture suggests this in the progression that "our gospel came to you" and then "rang out from you" (1 Thess. 1:5,8). In this way, the gospel creates the church which spreads the gospel which creates more churches in a continuous chain-reaction. Moreover, what Scripture teaches, strategy confirms. Each local church must evangelize the district in which it is situated, and has the resources to do so.

We recommend every congregation to carry out regular studies not only of its own membership and program but of its local community in all its particularity, in order to develop appropriate strategies for mission. Its members might decide to organize a visitation of their whole area, to penetrate for Christ a particular place where people assemble, to arrange a series of evangelistic meetings, lectures or concerts, to work with the poor to transform a local slum, or to plant a new church in a neighboring district or village. At the same time, they must not forget the church's global task. A church which sends our missionaries must not neglect its own locality, and a church which evangelizes its neighborhood must not ignore the rest of the world.

In all this each congregation and denomination should, where possible, work with others, seeking to turn any spirit of competition into one of cooperation. Churches should also work with para-church organizations, especially in evangelism, discipling and community service, for such agencies are part of the Body of Christ, and have valuable, specialist expertise from which the church can greatly benefit.

The church is intended by God to be a sign of his kingdom, that is, an indication of what human community looks like when it comes under his rule of righteousness and peace. As with individuals, so with churches, the gospel has to be embodied if it is to be communicated effectively. It is through our love for one another that the invisible God reveals himself today (1 Jn. 4:12), especially when our fellowship is expressed in small groups, and when it transcends the barriers of race, rank, sex and age which divide other communities.

We deeply regret that many of our congregations are inward-looking, organized for maintenance rather than mission, or preoccupied with church-based activities at the expense of witness. We determine to turn our churches inside out, so that they may engage in continuous outreach, until the Lord adds to them daily those who are being saved (Acts 2:47).

9. Cooperation in Evangelism

Evangelism and unity are closely related in the New Testament. Jesus prayed that his people's oneness might reflect his own oneness with the Father, in order that the world might believe in him (Jn. 17:20,21), and Paul exhorted the Philippians to "contend as one person for the faith of the gospel" (Phil. 1:27). In contrast to this biblical vision, we are ashamed of the suspicions and rivalries, the dogmatism over non-essentials, the power-struggles and empire-building which spoil our evangelistic witness. We affirm that cooperation in evangelism is indispensable, first because it is the will of God, but also because the gospel of reconciliation is discredited by our disunity, and because, if the task of world evangelization is ever to be accomplished, we must engage in it together.

"Cooperation" means finding unity in diversity. It involves people of different temperaments, gifts, callings and cultures, national churches and mission agencies, all ages and both sexes working together.

We are determined to put behind us once and for all, as a hangover from the colonial past, the simplistic distinction First World sending and Two-Thirds World receiving countries. For the great new fact of our era is the internationalization of missions. Not only are a large majority of all evangelical Christians now non-western, but the number of Two-Thirds World missionaries will soon exceed those from the West. We believe that mission teams, which are diverse in composition but united in heart and mind, constitute a dramatic witness to the grace of God.

Our reference to "the whole church" is not a presumptuous claim that the universal church and the evangelical community are synonymous. For we recognize that there are many churches which are not part of the evangelical movement. Evangelical attitudes to the Roman Catholic and Orthodox Churches differ widely. Some evangelicals are praying, talking, studying Scripture and working with these churches. Others are strongly opposed to any form of dialogue or cooperation with them. All evangelicals are aware that serious theological differences between us remain. Where appropriate, and so long as biblical truth is not compromised, cooperation may be possible in such areas as Bible translation, the study of contemporary theological and ethical issues, social work and political action. We wish to make it clear, however, that common evangelism demands a common commitment to the biblical gospel.

Some of us are members of churches which belong to the World Council of Churches and believe that a positive yet critical participation in its work is our Christian duty. Others among us have no link with the World Council. All of us urge the World Council of Churches to adopt a consistent biblical understanding of evangelism.

We confess our own share of responsibility for the brokenness of the Body of Christ, which is a major stumbling-block to world evangelization. We determine to go on seeking that unity in truth for which Christ prayed. We are persuaded that the right way forward towards closer cooperation is frank and patient dialogue on the basis of the Bible, with all who share our concerns. To this we gladly commit ourselves.

C. THE WHOLE WORLD

The whole gospel has been entrusted to the whole church, in order that it may be made known to the whole world. It is necessary, therefore, for us to understand the world into which we are sent.

10. The Modern World

Evangelism takes place in a context, not in a vacuum. The balance between gospel and context must be carefully maintained. We must understand the context in order to address it, but the context must not be allowed to distort the gospel.

In this connection we have become concerned about the impact of "modernity," which is an emerging world culture produced by industrialization with its technology and urbanization with its economic order. These factors combine to create an environment, which significantly shapes the way in which we see our world. In addition, secularism has devastated faith by making God and the supernatural meaningless; urbanization has dehumanized life for many; and the mass media have contributed to the devaluation of truth and authority, by replacing word with image. In combination, these consequences of modernity pervert the message which many preach and undermine their motivation for mission.

In AD 1900 only 9% of the world's population lived in cities; in AD 2000 it is thought that more than 50% will do so. This worldwide move into the cities has been called "the greatest migration in human history"; it constitutes a major challenge to Christian mission. On the one hand, city populations are extremely cosmopolitan, so that the nations come to our doorstep in the city. Can we develop global churches in which the gospel abolishes the barriers of ethnicity? On the other hand, many city dwellers are migrant poor who are also receptive to the gospel. Can the people of God be persuaded to relocate into such urban poor communities, in order to serve the people and share in the transformation of the city?

Modernization brings blessings as well as dangers. By creating links of communication and commerce around the globe, it makes unprecedented openings for the gospel, crossing old frontiers and penetrating closed societies, whether traditional or totalitarian. The Christian media have a powerful influence both in sowing the seed of the gospel and in preparing the soil. The major missionary broadcasters are committed to a gospel witness by radio in every major language by the year AD 2000.

We confess that we have not struggled as we should to understand modernization. We have used its methods and techniques uncritically and so exposed ourselves to worldliness. But we determine in the future to take these challenges and opportunities seriously, to resist the secular pressures of modernity, to relate the lordship of Christ to the whole of modern culture, and thus to engage in mission in the modern world without worldliness in modern mission.

11. The Challenge of AD 2000 and Beyond

The world population today is approaching 6 billion. One third of them nominally confess Christ. Of the remaining four billion half have heard of him, and the other half have not. In the light of these figures, we evaluate our evangelistic task by considering four categories of people.

First, there is the potential missionary work force, *the committed.* In this century this category of Christian believers has grown from about 40 million in 1900 to about 500 million today, and at this moment is growing over twice as fast as any other major religious group.

Secondly, there are *the uncommitted.* They make a Christian profession (they have been baptized, attend church occasionally and even call themselves Christians), but the notion of a personal commitment to Christ is foreign to them. They are found in all churches throughout the world. They urgently need to be re-evangelized.

Thirdly, there are *the unevangelized.* These are people who have a minimal knowledge of the gospel, but have had no valid opportunity to respond to it. They are probably within reach of Christian people if only these will go to the next street, road, village or town to find them.

Fourthly, there are *the unreached.* These are the two billion who may never have heard of Jesus as Savior, and are not within reach of Christians of their own people. There are, in fact, some 2,000 peoples or nationalities in which there is not yet a vital, indigenous church movement. We find it helpful to think of them as belonging to smaller "people groups" which perceive themselves as having an affinity with each other (e.g. a common culture, language, home or occupation). The most effective messengers to reach them will be those believers who already belong to their culture and know their language. Otherwise, cross-cultural messengers of the gospel will need to go, leaving behind their own culture and sacrificially identifying with the people they long to reach for Christ.

There are now about 12,000 such unreached people groups within the 2,000 larger peoples, so that the task is not impossible. Yet a present only 7% of all missionaries are engaged in this kind of outreach, while the remaining 93% are working in the already evangelized half of the world. If this imbalance is to be redressed, a strategic redeployment of personnel will be necessary.

A distressing factor that affects each of the above categories is that of inaccessibility. Many countries do not grant visas to self-styled missionaries, who have no other qualification or contribution to offer. Such areas are not absolutely inaccessible, however. For our prayers can pass through every curtain, door and barrier. And Christian radio and television, audio and video cassettes, films and literature can also reach the otherwise unreachable. So can so-called "tent-makers" who like Paul earn their own living. They travel in the course of their profession (e.g. business people, university lecturers, technical specialists and language teachers), and use every opportunity to speak of Jesus Christ. They do not enter a country under false pretenses, for their work genuinely takes them there; it is simply that witness is an essential component of their Christian life-style, wherever they may happen to be.

We are deeply ashamed that nearly two millennia have passed since the death and resurrection of Jesus, and still two-thirds of the world's population have not yet acknowledged Him. On the other hand, we are amazed at the mounting evidence of God's power even in the most unlikely places of the globe.

Now the year 2000 has become for many a challenging milestone.

Can we commit ourselves to evangelize the world during the last decade of this millennium? There is nothing magical about the date, yet should we not do our best to reach this goal? Christ commands us to take the gospel to all peoples. The task is urgent. We are determined to obey him with joy and hope.

12. Difficult Situations

Jesus plainly told his followers to expect opposition. "If they persecuted me," he said, "they will persecute you" (Jn. 15:20). He even told them to rejoice over persecution (Mt. 5:12), and reminded them that the condition of fruitfulness was death (Jn. 12:24).

These predictions, that Christian suffering is inevitable and productive, have come true in every age, including our own. There have been many thousands of martyrs. Today the situation is much the same. We earnestly hope that *glasnost* and *perestroika* will lead to complete religious freedom in the Soviet Union and other Eastern bloc nations, and that Islamic and Hindu countries will become more open to the gospel. We deplore the recent brutal suppression of China's democratic movement, and we pray that it will not bring further suffering to the Christians. On the whole, however, it seems that ancient religions are becoming less tolerant, expatriates less welcome, and the world less friendly to the gospel.

In this situation we wish to make 3 statements to governments which are reconsidering their attitude to Christian believers.

First, Christians are loyal citizens, who seek the welfare of their nation. They pray for its leaders and pay their taxes. Of course, those who have confessed Jesus as Lord cannot also call other authorities Lord, and if commanded to do so, or to do anything which God forbids, must disobey. But they are conscientious citizens. They also contribute to their country's well-being by the stability of their marriages and homes, their honesty in business, their hard work and their voluntary activity in the service of the handicapped and needy. Just governments have nothing to fear from Christians.

Secondly, Christians renounce unworthy methods of evangelism.

Though the nature of our faith requires us to share the gospel with others, our practice is to make an open and honest statement of it, which leaves the hearers entirely free to make up their own minds about it. We wish to be sensitive to those of other faiths, and we reject any approach that seeks to force conversion on them.

Thirdly, Christians earnestly desire freedom of religion for all people, not just freedom for Christianity. In predominantly Christian countries, Christians are at the forefront of those who demand freedom for religious minorities. In predominantly non-Christian countries, therefore, Christians are asking for themselves no more than they demand for others in similar circumstances. The freedom to 'profess, practise and propagate' religion, as defined in the Universal Declaration of Human Rights, could and should surely be a reciprocally granted right.

We greatly regret any unworthy witness of which followers of Jesus may have been guilty. We determine to give no unnecessary offense in anything, lest the name of Christ be dishonored. However, the offense of the cross we cannot avoid. For the sake of Christ crucified we pray that we may be ready, by His grace, to suffer and even to die. Martyrdom is a form of witness which Christ has promised especially to honor.

CONCLUSION: PROCLAIM CHRIST UNTIL HE COMES

"Proclaim Christ until he comes." That has been the theme of Lausanne II. Of course we believe that Christ has come; he came when Augustus was Emperor of Rome. But one day, as we know from his promises, he will come again in unimaginable splendor to perfect his kingdom. We are commanded to watch and be ready. Meanwhile, the gap between his two comings is to be filled with the Christian missionary enterprise. We have been told to go to the ends of the earth with the gospel, and we have been promised that the end of the age will come only when we have done so. The two ends (of earth space and time) will coincide. Until then he has pledged to be with us.

So the Christian mission is an urgent task. We do not know how long we have. We certainly have no time to waste. And in order to get on urgently with our responsibility, other qualities will be necessary, especially unity (we must evangelize together) and sacrifice (we must count and accept the cost). Our covenant at Lausanne was "to pray, to plan and to work together for the evangelization of the whole world." Our manifesto at Manila is that the whole church is called to take the whole gospel to the whole world, proclaiming Christ until he comes, with all necessary urgency, unity and sacrifice.

Appendix D

⌒⌒⌒

THE AMSTERDAM DECLARATION

A CHARTER FOR EVANGELISM IN THE 21ST CENTURY
©2000 BGEA

The Amsterdam Declaration is presented as a joint report of the three task groups of mission strategists, church leaders, and theologians gathered at Amsterdam 2000. It has been reviewed by hundreds of Christian leaders and evangelists from around the world. It is commended to God's people everywhere as an expression of evangelical commitment and as a resource for study, reflection, prayer, and evangelistic outreach.

PREAMBLE

As a renewal movement within historic Christian orthodoxy, trans-denominational evangelicalism became a distinct global reality in the second half of the twentieth century. Evangelicals come from many churches, languages and cultures but we hold in common a shared understanding of the gospel of Jesus Christ, of the church's mission, and of the Christian commitment to evangelism. Recent documents that express this understanding include the Berlin Statement (1966), the Lausanne Covenant (1974), the Amsterdam Affirmations (1983), the Manila Manifesto (1989), and The Gospel of Jesus Christ: An Evangelical Celebration (1999).

At the invitation of Dr. Billy Graham, some 10,000 evangelists, theologians, mission strategists and church leaders from more than 200 countries have assembled in Amsterdam in the year 2000 to listen, pray, worship and discern the wisdom of the Holy Spirit for the unfinished task of world evangelization. We are stirred and encouraged by the challenges we have heard and the fellowship we have shared with so many brothers and sisters in Christ. More than ever, we are resolved to make Christ known to all persons everywhere.

This Amsterdam Declaration has been developed as a framework to surround the many action plans that are being made for the evangelization of the world. It is based on the principles set forth in the documents referred to above, and includes these three parts: A charter of commitments, definitions of key theological terms used in the charter, and a prayer of supplication to our Heavenly Father.

CHARTER OF COMMITMENTS

This charter is a statement of tasks, goals and ideals for evangelism in the 21st century. The order of topics reflects the range of our concerns, not the priority of these themes.

1. Mission Strategy and Evangelism

The mission of the church has at its heart world evangelization. We have from our Lord a mandate to proclaim the good news of God's love and forgiveness to everyone, making disciples, baptizing, and teaching all peoples. Jesus made it clear in his last teachings that the scope of this work of evangelism demands that we give attention not only to those around us but also to the despised and neglected of society and to those at the ends of the earth. (Matthew 28:19; Acts 1:8) To do anything less is disobedience. In addition, we affirm the need to encourage new initiatives to reach and disciple youth and children worldwide; to make fuller use of media and technology in evangelism; and to stay involved personally in grass-roots evangelism so that our presentations of the biblical gospel are fully relevant and contextualized. We think it urgent to work toward the evangelization of every remaining unreached people group.

We pledge ourselves to work so that all persons on earth may have an opportunity to hear the gospel in a language they understand, near where they live. We further pledge to establish healthy, reproducing, indigenous churches among every people, in every place, that will seek to bring to spiritual maturity those who respond to the gospel message.

2. Leadership and Evangelism

We affirm that leadership is one of Christ's gifts to the church. It does not exist for itself; it exists to lead the people of God in obedience to our Heavenly Father. Leaders must submit themselves in humility to Christ, the Head of the church, and to one another. This submission involves the acceptance of the supreme authority of Scripture by which Christ rules in his church through his Spirit. The leaders' first task is to preserve the biblical integrity of the proclamation of the church and serve as vision carriers of its evangelistic vocation. They are responsible to see that vocation implemented by teaching, training, empowering and inspiring others. We must give special attention to encouraging women and young leaders in their work of evangelism. Leaders must always be careful not to block what God is doing as they exercise their strategic stewardship of the resources which Christ supplies to his body. (Ephesians 4:11-13; Mark 10:42-45; Colossians 1:18)

We pledge ourselves to seek and uphold this model of biblical servant-leadership in our churches. We who are leaders commit ourselves afresh to this pattern of leadership.

3. Theology and Evangelism

Christian theology is the task of careful thinking and ordering of life in the presence of the triune God. In one sense, all Christians are theologians and must labor to be good ones rather than bad ones. This means that everyone's theology must be measured by biblical teaching from which alone we learn God's mind and will. (Mark 7:13; II Timothy 2:15; 3:16) Those called to the special vocations of evangelism, theology, and pastoral ministry must work together in the spread of the gospel throughout the world. Evangelists and pastors can help theologians maintain an evangelistic motivation, reminding them that true theology is always done in the service of the church. Theologians can help to clarify and safeguard God's revealed truth, providing resources for the training of evangelists and the grounding of new believers in the faith. (I Timothy 6:20; II Timothy 1:14)

We *pledge ourselves* to labor constantly in 'learning and teaching the faith according to the Scriptures, and in seeking to ensure (1) that all who preach the gospel are theologically equipped and resourced in adequate ways for the work' they have in hand, and (2) that all professional teachers of the faith share a common concern for evangelism.

4. Truth and Evangelism

Under the influence of modern rationalism, secularism, and humanism (modernity), the Western intellectual establishment has largely reacted into a relativistic denial that there is any global and absolute truth (postmodernity). This is influencing popular culture throughout the world. (Romans 15:16) By contrast, (Galatians 1:7; 2:14) the gospel (which is the authoritative word of the one, true and living God) comes to everyone everywhere at all times as truth in three senses: its affirmations are factually true, as opposed to false; it confronts us at every point with reality, as opposed to illusion; and it sets before us Jesus Christ, the co-Creator, Redeemer, and Lord of the world, as the Truth (that is, the one universally, real, accessible, authoritative, truth-telling, trustworthy Person), for all to acknowledge. (I Corinthians 9:12; II Thessalonians 1:8) There is a suspicion that any grand claim that there is one truth for everyone is inevitably oppressive and violent. But the gospel sets before us one who, though he was God, became man and identified with those under the bondage of sin to set them free from its enslavement. This gospel of God is both true for everyone and truly sets people free. (John 8:31-32) It is therefore to be received in trust, not suspicion.

> *We pledge ourselves* to present and proclaim the biblical gospel and its Christ, always and everywhere, as fully sufficient and effective for the salvation of believers. Therefore, we oppose all skeptical and relativizing or syncretizing trends, whether rationalist or irrationalist, that treat that gospel as not fully true, and so unable to lead believers into the new divine life that it promises them. We oppose all oppressive and destructive uses of God's wonderful truth.

5. Human Need and Evangelism

Both the law and the gospel uncover a lost human condition that goes beyond any feelings of pain, misery, frustration, bondage, powerlessness, and discontent with life. The Bible reveals that all human beings are constitutionally in a state of rebellion against the God who made them, and of whom they remain dimly aware; they are alienated from him, and cut off from all the enjoyment of knowing and serving him that is the true fulfillment of human nature. (Romans 1:18-32; 5:12; 18a; I Corinthians 15:22) We humans were made to bear God's image (Genesis 1:26) in an endless life of love to God and to other people, but the self-centeredness of our fallen and sinful hearts makes that impossible. Often our dishonesty leads us to use even the observance of religion to keep God at a distance, so that we can avoid having him deal with us about our ungodly self-worship. Therefore all human beings now face final condemnation by Christ the Judge, and eternal destruction, separated from the presence of the Lord. (II Thessalonians 1:9)

> *We pledge ourselves* to be faithful and compassionate in sharing with people the truth about their present spiritual state, warning them of the judgment and hell that the impenitent face, and extolling the love of God who gave his Son to save us.

6. Religious Pluralism and Evangelism

Today's evangelist is called to proclaim the gospel in an increasingly pluralistic world. In this global village of competing faiths and many world religions, it is important that our evangelism be marked both by faithfulness to the good news of Christ and humility in our delivery of it. Because God's general revelation extends to all points of his creation, there may well be traces of truth, beauty and goodness in many non-Christian belief systems. (Romans 1:18-20) But we have no warrant for regarding any of these as alternative gospels or separate roads to salvation. (John 14:6; Acts 4:12) The only way to know God in peace, love and joy is through the reconciling death of Jesus Christ the risen Lord. As we share this message with others, we must do so with love and humility shunning all arrogance, hostility and disrespect. (Mark 10:41-45; James 1:20) As we enter into dialogue with adherents of other religions, we must be courteous and kind. But such dialogue must not be a substitute for proclamation. Yet because all persons are made in the image of God, (Genesis 1:26) we must advocate religious liberty and human rights for all.

> We pledge ourselves to treat those of other faiths with respect and faithfully and humbly serve the nation in which God has placed us, while affirming that Christ is the one and only Savior of the world.

7. Culture and Evangelism.

By the blood of the Lamb, God has purchased saints from every tribe and language and people and nation. (Revelation 5:9; I Corinthians 6:19) He saves people in their own culture. World evangelization aims to see the rise of churches that are both deeply rooted in Christ and closely related to their culture. Therefore, following the example of Jesus and Paul, those who proclaim Christ must use their freedom in Christ to become all things to all people. (I Corinthians 9:19-23) This means appropriate cultural identification while guarding against equating the gospel with any particular culture. Since all human cultures are shaped in part by sin, the Bible and its Christ are at key points countercultural to everyone of them.

We pledge ourselves to be culturally sensitive in our evangelism. We will aim to preach Christ in a way that is appropriate for the people among whom we witness and which will enrich that culture in all appropriate ways. Further, as salt and light we will seek the transforming of culture in ways that affirm gospel values.

8. Scripture and Evangelism

The Bible is indispensable to true evangelism. The Word of God itself provides both the content and authority for all evangelism. Without it there is no message to preach to the lost. (I Thessalonians 2:13; Acts 2:14-39; 13:16-41) People must be brought to an understanding of at least some of the basic truths contained in the Scriptures before they can make a meaningful response to the gospel. Thus we must proclaim and disseminate the Holy Scriptures in the heart language of all those we are called to evangelize and disciple.

We pledge ourselves to keep the Scriptures at the very heart of our evangelistic outreach and message, and to remove all language and cultural barriers to a clear understanding of the gospel on the part of our hearers.

9. The Church and Evangelism

There is no dispute that in established congregations regular teaching for believers at all stages in their pilgrimage must be given, and appropriate pastoral care must be provided. (I Corinthians 14:13-17) But these concerns must not displace ongoing concern for mission, which involves treating evangelistic outreach as a continuing priority. Pastors in conjunction with other qualified persons should lead their congregations in the work of evangelism. Further, we affirm that the formation of godly, witnessing disciples is at the heart of the church's responsibility to prepare its members for their work of service. (Matthew 28:19; II Timothy 2:2) We affirm that the church must be made a welcoming place for new believers.

We pledge ourselves to urge all congregations in and with which we serve to treat evangelism as a matter of priority at all times, and so to make it a focus of congregational praying, planning, training and funding.

10. Prayer and Evangelism

God has given us the gift of prayer so that in his sovereignty he may respond in blessing and power to the cries of his children. Prayer is an essential means God has appointed for the awakening of the church and the carrying of the gospel throughout the world. From the first days of the New Testament church, God has used the fervent, persistent praying of his people to empower their witness in the Spirit, overcome opposition to the Lord's work and open the minds and hearts of those who hear the message of Christ. (Acts 1:14; 2:42; 4:23-30; 6:4; 12:5) At special times in the history of the church, revivals and spiritual breakthroughs have been preceded by the explicit agreement and union of God's people in seasons of repentance, prayer and fasting. Today, as we seek to carry the gospel to unreached people groups in all the world, we need a deeper dependence upon God and a greater unity in prayer. (Ephesians 6:18)

We pledge ourselves to pray faithfully to the Lord of the harvest to send out workers for his harvest field. (Matthew 9:37-38) We also pray for all those engaged in world evangelization and to encourage the call to prayer in families, local churches, special assemblies, mission agencies and transdenominational ministries.

11. Social Responsibility and Evangelism

Although evangelism is not advocacy of any social program, it does entail social responsibility for at least two reasons. First, the gospel proclaims the kingship of the loving Creator who is committed to justice, human life and the welfare of his creation. (Psalm 47:7; I Timothy 6:15; Revelation 17:14) So evangelism will need to be accompanied by obedience to God's command to work for the good of all in a way that is fitting for the children of the Father who makes his sun shine on the evil and the good and sends his rain on the righteous and the unrighteous alike. (Galatians 6:10; Matthew 5:45) Second, when our evangelism is linked with concern to alleviate poverty, uphold justice, oppose abuses of secular and economic power, stand against racism, and advance responsible stewardship of the global environment, it reflects the compassion of Christ and may gain an acceptance it would not otherwise receive. (Deuteronomy 24:10-13, 14-15; Luke 1:52-53; 4:18-19; James 5:1-6)

We pledge ourselves to follow the way of justice in our family and social life, and to keep personal, social and environmental values in view as we evangelize.

12. Holiness and Evangelism

The servant of God must adorn the gospel through a holy life. (I Timothy 3:2-13; Titus 1:6-9) But in recent times God's name has been greatly dishonored and the gospel discredited because of unholy living by Christians in leadership roles. Evangelists seem particularly exposed to temptations relating to money, sex, pride, power, neglect of family and lack of integrity. The church should foster structures to hold evangelists accountable for their lives, doctrine and ministries. The church should also ensure that those whose lives dishonor God and the gospel will not be permitted to serve as its evangelists. The holiness and humility of evangelists gives credibility to their ministry and leads to genuine power from God and lasting fruit. (I Corinthians 5:1-13; II Thessalonians 3:14-15; I Timothy 5:11-13, 19-20)

We pledge ourselves to be accountable to the community of faith for our lives, doctrine and ministry, to flee from sin, and to walk in holiness and humility. (I Corinthians 6:18; II Timothy 2:2)

13. Conflict, Suffering and Evangelism

The records of evangelism from the apostolic age, the state of the world around us today, and the knowledge of Satan's opposition at all times to the spread of the gospel, combine to assure us that evangelistic outreach in the twenty-first century will be an advance in the midst of opposition. (Acts 13:6-12; Ephesians 6:11-13) Current forms of opposition, which Satan evidently exploits, include secular ideologies that see Christian faith as a hindrance to human development; political power structures that see the primacy of Christians' loyalty to their Lord as a threat to the regime; and militant expressions of non-Christian religions that are hostile to Christians for being different. We must expect, and be prepared for, many kinds of suffering as we struggle not against enemies of blood and flesh, but against the spiritual forces of evil in the heavenly places. (Ephesians 6:14-18)

> We *pledge ourselves* ever to seek to move forward wisely in personal evangelism, family evangelism, local church evangelism, and cooperative evangelism in its various forms, and to persevere in this despite the opposition we may encounter. We will stand in solidarity with our brothers and sisters in Christ who suffer persecution and even martyrdom for their, faithful gospel witness.

14. Christian Unity and Evangelism

Jesus prayed to the Heavenly Father that his disciples would be one so that the world might believe. (Ephesians 4:1-6; John 17:21-23) One of the great hindrances to evangelism worldwide is the lack of unity among Christ's people, a condition made worse when Christians compete and fight with one another rather than seeking together the mind of Christ. We cannot resolve all differences among Christians because we do not yet understand perfectly all that God has revealed to us. (Romans 11:24; II Peter 3:15) But in all ways that do not violate our conscience, we should pursue cooperation and partnerships with other believers in the task of evangelism, practicing the well-tested rule of Christian fellowship: "In necessary things, unity; in non-essential things, liberty; in all things, charity." (Romans 14:14, 23)

> We *pledge ourselves* to pray and work for unity in truth among all true believers in Jesus and to cooperate as fully as possible in evangelism

with other brothers and sisters in Christ so that the whole church may take the whole gospel to the whole world.

DEFINITIONS OF KEY TERMS

The message we proclaim has both a propositional and an incarnational dimension—"the Word became flesh." (John 1:14) To deny either one is to bear false witness to Christ. Because the relation between language and reality is much debated today, it is important to state clearly what we mean by what we say. To avoid confusion and misunderstanding, then, we here define the following key words used in this Declaration. The definitions are all Trinitarian, Christocentric, and Bible-based.

1. God

The God of whom this Declaration speaks is the self-revealed Creator, Upholder, Governor and Lord of the universe. (Genesis 1:1; Exodus 20:11; Psalm 24:1-2; 33:6; Acts 4:24-30) This God is eternal in his self-existence and unchanging in his holy love, goodness, justice, wisdom, and faithfulness to his promises. (Psalm 90:2; 119:42) God in his own being is a community of three co-equal and co-eternal persons, who are revealed to us in the Bible as the Father, the Son, and the Holy Spirit. (Matthew 28:19; II Corinthians 13:14) Together they are involved in an unvarying cooperative pattern in all God's relationships to and within this world. God is Lord of history, where he blesses his own people, overcomes and judges human and angelic rebels against his rule, and will finally renew the whole created order. (Daniel 7:1-28; Acts 2:23-24; 4:28; Ephesians 1:9-10)

2. Jesus Christ

The Declaration takes the view of Jesus that the canonical New Testament sets forth and the historic Christian creeds and confessions attest. He was, and is, the second person of the triune Godhead, now and forever incarnate. He was virgin-born, lived a life of perfect godliness, died on the cross as the substitutionary sacrifice for our sins, was raised bodily from the dead, ascended into heaven, reigns now over the universe and will personally return for judgment and the renewal of all things. As the God-man, once crucified, now enthroned, he is the Lord and Savior who in love fulfills towards us the threefold mediational ministry of prophet, priest and king. His title, "Christ," proclaims him the anointed servant of God who fulfills all the Messianic hopes of the canonical Old Testament. (Romans 9:5; Titus 2:13; Hebrews 1:8; John 1:1-14; Hebrews 4:15; Romans 3:21-26; II Corinthians 5:21; I Corinthians 15:3-4; I Timothy 3:16; Philippians 2:9-11; II Thessalonians 1:7-10; Acts 2:26; Romans 1:1-3)

3. Holy Spirit

Shown by the words of Jesus to be the third divine person, whose name, "Spirit," pictures the energy of breath and wind, the Holy Spirit is the dynamic personal presence of the Trinity in the processes of the created world, in the communication of divine truth, in the attesting of Jesus Christ, in the new creation through him of believers and of the church, and in ongoing fellowship and service. (John 3:8; 14:16-17, 26; 16:13-15) The fullness of the ministry of the Holy Spirit in relation to the knowledge of Christ and the enjoyment of new life in him dates from the Pentecostal outpouring recorded in Acts 2. As the divine inspirer and interpreter of the Bible, the Spirit empowers God's people to set forth accurate, searching, life-transforming presentations of the gospel of Jesus Christ, and makes their communication a fruitful means of grace to their hearers. (Acts 2:14; II Timothy 3:16; II Peter 1:21; I Thessalonians 1:5) The New Testament shows us the supernatural power of the Spirit working miracles, signs and wonders, bestowing gifts of many kinds, and overcoming the power of Satan in human lives for the advancement of the gospel. (Acts 2:43; 5:12; 6:8; 14:3; 15:12) Christians agree that the power of the Holy Spirit is vitally necessary for evangelism and that openness to his ministry should mark all believers.

4. Bible

The 66 books of the Old and New Testaments constitute the written Word of God. As the inspired revelation of God in writing, the Scriptures are totally true and trustworthy, and the only infallible rule of faith and practice. In every age and every place, this authoritative Bible, by the Spirit's power, is efficacious for salvation through its witness to Jesus Christ. (II Timothy 3:16; II Peter 1:21; Luke 1:1-4; John 14:26; I John 1:3)

5. Kingdom

The kingdom of God is his gracious rule through Jesus Christ over human lives, the course of history, and all reality. (Daniel 7:14; Luke 11:20) Jesus is Lord of past, present, and future, and Sovereign ruler of everything. (Hebrews 13:8) The salvation Jesus brings and the community of faith he calls forth are signs of his kingdom's presence here and now, though we wait for its complete fulfillment when he comes again in glory. (Luke 22:29) In the meantime, wherever Christ's standards of peace and justice are observed to any degree, to that degree the kingdom is anticipated, and to that extent God's ideal for human society is displayed. (Luke 6:20; Matthew 5:3)

6. Gospel

The gospel is the good news of the Creator's eternal plan to share his life and love with fallen human beings through the sending of his Son Jesus Christ, the one and only Savior of the world. As the power of God for salvation, the gospel centers on the life, death, resurrection and return of Jesus and leads to a life of holiness, growth in grace and hope-filled though costly discipleship in the fellowship of the church. (Romans 1:16-17; I Corinthians 15:2; Acts 2:14-39; 13:16-41; Romans 1:1-5) The gospel includes the announcement of Jesus' triumph over the powers of darkness and of his supreme lordship over the universe. (Colossians 2:15; I Peter 3:22)

7. Salvation

This word means rescue from guilt, defilement, spiritual blindness and deadness, alienation from God, and certainty of eternal punishment in hell, that is everyone's condition while under sin's dominion. This deliverance involves present justification, reconciliation to God and adoption into his family, with regeneration and the sanctifying gift of the Holy Spirit leading to works of righteousness and service here and now, and a promise of full glorification in fellowship with God in the future. This involves in the present life joy, peace, freedom and the transformation of character and relationships and the guarantee of complete healing at the future resurrection of the body. We are justified by faith alone and the salvation faith brings is by grace alone, through Christ alone, for the glory of God alone. (Ephesians 2:8-9; Romans 5:9; 3:21-26; 8:30; Ephesians 2:10; Philippians 2:12-13; 3:21; I Corinthians 15:43; II Thessalonians 1:9-10; Mark 4:42-48; Romans 4:4-6; Ephesians 2:8-9; Titus 3:4-7; Romans 11:36; 15:9; Philippians 1:11)

8. Christian

A Christian is a believer in God who is enabled by the Holy Spirit to submit to Jesus Christ as Lord and Savior in a personal relation of disciple to master and to live the life of God's kingdom. (Acts 11:26; 26:28) The word Christian should not be equated with any particular cultural, ethnic, political, or ideological tradition or group. (I Peter 4:16) Those who know and love Jesus are also called Christ-followers, believers and disciples.

9. Church

The church is the people of God, the body and the bride of Christ, and a temple of the Holy Spirit. The one, universal church is a transnational, transcultural, transdenominational and multi-ethnic family, the household of faith. (I Corinthians 12:27; Ephesians 5:25-27, 32) In the widest sense, the church includes all the redeemed of all the ages, being the one body of Christ extended throughout time as well as space. (Matthew 28:19; Romans 3:27-30; Revelation 7:9-10) Here in the world, the church becomes visible in all local congregations that meet to do together the things that according to Scripture the church does. (I Corinthians 1:2) Christ is the head of the church. Everyone who is personally united to Christ by faith belongs to his body and by the Spirit is united with every other true believer in Jesus.

10. *Mission*

Formed from *missio*, the Latin word for "sending," this term is used both of the Father's sending of the Son into the world to become its Savior and of the Son's sending the church into the world to spread the gospel, perform works of love and justice, and seek to disciple everyone to himself. (John 17:18; 20:21)

11. *Evangelism*

Derived from the Greek word *euangelizesthai*, "to tell glad tidings," this word signifies making known the gospel of Jesus Christ so that people may trust in God through him, receiving him as their Savior and serving him as their Lord in the fellowship of his church. (Luke 4:18; Romans 1:15-17) Evangelism involves declaring what God has done for our salvation and calling on the hearers to become disciples of Jesus through repentance from sin and personal faith in him.

12. *Evangelist*

All Christians are called to play their part in fulfilling Jesus' Great Commission, but some believers have a special call to, and a spiritual gift for, communicating Christ and leading others to him. These we call evangelists, as does the New Testament. (II Timothy 4:5; Ephesians 4:11)

PRAYER

Gracious God, our Heavenly Father, we praise you for the great love that you have shown to us through the redeeming death and triumphant resurrection of your Son, our Lord Jesus Christ. We pray that you would enable us by the power of your Holy Spirit to proclaim faithfully the good news of your kingdom and your love. Forgive us for failing to take the gospel to all the peoples of the world. Deliver us from ignorance, error, lovelessness, pride, selfishness, impurity, and cowardice. Enable us to be truthful, kind, humble, sympathetic, pure, and courageous. Salvation belongs to you. O God, who sits on the throne, and to the Lamb. We ask you to make our gospel witness effective. Anoint our proclamation with the Holy Spirit; use it to gather that great multitude from all nations who will one day stand before you and the Lamb giving praise. This we ask by the merits of our Lord Jesus Christ. Amen. (Revelation 7:9-10)

Appendix E

Corporate Statements of the BGEA

FINANCIAL INTEGRITY

How can we be sure that our organization will remain true and authentic in the matter of financial integrity? That question is asked constantly at the Billy Graham Evangelistic Association

Given our biblical understanding of the fallen nature of humankind, there is no way to be absolutely certain of achieving this worthy goal. But there are some very specific things we've done at BGEA (which can be done by almost any organization big or small) in order to maximize our oversight of finances with the greatest care.

At a prayer day retreat in Modesto, California, early in the Team's history, Mr. Graham, Mr. Barrows, and Mr. Shea prayed and discussed the great problems that evangelists had been plagued by: immorality, greed, lies by overstatements, and a proud, critical spirit. So, they formed what is now referred to as "The Modesto Manifesto." It has four parts:

1. We will never criticize, condemn, or speak negatively about other pastors, churches, or other Christian workers.

2. We will be accountable, particularly in handling finances, with integrity according to the highest business standards.

3. We will tell the truth and be thoroughly honest, especially in *reporting* statistics.

4. We will be exemplary in morals—clear, clean, and careful to avoid the very appearance of any impropriety.

While all of these points are a part of our corporate culture, financial accountability is one of the major issues. Here are some of the things we've done to develop a high level of confidence and integrity:

Board of Directors:

All of BGEA is accountable to a strong Board which has full authority to control the financial operations, including the ability to say "no" when necessary and enforce that decision. The thirty-one members are made up of executives and businessmen, balanced by ministers; a limited number of Team employees; and including members with diversity in race, gender, geographical region and theological viewpoints.

Executive Committee:

Comprised of all outside Board Members (with no employees—including Mr. Graham, who is not on the Executive), the finances are under the control of the Executive Committee with recommendations and oversight of a strong Finance Committee.

Audit Review Committee of the Board:

An active Committee that recommends the engagement of outside auditors each year, meets with them independent of management and reviews every conceivable issue which could allow some difficulty. Minutes are maintained and circulated to appropriate Board members so that all are apprised of their activity.

Annual Report:

Publication of the full, audited statement for the Association is made available to all who request it. Though not required by law, it is another step toward accountability in full disclosure of all the Association's finances.

Outside Auditors:

A "big eight" firm of professionals is engaged each year to audit the Association and its affiliates. Their statement is another verification that appropriate accounting and business practices are being practiced and that BGEA is fully accountable.

Internal Auditor:

A full-time employee, answerable directly and independently to the Audit Review Committee, assures the Board and Management of the highest levels of accountability. Efficiency and effectiveness are constantly scrutinized and improved in the still-expanding experience of the ministry.

Checks-and-Balances:

Procedures within the day-to-day operations of BGEA reveal the same sensitivity to avoiding the appearances of wrong by providing for the normal business checks and balances. This allows for constant, daily accountability to one another within the work teams and provides for protective safeguards in the full range of prudent activities. Examples of this principle are independent verifications by persons not in the regular functional process, dual signers required, etc.

Other Ideas:

Management constantly monitors our systems and watches for exposures. Regular compliance testing is a way of life using such concepts as surveillance cameras, security systems, field tests, employee training, and professional monitoring services.

Commitment Authority Policy:

Making spending commitments in line with the preapproved budget is done by policy at four levels and by those designated on an annually approved listing of management personnel. Specific authorization is by policy with an established procedure that incorporates the best control and flow techniques.

Conflict of Interest Policy:

BGEA asks its Board and employees to sign a disclosure statement each year. Carefully reviewed by management and the Audit Review Committee, the policy requires disclosures and avoidance of perceptions of conflict in all transactions.

Policies:

Financial policy is taken seriously, and while too extensive to report fully in this document, here are some of the most important matters for which we have established policy guidelines.

We do *not borrow money* but are committed to operate with the funding which the Lord's people provide in support of our objectives. Also, we do not loan money.

We do *not use professional fund-raisers* nor their techniques. We do not pay commission for funds received, use a "gift of" for a premium, ask for upgraded percentage increases, telephone calling pressure tactics, nor any of the product-commissions-type schemes such as percentage of royalties, percent of phone calls, etc. We avoid these to be totally non-commercial and to be completely dependent on God's supply from His people.

We have a *graded scale of compensation* and job evaluations . . . along with a *Corporate Compensation Committee* of the Board. All officers are elected by the Board and *officers' salaries are set* by the Executive Committee. There are no bonuses and *no salary incentive programs* for any employees or officers.

All employees are salaried and receive *reimbursement* for appropriate business expenses of their assignments. All business *travel is pre-approved* by the employee's supervisor before the expenses are paid. Full documentation is required from all employees and carefully monitored.

All "love gifts" and honoraria of the Evangelists, Associates, and officers are assigned to the Association, and *no individual* personally profits by those gifts. *All contributions are receipted* and accounted for on a daily basis.

BGEA does *not employ fundraisers* and thus does not pay outside consultants, firms, nor persons to represent the ministry to donors. Field staff assist donors when requested, but do not accept on-the-spot gifts of cash.

Investments:

Our Board has an annual appointment of a committee that drafts our Investment Policy; then the Investment Committee monitors the performance and compliance of outside professional management firms who handle investments for the Association.

We do not co-mingle investment funds but maintain simpler records of each investment source for increased accountability.

Budgets:

Funding allocations are approved by the Board in the annual Operating Budget and an annual Capital Budget. Monthly reports to the Board track the compliance to the approved budget and variances are dealt with by the Board.

IRS Audit:

We have more than once had agents of the Internal Revenue Service call on us at BGEA and carefully audited our records. Everything has been found to be fully disclosed, appropriately reported and accounted for to their satisfaction.

Organizations:

BGEA is a member in good standing with the Evangelical Council for Financial Accountability (ECFA) and with the Christian Charitable Council in Canada (CCCC). We are locally members of the Chamber of Commerce and other regional and professional groups. Additionally, our executive management team are encouraged to belong to professional associations in their specialized field.

VALUES

INCLUSIVE FELLOWSHIP

1. Capacity to convene God's people.

There is a magnetism that God has given to draw the Lord's people together under the ministry of Mr. Graham and the BGEA. It is partly the heritage of trust built up over years of consistency. BGEA has been able to get the people of God to rally together and put their distinctives aside in order to accomplish a greater good together. To convene for evangelistic purposes is a divine gift to BGEA.

2. True to biblical fundamentals yet openly including those sincerely holding different theological positions.

Broad acceptance of God's people and a willingness to work practically with people who were willing to work with us . . . that is part of the Graham movement. Not insisting on a theological consensus but rather maintaining the personal privilege to speak the truth as Mr. Graham understood it without apology, but also without rancor. Maintaining his own belief in the fundamental truths of the Scripture and declaring the gospel authoritatively was the evangelist's job. Not squeezing all others in the same mold and allowing the Holy Spirit to work in His time — this permitted the inclusion of many and the hostility of few.

3. Stay inclusive on race, gender, politics, ideology, theology and sociological issues.

Beyond being "politically correct," there is concern to balance the matters in such a way that all feel a part and none are excluded. As much as possible, BGEA strives to be non-offensive in the questions of the day and issues of the times.

4. Loyalty to old friends in time, commitments.

Mr. Graham has a special love and loyalty to friends of long standing. They are not forgotten, nor easily forsaken in the heat of the battle. Time is committed to old friends even when busy. Appointments are undertaken and events committed to the schedule often (not on the merits of the activity) because of the old friend who requested it. Loyalty to those who helped in the past is a part of the Graham Team. Friends are remembered and cherished, honored and respected.

MORAL PURITY

5. Avoid even the appearance of evil in morals/sexual matters.

Constant watchfulness and careful attention to appearances are daily alerts for all BGEA. Care is taken to eliminate situations where persons could be suspected of any impropriety between the sexes. Avoiding the situations by which rumors and suspicions could be spawned has been a regular watchword for BGEA.

6. Pursue righteousness; be intolerant of evil.

It is our corporate intent to follow not only the letter of the law but also the spirit of that law. We want to be as close as we can to righteousness and pro-actively seek ways to be conformed to His ways. While avoiding the showy patterns in order to be seen by men, we know we are accountable to God and to one another. When evil exists, we purpose to repent, to correct, and to purge out the leaven of wickedness, to cleanse ourselves of all unrighteousness of the soul and spirit, perfecting holiness in the sight of God. Rigid watchfulness in little things keeps us from being scandalized in major matters.

7. Be careful/conservative in reporting statistics.

We choose to err on the down side whenever numbers are reported. Recognizing that bigness is not the same as godliness, BGEA would report numbers on the conservative side, especially as regards crowd sizes and estimated results.

8. *Money is handled by local committee, not by Team.*

Financial policies that create integrity by process, disclosure, reporting, and accountability. Early on it was the goal to leave no sad questions about finances. Among the helpful steps: commitment to have the finances handled by the local committee, put the Team on salary instead of the traditional "love gifts," and the adoption of many good common-sense business practices. With money not a driving force of motivation, the Team were free to serve the Lord without the pressure of finding ways to pay the bills on a day-to-day basis.

SINCERE SPIRITUALITY

9. *Prayer is the priority.*

Prayer has received more than lip-service attention. It has been given prominence in what is said about ministry activities, but more than that it has pervaded offices, committees, boards, conferences, consultations, etc., as well as constantly utilized individually, in groups, and in every conceivable method.

10. *Centrality of Christ.*

The banner of most Crusades was "Jesus said, 'I am the Way, the Truth, and the Life.'" Christianity is Christ, His uniqueness as Savior and His sufficiency as Lord of All, Head of His Church. Truth issues are all related to Him and our lives and ministry anchored by our being "in Christ."

11. *Authority and use of Scripture.*

"The Bible Says" became a characteristic phrase of Mr. Graham's preaching. Full authority of Scripture as our rule of faith, beliefs, and for our practical directions has provided solid rock foundation to BGEA ministry. Not only has Mr. Graham preached the Word, but we have published copies of the Bible and Bible portions, Bible studies, guides, commentaries, and study helps to saturate our own hearts and minds with the treasures of God's Word.

12. A sense of urgency — imminency of return of Christ.

In the beginning, the imminent return of Christ had high profile. Mr. Graham's preaching over the years on the coming of Christ holds the concern for the immediate possibility that He will come today. Urgency to bring others to the Savior is motivated by the sense that we are at the end of times—the night cometh when no man can work. Mr. Graham once commented about a struggling evangelist, "he may not have a sense of urgency" (thought to be a qualifying necessity for an evangelist).

13. Single-minded concentration to evangelism in all ways.

Focus on the primary task and specific calling of the Evangelist has been maintained. Determined and dogged pursuit of one calling of God has not wavered: to evangelize. Temptations have come along the way to make major commitments for education, churchmanship, entertainment, business enterprise, youth specialization, etc. Part of the BGEA culture is to stay in a focused, single-minded, this-one-thing-I-do mode for evangelistic outreach. Everything else is secondary to this consuming passion and concentration.

14. Global perspective from the outset.

National vision was clearly not enough. Mr. Graham had a world on his heart from the start. The Switzerland conference and the world conferences evidence this heartbeat. Perhaps the early trips to England in the 40s and the World War's end had its impact upon the Team, but global concerns have been a part of the Graham ministry.

15. Contemporary issues awareness.

Early *Hour of Decision* broadcast messages began with a reflection of current news items that led to Mr. Graham's sermon week after week. Matters of public concern have often formed the basis for capturing attention and leading on to the deeper issues of spiritual life.

Avoiding controversy for controversy's sake, steering clear of political issues, etc., the Team have always tried to keep abreast of issues of the day and use them to bring attention to the gospel facts.

16. "Team" effort instead of individual stars.

Billy Graham is the acknowledged personality of the ministry—there is no other rivaling his stature. But it is his desire and deference that, supporting all BGEA activities, the whole "team" effort of cooperation should be acknowledged and acclaimed. Much positive testimony has been born to a watching world by the positive, affirming, and loving relationship of being "team" players together in the Lord's harvest.

PERFORMANCE QUALITY OF EXCELLENCE

17. Business-like operations.

Recognizing the spiritual gifts to God's servants, the business of the BGEA has been guided by common sense and normal, wise practices of the commercial world. Refusing to allow slip-shod or spiritualized excuses for sloppiness has resulted in crisp, clear, clean operations that achieve with professionalism and excellence. Business, as well as programs, are part of the ministry of pleasing our Lord.

18. Commit to personnel and trust them to operate.

Beginning with Mr. Graham himself and throughout the company, workers are given responsibility and then, without undue interference, allowed to operate in a highly trusted, though accountable, fashion. It is a satisfying relationship for the employee and an effective pattern for achievement.

19. Quality first-class whenever prudent.

The resources are guided toward use of excellence in all forms. This applies to use of talented personnel and to the use of physical equipment and practical means for our work and ministry. Our choice is for quality over quantity whenever a decision between the two must be made.

20. *Media have a unique power we can benefit from.*

Media have been both favorable and adversarial to BGEA over the years—with far more positive coverage given. Care is taken to accommodate the news media. Recognizing the powerful impact of the general population hearing about the ministry through news outlets, BGEA seeks to harness and aid the news media personnel in getting their story. And, we have been careful to see that activities would be non-offending if reported so that there is no fear of the truth being told.

21. *Willingness to risk at all levels.*

Flamboyant Youth for Christ "stunts" were considered and utilized. Media was a risk for a young team. In later years, the new use of youth-oriented music is risky . . . not only on the platform, but in the sites, preparations, programs of involvement, and personalities. Capacity to put achievement ahead of reputation and status quo have led the Team to significant strides of progress and success.

22. *Use of non-team top-quality talent personnel.*

Teams have been close-knit family in spirit. But, outside guests are used only when their talented competence is matched with spiritual integrity. High-quality ability and achievement must be paralleled by a corresponding quality of character development. If a testimony is blurred or non-established, BGEA has elected to present only those whose witness is verified and firm.

23. *Diversification into radio, film, TV, magazine, etc.*

From the beginning, technology and varied methods have been used to communicate the message and to expand the scope of proclaiming the Word. National radio programs were few when the *Hour of Decision* began. Christian western musicals in films were unheard of when Mr. Texas came from the Graham ministry. Television, computers, satellite, etc., are all utilized in a Global Mission strategy.

The capacity to innovate and utilize new technology is a hallmark of the BGEA.

24. *Use of modern transportation — flights, Europe.*

Travel by air was rather rare as Mr. Graham began. Trains, autos, and buses were much more common for travel, The capacity to fly across the country, and across the ocean to Europe, greatly enhanced his itinerating evangelism. Now as resources allow the Team to fly to appointments freely, a standard of travel prevails that is foreign to most evangelists in our time.

25. *Association with greatness — places, people, possessions.*

A relationship with popular and well-known persons began with the celebrities finding the Lord in LA '49. It continued with well-known places such as the early rally on the steps of the United States Capitol. Political personalities all the way to Presidents. Hollywood types such as Cecil B. DeMille, etc. and sports stars, media magnets, educators, philanthropists, business leaders: Most did very little directly for the Graham work, but their association with the Team gave an aura of success and credibility in the early days.

TO HONOR THE LOCAL CHURCH

26. *Non-competitive with the local church.*

We always begin from the perspective of the local congregation as a source of the force for evangelism and end with the benefit being incorporated into the local body of believers. BGEA does nothing that denigrates or minimizes the local church, but rather honors her place as God's institution without being *dominated* by any single congregation.

27. *Origins: By invitation only of the total local church.*

Much has been gained by the insistence of beginning with the local invitation. BGEA does not superimpose its program upon the community nor its churches. Rather, Billy Graham comes only upon their invitation. At times, BGEA has had to work to develop that local consensus, but without it, we are not able to proceed with effectiveness.

28. Full recognition of God's place for church — Temporary permanency.

BGEA remains non-competitive with the permanent organizations of a community. Organizational structures and program entities are temporary. This allows temporary subjugation of distinctives within the Body while the cooperative effort of BGEA is achieved. Knowing that the BGEA event is temporary encourages local bodies to participate for the short-term. They know from years of track record, that BGEA will not continue to be there to draw away resources and attention for the continual longer term. Temporary permanence is really limited permanence for the extent of the *ministry* event of BGEA—after that, the local structures and BGEA-supporting bodies will incorporate the harvest into the mainstream of church/community life.

29. Non-critical of other servants or institutions.

Our policy is that we do not comment on other organizations nor other Christian workers. Especially, we avoid criticism of them, their methods, and their ministries. We seek to never speak negatively of others.

Mr. Graham's personal temperament is non-confrontive, and so for BGEA. We are not lighters . . . even to "defend" ourselves . . . not because we are gutless, but because we desire to "live peaceably with all men" for "as much as you can."

30. Total concept of evangelism through discipleship and follow-up.

Decisions alone are not the objective . . . rather, fulfillment of the Great Commission in its broader and fuller implications. Disciples are the goal— believers incorporated into the life of the Church and making a wholesome contribution to the development of His Body. We have believed that evangelism is not complete until the evangelized become evangelistic. Care is taken to see that appropriate follow-up and "linking" activity takes place so that evangelism is integrated into mainstream church life. It is thought to be irresponsible to win 'em and leave 'em.

FINANCIAL INTEGRITY

31. High integrity in fund-raising.

No gimmicks to fund-raising. No professional fundraisers are used. No cheap-shot offers. No pressure tactics such as the telemarketing phone callers. No "for-a-gift-of" offers. Premiums have been kept to ministry items that are valid messages by themselves. No one has a job description that includes the task of raising funds.

32. Full disclosure on finances.

Openness to discuss and reveal financial matters has added to the respect for Mr. Graham. Willingness to disclose his own personal situation of salary, organizational accountability and public reporting, even beyond what is legally required, has resulted in the aura of financial integrity.

33. Pay as you go — no debt.

Believing that God's work done in God's way does not want for God's supply, debt is unnecessary. By avoiding the pressures of financial bonds, the ministry has the freedom to be immediate, free and spontaneous.

34. Be generous in giving to others.

BGEA has shown generosity from the outset in providing (sharing) funding for other organizations' benefit. Whatever we have, personnel, funds, expertise, information, has been shared most freely. It has been "give and it shall be given unto you." Like Mr. Graham, the organization has never been stingy, though often restrained by necessity.

Notes

⸎

Foreword

1. Billy Graham, *Just As I Am* (San Francisco: HarperCollins, 1997), 160.

2. See *Making Christ Known: Historic mission documents from the Lausanne Movement, 1974–1989*, ed. John Stott (Grand Rapids, MI: Eerdmans, 1996), xiv.

3. Ibid., 240.

Chapter 1: An Epic Begins

1. John Pollock, *Billy Graham: The Authorized Biography* (Grand Rapids, MI: Zondervan, 1966), 55.

2. Ibid., 12.

3. Ibid., 55.

4. Ibid., 56–59.

5. Ibid., 59–60.

6. Ibid., 60.

7. Ibid.

8. Ibid., 64.

9. Timothy Dudley-Smith, *John Stott: The Making of a Leader* (Downers Grove, IL: InterVarsity Press, 1999), 15.

10. The term "evangelical" is colored with different shadings in various parts of the world. In North America until very recently, it was used to refer to Christians who are loyal to both a formal principle and a material principle. The formal principle is the truth, authority, and finality of the Bible. The material principle is the gospel as understood in historic evangelical Protestantism. While not wanting to minimize the theological and ecclesiastical differences in that heritage, we might summarize that heritage in terms such as these: We insist that salvation is gained exclusively through personal faith in the finished cross-work of Jesus Christ, who is both God and man. His atoning death planned and brought about by His heavenly Father, expiates our sin, vanquishes Satan, propitiates the Father, and inaugurates the promised kingdom. In the ministry, death, resurrection, and exaltation of Jesus, God Himself is supremely revealed, such that rejection of Jesus, or denials of what the Scriptures tell us about Jesus, constitute nothing less than rejection of God Himself. In consequence of His triumphant cross work, Christ has bequeathed the Holy Spirit, Himself God, as the down payment of the final inheritance that will come to Christ's people when He Himself returns. The saving and transforming power of the Spirit displayed in the lives of Christ's people is the product of divine grace, grace alone—grace that is apprehended by faith alone. The knowledge of God that we enjoy becomes for us an impetus to missionary outreach characterized by urgency and compassion.

   This summary, or something like it, most evangelicals would happily espouse. This sort of approach tightly ties "evangelical" to "evangel" . . . the gospel of Jesus Christ.

11. D. A. Carson, *The Gagging of God* (Grand Rapids, MI: Zondervan, 1996), 445.

Chapter 2: The Holy Spirit

1. Billy Graham, *The Holy Spirit* (Nashville: Word Publishing, 1978), 11.

2. Ibid., 11.

3. Ibid., 12.

4. Ibid., 23.

5. Ibid., 28.

6. Ibid., 29.

7. David Frost, *Billy Graham: Personal Thoughts of a Public Man* (Colorado Springs, CO: Chariot Victor, 1997), 64.

8. Graham, *How to Be Born Again* (Nashville: Word Books, 1977), 163.

9. Trudy S. Settel, *The Faith of Billy Graham* (New York: Wing Books, 1995), 72.

10. Billy Graham, *Unto the Hills* (Dallas: Word, 1996), 401.

11. George Beasley-Murray, *Word Biblical Commentary*, vol. 36, *John* (Dallas: Word, 1987), 271.

12. Graham, *Just As I Am*.

13. Billy Graham, *Approaching Hoofbeats: The Four Horsemen of the Apocalypse* (Dallas: Word Books, 1983), 233.

14. Billy Graham, *A Biblical Standard for Evangelists* (Minneapolis: World Wide Publications, 1984), 65.

15. Graham, *Holy Spirit*, 65.

16. Ibid., 71.

17. Ibid., 97.

18. Billy Graham and Charles Ward, eds., *The Billy Graham Christian Worker's Handbook* (Minneapolis: World Wide Publications, n.d.), 293.

19. Graham, *Holy Spirit*, 106.

20. Billy Graham, *Hope for the Troubled Heart* (Nashville: Word Books, 1991), 173.

21. Billy Graham, interview with Lewis Drummond, Montreat, NC, October 2000.

22. Graham, *Holy Spirit*, 106.

23. Ibid., 119.

24. W. H. Griffith Thomas, *The Holy Spirit of God* (Grand Rapids, MI: Eerdmans, 1955), 196–97.

Chapter 3: The Full and True Gospel

1. Billy Graham, *Death and the Life After* (Nashville: Word Books, 1995), 128.

2. Graham, interview, Oct. 2000.

3. C. H. Dodd, *The Apostolic Preaching and Its Development* (London: Hodder and Stoughton, 1936), 8.

4. Ibid., 24.

5. Billy Graham, *Peace with God* (New York: Pocket Books, 1963), 96.

6. Graham and Ward, *Christian Worker's Handbook*, 61.

7. Graham, *Approaching Hoofbeats*, 30.

8. Billy Graham, *Billy Graham Answers Your Questions* (Minneapolis: World Wide Publications, n.d.), 230.

9. Billy Graham, *Answers to Life's Problems* (Nashville: Word Publishing, 1988), 284.

10. Graham, interview, Oct. 2000.

11. Graham, *Peace with God*, 51–52.

12. Billy Graham, *How to Be Born Again* (Nashville: Word Publishing, 1980), 131–32.

13. Ibid., 133.

14. Ibid.

15. Ibid., 137.

16. Ibid.

17. Graham and Ward, *Christian Worker's Handbook*, 183.

18. Graham, *Peace with God*, 219–20.

19. Ibid., 119.

20. Ibid., 121.

21. Ibid.

22. Ibid., 136.

23. Ibid., 114.

24. Graham, *How to Be Born Again*, 171–72.

25. Graham and Ward, *Christian Worker's Handbook*, 155–56.

26. Billy Graham, *The Secret of Happiness*, (New York: Doubleday, 1995), 201–2.

27. Billy Graham, *Death and the Life After*, 159.

28. Ibid., 160.

29. Ibid., 164.

30. Ibid.

31. Ibid.

32. Ibid., 169.

33. Ibid., 175.

34. Ibid., 178.

35. Ibid., 180–81.

36. Billy Graham, *The Challenge: Sermons from Madison Square Garden* (Garden City, NJ: Doubleday, 1969), 157.

37. Ibid., 153.

38. Graham, *Peace with God*, 71.

39. Graham, *How to Be Born Again*, 90.

40. Graham, *Answers to Life's Problems*, 151.

41. Graham, *Peace with God*, 44–47.

42. Ibid., 51–53.

43. Ibid., 53.

44. Billy Graham, *Billy Graham Talks to Teenagers* (Grand Rapids, MI: Zondervan, 1958), 64.

45. Graham, *Billy Graham Answers Your Questions*, 228.

Chapter 4: The Sovereignty of God

1. Graham, interview, Oct. 2000.

2. Ibid.

3. Graham, *Approaching Hoofbeats*, 37.

4. John Pollock, *Crusades: 20 Years with Billy Graham* (Minneapolis: World Wide Publications, 1969), 276.

5. Pollock, *Billy Graham*, 252.

6. Ibid., 253.

7. Pollock, *Crusades*, 190.

8. Graham, *Unto The Hills*, 180.

9. Graham, *Peace with God*, 140.

10. Graham, *World Aflame*, 142.

11. Pollock, *Billy Graham*, 125.

12. Graham, *The Messages 2* (Minneapolis: World Wide Publications, n.d.), 4–5.

13. Graham, *Just As I Am*, 235.

14. Marshall Frady, *A Parable in American Righteousness* (Boston: Little, Brown, 1979), 315.

15. Frost, *Billy Graham: Personal Thoughts*, 166–67.

16. Graham, *Billy Graham Answers Your Questions*, 207.

17. Ibid., 213.

18. Graham, *Holy Spirit*, 75.

19. Graham, *Peace with God*, 25.

20. Ibid., 30–31.

21. Wayne Stanley Bonde, "The Rhetoric of Billy Graham: A Description, Analysis, and Evaluation" (PhD. diss., Southern Illinois University, 1973), 45.

22. Quoted in ibid., 48–49.

23. Ibid., 45.

24. Graham, *Death and the Life After*, 38.

25. Ibid., 54.

26. Graham, *World Aflame* (New York: Doubleday, 1965), 139.

27. Ibid., 85.

28. Graham, *Just As I Am*, 213.

29. Ibid., 225.

30. Graham, *Just As I Am*, 680.

31. Frost, *Billy Graham: Personal Thoughts*, 64.

32. Graham, *Just As I Am*, 225.

33. John Pollock, *Billy Graham: Evangelist to the World* (San Francisco: Harper & Row, 1979), 111.

34. Pollock, *Billy Graham: Evangelist*, 251.

35. Pollock, *Crusades*, 145.

36. Graham, *Just As I Am*, 246.

Chapter 5: The Centrality of Christ

1. Billy Graham, *Storm Warning* (Nashville: Word Books, 1992), 80.

2. David Lockard, *The Unheard Billy Graham* (Nashville: Word Publishers, 1971), 35.

3. Graham, *Storm Warning*, 80.

4. Billy Graham, "Jesus Christ, Superstar," sermon delivered at Birmingham, AL, 16 May 1972.

5. Graham, *Storm Warning*, 76.

6. Graham, *Answers to Life's Problems*, 156–57.

7. Janet Lowe, *Billy Graham Speaks* (New York: Wiley & Sons, 1999), 39.

8. Billy Graham, *World Aflame*, 111.

9. William Martin, *A Prophet With Honor: The Billy Graham Story* (New York: William Morrow, 1991), 407.

10. Graham, *The Secret of Happiness* (New York: Doubleday, 1955), 10.

11. Graham, *Death and the Life After*, 37.

12. Ibid.

13. Graham, *Peace with God*, 93.

14. Ibid.

15. Graham, *Death and the Life After*, 38.

16. Graham, "Jesus Christ, Superstar."

17. Ibid.

18. Ibid.

19. Graham, *Secret of Happiness*, 12.

20. John R. W. Stott, *The Cross of Christ* (Downers Grove, IL: InterVarsity Press, 1986), 89.

21. Billy Graham's sermon preached in Nashville, TN, crusade on 9 September 1954.

22. Ibid.

23. Sermon, "Did Christ Die for You?" quoted in William Dale Apel, "The Understanding of Salvation and the Evangelistic Message of Billy Graham" (Ph.D. diss., Northwestern University, 1993), 91.

24. Billy Graham, *America's Hour of Decision* (Wheaton, IL: Van Kampen Press, 1951), 124.

25. *Decision* magazine, April 1999: 1.

26. Ibid.

27. Ibid.

28. Billy Graham, *Sick Society* (Minneapolis: World Wide Publications, 1967), 8.

29. Ibid.

30. Ibid.

31. Settel, *Faith of Billy Graham*, 18.

Chapter 6: The "Social Gospel"

1. Martin, *Prophet with Honor*, 145.

2. Pollock, *Crusades*, 281.

3. Graham, *World Aflame*, 142.

4. "Graham Now Favors War on Poverty," *The Baptist Standard*, 21 June 1967: 17.

5. Stanley High, *Billy Graham: The Personal Story of the Man, His Message, and His Mission* (New York: McGraw-Hill, 1956), 61.

6. Graham, *World Aflame*, 177.

7. Lockard, *Unheard Billy Graham*, 92.

8. Ibid., 8.

9. Ibid., 27.

10. Graham, *Storm Warning*, 51.

11. Graham, *Approaching Hoofbeats*, 129.

12. T. B. Maston, *Christianity and World Issues* (New York: Macmillan, 1957), 326–27.

13. Graham, *World Aflame*, 142.

14. Ibid., 187.

15. Graham, *Billy Graham Answers Your Questions*, 125.

16. Ibid., 128.

17. Martin, *Prophet with Honor*, 249–50.

18. Ibid.

Chapter 7: Billy Graham and Suffering

1. John Corts, interview with Lewis Drummond, Jacksonville, FL, October 2000.

2. Graham, *Storm Warning*, 28.

3. Graham, *Approaching Hoofbeats*, 92.

4. Graham, *Secret of Happiness*, 83.

5. Ibid., 94.

6. Ibid., 184.

7. Curtis Mitchell, *Billy Graham: Saint or Sinner?* (Old Tappan, NJ: Fleming Revell, 1979), 66.

8. Graham, *Secret of Happiness*, 190.

9. Ibid., 188–89.

10. High, *Billy Graham*. 64.

11. Graham, *Secret of Happiness*, 190–91.

12. Ibid., 192.

13. Ibid.

14. Ibid.

15. Ibid., 193.

16. Ibid.

17. Grady Wilson, *Count It All Joy* (Nashville: Broadman & Holman, 1984), Introduction.

18. John Stott, interview with Lewis Drummond, Amsterdam, Netherlands, July 2000.

19. Martin, *Prophet with Honor*, 218.

20. Ibid., 317–18.

21. Lowe, *Billy Graham Speaks*, 164.

22. Graham, *Hope for the Troubled Heart*, 115.

23. Ibid., 47.

24. Martin, *Prophet with Honor*, 335.

25. Lowe, *Billy Graham Speaks*, 135.

26. Ibid., 49.

27. Pollock, *Billy Graham: Evangelist*, 78.

28. Ibid., 225.

29. Pollock, *Crusades*, 172.

30. Graham, *Unto the Hills*, 137.

31. Graham, *Just As I Am*, 187.

32. Martin, *Prophet with Honor*, 175.

33. Ibid.

34. Graham, *Just As I Am*, 249–50.

35. Frank Harbor, interview with Lewis Drummond, Amsterdam, Netherlands, July 2000.

36. Graham, *Hope for the Troubled Heart*, 118.

37. Frost, *Billy Graham: Personal Thoughts*, 156.

38. Ibid., 87–88.

39. Graham, *Storm Warning*, 111–12.

40. Frost, *Billy Graham: Personal Thoughts*, 83–84.

41. Ibid., 86.

42. Ibid., 354.

43. Frost, *Billy Graham: Personal Thoughts*, 87–88.

44. Graham, *Secret of Happiness*, 186–87.

45. Mitchell, *Billy Graham: Saint*, 216.

Chapter 8: A Man of the Bible

1. Roland H. Bainton, *Here I Stand: A Life of Martin Luther* (New York: Abingdon-Cokesbury Press, 1950), 185.

2. Timothy George, *The Theology of the Reformers* (Nashville: Broadman & Holman, 1988), 53.

3. Graham, interview, Oct. 2000.

4. Ibid.

5. Graham, *World Aflame*, 40.

6. Roger Elwood, ed., *To God Be the Glory* (New York: Walker, 1984), 31.

7. Graham, *How to be Born Again*, 26.

8. Graham, *Answers Your Questions*, 132.

9. Lowe, *Billy Graham Speaks*, 141.

10. Frost, *Billy Graham: Personal Thoughts*, 73.

11. Graham, *Answers Your Questions*, 130.

12. Martin Luther, *Commentary on Genesis* (Grand Rapids, MI: Zondervan, 1958), 150.

13. Billy Graham, "Why I believe the Bible is the Word of God," *Decision*, November 1968: 14.

14. John Calvin, *Institutes of the Christian Religion*, trans. F. L. Battles Collins, 1986, Vol. 4, 8,9.

15. Stott, interview, July 2000.

16. Graham, *Holy Spirit*, 42.

17. Graham, *Just As I Am*, 46.

18. Graham, *Holy Spirit*, 39.

19. Donald W. Waite, "Evangelistic Preaching of Billy Graham" (Ph.D. diss., Purdue University, 1961).

20. Graham, *World Aflame*, 99.

21. Billy Graham, "Ambassadors," *Decision* magazine, May 1977: 3.

22. Graham, interview, Oct. 2000.

23. Graham, *Holy Spirit*, 43.

24. Ibid., 40.

25. Graham, *Holy Spirit*, 44.

26. Ibid.

27. Ibid.

28. Ibid., 47.

29. Curtis Mitchell, *Billy Graham: The Making of a Crusader* (Philadelphia: Chilton Publishers, 1966), 54.

30. Cort R. Flint, *The Faith of Billy Graham* (Anderson, SC: Drake House, 1968), 28.

31. Ibid., 40.

32. Billy Graham, "Can God Bring Revolution to Your Heart?" *Decision*, 7 July 1981.

33. Graham, interview, Oct. 2000.

34. Graham, *How to Be Born Again*, 39.

35. Rich Marshall, interview with Lewis Drummond, St. Louis, MO, October 1999.

36. Graham, "Ambassadors," 26.

37. Elwood, *To God Be the Glory*, 31.

38. Flint, *Faith of Billy Graham*, 28.

39. Graham, *Holy Spirit*, 47.

40. Graham, *Billy Graham Answers Your Questions*, 156.

41. Tom Phillips, interview with Lewis Drummond, Warsaw, Poland, September 1999.

42. Ibid.

43. Graham, interview, Oct. 2000.

44. Graham, *Just As I Am*, 126.

45. Larry Walker, interview with Lewis Drummond, Amsterdam, Netherlands, July 2000.

46. Graham, "Your Spiritual Survival Kit," *Decision*, November 2000.

47. Ben Siamlie, "I Can Go No Further," *Christianity Today*, 26 September 1966: 53.

48. Larry Davis, "Interpretation of Scripture in the Evangelistic Preaching of William Franklin Billy Graham" (Ph.D. diss., Southern Baptist Theological Seminary, 1986.)

49. Luther, *Commentary on Genesis*, 155.

50. Graham, *World Aflame*, xiv.

51. Graham, *Unto the Hills*, 313.

52. Robert Ferm, *Persuaded to Live* (Westwood, NJ: Fleming Revell, 1958), 192.

Chapter 9: Boldness

1. Funk and Wagnall's Desk Standard Dictionary.

2. Joseph Henry Thayer, *Greek-English Lexicon of the New Testament* (New York, NY: American Book, n.d.), 491.

3. Graham, *Just As I Am*, 172.

4. Frost, *Billy Graham: Personal Thoughts*, 132.

5. Martin, *Prophet with Honor*, 402.

6. Ibid., 403.

7. Ibid., 406.

Chapter 10: Godliness

1. Pollock, *Billy Graham*, 4.

2. Graham, *Just As I Am*, 37.

3. Graham, *Unto the Hills*, 65.

4. Ibid.

5. Ibid., 38.

6. Ibid., 43.

7. Ibid., 69.

8. Graham, *Secret of Happiness*, 103.

9. Billy Graham, "You Can't Cover Up Sin," *Decision*, September 1999.

10. Frost, *Billy Graham: Personal Thoughts*, 145.

11. Ibid.

12. Graham, interview, Oct. 2000.

13. Billy Graham, "The Power of Prayer: Turning the Tide of History," *Decision*, July/August 1999.

14. Ibid.

15. Ibid.

16. Ibid.

17. Cliff Barrows, interview with Lewis Drummond, Birmingham, AL, 1999.

18. Graham, *Secret of Happiness*, 208.

19. Graham, *Biblical Standard for Evangelists*, 74.

20. Martin, *Prophet with Honor*, 107.

21. Barrows, interview, Oct. 1999.

22. Sterling Houston, interview with Lewis Drummond, Indianapolis, IN, June 1999.

23. Amsterdam 2000 "List of Evangelist Standards" (Minneapolis: BGEA, 2000).

24. Graham, *Biblical Standard for Evangelists*, 109.

25. Ibid., 110.

26. Frost, *Billy Graham: Personal Thoughts*, 71–72.

27. Ibid., 173.

Chapter 11: Revival

1. Martin, *Prophet with Honor*, 173.

2. Billy Graham, *America's Lost Frontier* (Minneapolis: World Wide Publications, 1962).

3. Graham, *Storm Warning*, 307–8.

4. Lowe, *Billy Graham Speaks*, 31.

5. James Burns, *Revivals: Their Laws and Leader* (Grand Rapids, MI: Baker Book House, 1960), 310–11.

6. Graham, *Biblical Standard for Evangelism*, 124.

7. Ibid.

8. Waite, "Evangelistic Preaching," 91.

9. Sermon preached at the Harringay Crusade, London, England, 1954.

10. Ibid.

11. Billy Graham, *Revival in Our Time* (Wheaton, IL: Van Kampen Press, 1950), 73.

12. Ibid., 77.

13. Pollock, *Billy Graham*, 217.

14. Martin, *Prophet with Honor*, 124.

15. Sermon preached in Japan, 1994.

16. Frost, *Billy Graham: Personal Thoughts*, 23.

17. Anne Graham Lotz, interview with Lewis Drummond, St. Louis, MO, Oct. 1999.

18. William D. Apel, "Understanding of Salvation," 41.

19. Graham, *Unto the Hills*, 178.

20. Graham, *Biblical Standard for Evangelists*, 178.

21. Melvin Graham, interview with Lewis Drummond, St. Louis, MO, Oct. 1999.

22. Graham, *Storm Warning*, 200.

23. Ibid.

24. Graham, *World Aflame*, 23–24.

Chapter 12: A Worldwide Ministry

1. Graham, *Just As I Am*, 735.

2. William Deckard, ed., *Breakfast with Billy Graham*, 38.

3. Martin, *Prophet with Honor*, 439.

4. Maurice Rowlandson, *Life with Billy* (London: Hodder & Stoughton, 1992), 254.

5. Billy Graham, "Extending the Kingdom of God," *Decision*, October 2000: 4.

6. Graham, *Just As I Am*, 453.

7. Graham, interview Oct. 2000.

8. Pollock, *Crusades*, 168.

Chapter 13: The Church

1. Graham, *Peace with God*, 188.

2. Ralph Bell, interview with Lewis Drummond, Indianapolis, IN, 1999.

3. Ibid.

4. Graham, *Billy Graham Answers Your Questions*, 73.

5. Letter to Allison Barker, Christian Guidance Department of the BGEA, April 13, 1999.

6. Ibid.

7. Ibid.

8. Graham, *Peace with God*, 190.

9. Ibid., 191–92.

10. Ibid., 194.

11. Ibid., 190.

12. Graham, *Answers to Life's Problems*, 68.

13. Ibid., 67.

14. Ibid., 69.

15. Ibid., 109.

16. Graham, *Peace with God*, 194.

17. Graham, *Answers to Life's Problems*, 109.

18. Ibid., 110.

19. Graham, *Peace with God*, 196.

20. Ibid.

21. Graham, *Approaching Hoofbeats*, 43.

22. Graham, *Challenge for Today's Church* (Minneapolis: World Wide Publications, n.d.), 4.

23. Graham, *Answers to Life's Problems*, 114.

24. Graham, *Peace with God*, 121.

25. Ibid., 186.

26. Graham, *Answers to Life's Problems*, 110.

27. Ibid., 118–19.

28. Ibid.

29. Graham, *Biblical Standard for Evangelists*, 90.

30. Graham, *Christian Workers Handbook*, 72.

31. Frost, *Personal Thoughts of a Public Man*, 74.

32. Charles Dullea, *A Catholic Looks at Billy Graham* (New York: Paulist Press, 1973).

33. Lowe, *Billy Graham Speaks*, 68.

Chapter 14: The Lasting Legacy

1. Martin, *Prophet with Honor*, 592.

2. Irwin Lutzer, phone interview with Barbara Kois, December 2000.

3. Martin, *Prophet with Honor*, 71.

4. Ibid., 78.

5. Russ Busby, *Billy Graham: God's Ambassador* (Del Mar, CA: Tehabi Books, 1999), 262.

6. Martin, *Prophet with Honor*, 538.

7. Ibid., 602.

8. Ibid., 451.

9. Ibid., 591.

10. Lon Allison, interview with Barbara Kois, 19 December 2000.

11. Martin, *Prophet with Honor*, 310.

12. John Yarbrough, phone interview with Barbara Kois, December 2000.

13. Martin, *Prophet with Honor*, 506.

14. Ibid., 524.

15. Busby, *Billy Graham: God's Ambassador*, 47.

16. Martin, *Prophet with Honor*, 472.

17. Ibid., 466.

18. Ibid., 472.

19. Busby, *Billy Graham: God's Ambassador*, 134.

20. Elmer L. Towns and Douglas Porter, *The Ten Greatest Revivals Ever* (Ann Arbor, MI: Servant Publications, 2000) Introduction, 10.

21. Martin, *Prophet with Honor*, 414.

22. Ibid., 171.

23. Yarbrough, interview, Dec. 2000.

24. Martin, *Prophet with Honor*, 220.

25. Ibid., 224.

26. Ibid., 212.

27. Busby, *Billy Graham God's Ambassador*, 8.

28. Ibid., 211.

29. Jim and Gretchen Reidel, interview with Barbara Kois, 14 December 2000.

30. George W. Bush and Karen Hughes, *A Charge to Keep* (New York: William Morrow, 1999).

31. Martin, *Prophet with Honor*, 616.

32. Ibid., 506.

33. Ibid., 616.

34. Stephen Olford, phone interview with Barbara Kois, December 2000.

35. Elmer Towns, phone interview with Barbara Kois, December 2000.

36. Martin, *Prophet with Honor*, 442.

37. Ibid., 445.

38. Ibid., 530.

39. Ibid., 541.

40. Lon Allison, interview with Barbara Kois, 19 December 2000.

41. Marie Little, interview with Barbara Kois, 27 December 2000.

42. Martin, *Prophet with Honor*, 609.

43. Graham, interview, Oct. 2000.

44. Ibid.

45. Ibid.

46. Ibid.

47. Ibid.

48. Lotz, interview, Oct. 1999.

49. Graham, interview, Oct. 2000.

50. Ibid.

51. Busby, *Billy Graham God's Ambassador*, 21.

52. Ibid., 271.

Appendix B: The Lausanne Covenant
1. The Lausanne Covenant is reprinted here by permission of Leighton Ford, Leighton Ford Ministries.

Appendix C: The Manila Manifesto
1. The Manila Manifesto is reprinted here by permission of Leighton Ford, Leighton Ford Ministries.